THE
COMPLETE BOOK
OF

THUNDERBIRDS™

CHRIS BENTLEY

The author would like to acknowledge the invaluable assistance provided by the following:
Gerry Anderson, Mary Anderson, Stephen Brown, Terry Curtis, Derek Dorking, Martin Gainsford,
Adrian Hinchliffe, David Lane, Lesley Levene, Jon Lucas and the designers at AdVantage,
Jenny Olivier, Andrew Pixley, Russell Porter, Robin Quinn, David Ross, Ralph Titterton, Ken Turner,
Nick Williams, Keith Wilson
and, above all, my mother, Joan Bentley.
Without their help, this book would not have been possible.

This book is dedicated to everyone at AP Films/Century 21 who was involved in bringing
THUNDERBIRDS to the screen, and especially to three individuals who are sadly no longer with us,
but whose contributions to the series were immeasurable:
Reg Hill, Christine Glanville and Derek Meddings.

FANDERSON is the Official Appreciation Society for the film and television productions of
Gerry Anderson. For further information and a membership application form, please write
(enclosing a stamped self-addressed envelope) to:
FANDERSON, PO Box 12, Bradford, West Yorkshire BD10 0YE
or visit the Fanderson website at www.fanderson.org.uk

Every effort has been made to acknowledge correctly and contact the source and/or copyright
holder of each picture, and Carlton Books Limited apologizes for any unintentional errors or
omissions which will be corrected in future editions of this book.

THIS IS A CARLTON BOOK

Published by Carlton Books Limited 2000
20 Mortimer Street
London
W1N 7RD

Reprinted in 2001

Text and design © 2000 Carlton Books Limited

™ and © 1965 and 1999. THUNDERBIRDS is a trademark of Carlton International Media Limited
and is used under licence.
THUNDERBIRDS is a Gerry Anderson Production.
Licensed by Carlton International Media Limited.
© 1999. The CARLTON logotype device is a trademark of Carlton International Media Limited.

A CIP catalogue for this book is available from the British Library.

ISBN 1 84222 092 6

Production: Garry Lewis

CONTENTS

FOREWORD

Although to date I have made some 600 episodes of entertainment using puppets, live action, stop motion and computer-generated images, I am mainly known as the man who made THUNDERBIRDS, and that's OK with me!

THUNDERBIRDS was filmed in 1964. It was the result of many years of development work, culminating in the Supermarionation process. THUNDERBIRDS was an instant success. When it was first screened there were rave reviews in the national press, the television ratings went through the roof and the merchandising was so successful that my company, the Century 21 Organization, bought a toy company to help cope with the demand. It is said today that THUNDERBIRDS sold to some sixty countries, although I seem to remember that it was sold to over a hundred!

Lew Grade, my ex-boss and managing director of Associated TeleVision, who financed THUNDERBIRDS and many of my other productions, had his own distribution company, Incorporated Television Company (ITC). When Lew was deposed ITC – which then owned THUNDERBIRDS – was sold to an Australian, Robert Holmes a Court. He died shortly afterwards and ITC was bought by another Australian, Alan Bond, who ended up in jail. ITC was then bought by the management of its New York subsidiary. From there it was sold to Polygram in Los Angeles and finally it was purchased by Carlton Communications. I cannot tell you how pleased I was that THUNDERBIRDS had, at long last, returned to the UK, where it rightfully belongs.

Some thirty-five years after THUNDERBIRDS was born it is being broadcast yet again. I am delighted to think that a whole new generation is about to share in the adventures of International Rescue. And what better companion could there possibly be, for fans new and old, than *The Complete Book of THUNDERBIRDS*!

In commissioning this book, Carlton Book's senior executive editor, Jenny Olivier, had to find a writer who really knew the inside story. She wisely chose Chris Bentley.

Chris is the chairman of Fanderson, a fan club that was formed some twenty years ago. The members produce merchandise, hold conventions, collect anything and everything to do with my work, including puppets and models from the shows, and publish a beautifully produced magazine called *FAB*. Their claim is: 'You read it here in *FAB* first.' A Fanderson website, www.fanderson.org.uk, gives the latest information about the work I am doing and my past shows.

Chris is a very hard-working and responsible person and the content of *The Complete Book of THUNDERBIRDS* reflects that. He already had extensive knowledge of THUNDERBIRDS but he conducted further research for the book and was able to call upon the members of the Fanderson committee for additional information. As a result he has produced the most comprehensive book about the series ever written.

If you enjoy THUNDERBIRDS, *The Complete Book of THUNDERBIRDS* is for you.

Gerry Anderson

Gerry Anderson
14 April 2000

OPPOSITE: *Design & Art Direction*: Chris Bentley; *Photography*: David Finchett; *Digital Composition*: The Magic Camera Company; *Thunderbird 2 Model*: Richard Gregory.

INTRODUCTION

'The rescue came sooner than anyone had thought possible at dawn this morning. The final stage was accomplished with a barely credible smoothness. It took two and a half hours from the moment the escape cylinder, empty, was lowered on a test run through the shaft, to the shout we heard from the inside of the chamber when the last man was safely above the ground – two and a half hours of tension that left one weak at the knees.'

Charles Wheeler, BBC Radio News
1 November 1963

At 8.00 p.m. on Friday 24 October 1963, 129 men were working the late shift at the Lengede iron mine near Brunswick in Lower Saxony, West Germany, when disaster struck. The dam holding water used in the processing of the iron ore collapsed and the mine was flooded, trapping the miners deep underground in pitch blackness. Seventy-nine of them managed to make their way in the dark to an air shaft and, over the next four hours, climbed ladders to the surface, but fifty men remained cut off hundreds of feet below the surface with little hope of rescue.

Over the next two weeks, the world was gripped by the unfolding events at Lengede as attempts to save the miners continued round the clock. The day after the disaster, rescue teams located seven men in a half-flooded gallery 110 feet down, and all were brought to the surface by a rescue party using rubber boats and frogmen's equipment. This left the forty-three men who had actually been working in the pit when the dam broke.

By drilling a narrow bore hole through a beet field on the surface, three men were discovered in a pocket of high-pressure air some 300 feet below; a fourth man who had been with them when the dam broke had died in the initial rush of flood water. The operation to rescue these men was complicated by the high pressure in the pocket: to prevent the men from contracting the 'bends' as they were brought to the surface, the shaft being drilled down to them had to be lined with concrete and secured with an air lock, so that normal air pressure could be gradually restored in a decompression chamber once the men were on the surface. Complications meant that it was early the following Saturday morning before the drill making the rescue shaft was able to break through the roof of the chamber in which the men were trapped, and another nine hours before they could be winched to the surface, one by one, in a rescue capsule.

Unwilling to give up on the other missing miners, the rescue teams took the advice of veteran miners to locate a further eleven survivors who were sheltering in a small inlet of the mine gallery 185 feet down, a dome-shaped cavity 20 feet long, 12 feet high and 9 feet wide. This cavity was above the level of the flood water and the men had been able to survive for ten days by drinking water dripping through the roof. The air pressure was normal but the roof was not shored up, so any rescue attempt risked burying the men under rubble as the drill bored down to them.

The rescuers' ingenious solution was to drill a 2-inch pilot bore and send down narrow steel piping so that the men could first build themselves a framework covered by synthetic material that would act as a protection from falling rock. A second shaft, three times wider than the first, was then drilled so that food supplies could be sent down, along with sturdier shoring material, tools and wood, but unfortunately this shaft missed the cavity by about 3 feet and it was too risky to disturb the surrounding rock by drilling another supply shaft. The drilling of the main rescue shaft continued and the world held its breath as the drill finally came down into one corner of the cavity. To everyone's relief, the roof held, the rescue shaft was quickly completed and, on 7 November, the last eleven survivors were brought to the surface in a rescue capsule after being trapped underground for fourteen days.

Twenty-nine miners lost their lives in the Lengede disaster, but had it not been for the remarkable perseverance and ingenuity of the rescue teams, another twenty-one would also have died. Only a rescue organization equipped with incredible advanced machinery far beyond the capabilities of current technology could possibly have saved them all.

THE MAKING OF THUNDERBIRDS

BEFORE THUNDERBIRDS

Towards the end of October 1963, television producer Gerry Anderson was faced with a dilemma. He and his colleagues at the AP Films Studios in Slough were coming to the end of filming on a thirty-nine-episode colour television series called STINGRAY. This series was the third that Anderson had produced for Lew Grade, the managing director of Associated TeleVision, and its international distribution arm ITC, using a sophisticated puppetry technique known as Supermarionation. Each series had been more successful than the last and this latest, a science-fiction adventure set under the sea in the middle of the twenty-first century, was one of only a handful of British television series that had, at that time, been made in colour. But now Anderson was fighting a deadline to come up with an idea for the series that would follow STINGRAY into production.

'We had a studio which had to be fed with product, so as one series was nearing completion, I knew that I had to think up what the next one was going to be about, in order to keep the production line going. Time was drawing close for Lew Grade to call me and say, "Gerry, come up and tell me what the next series is going to be about."

'At that time, there was a mine disaster in Germany and I was listening avidly on the radio to this. There were, as far as I remember, twenty or thirty men trapped 300 feet below ground in a flooded pit and the rescuers were drilling, first of all, a hole to supply them with air and food, and then a larger hole in order to pull them out. The only men that survived were those in air pockets. Having rescued the first three, these men reported that there were another dozen or so trapped in another part of the mine, and so this terrifying story unfolded.

'I not only felt sorry for the men, but was also fascinated by some of the news reports. For instance, the rescuers needed a huge drill that was big enough to hoist a man from 300 feet down below. Such a drill existed, but it was in Bremen, so it had to be brought by rail and was going to take eight hours to arrive. Little by little, I started to think that there really ought to be dumps around the world with rescue gear standing by, so that when a disaster happened, all these items of rescue equipment could be rushed to the disaster zone and used to help to get people out of trouble.

'At that point, I got a call from Lew to say, "Gerry, can you come up tomorrow morning and tell me about your new show?" So I drove up to see Lew and I was thinking, "Rescue, yes, rescue, but how to make it science fiction? What about an international rescue organization? They'll need to fly to the danger zone and they'll have

The entire THUNDERBIRDS crew on one of the AP Films puppet soundstages.

to have a transporter to bring the heavy equipment up. But villains will be after their equipment, so they'll have to be located in a secret location – an island in the Pacific that hasn't been mapped yet..." and by the time I got to Lew, I had the basis of the story.

'Lew, as always, was only interested in the key items in the proposed series: Did it have a good title? Was it action adventure? Was it exciting? Was it different? And if all those things got a yes, he would say, "Go ahead." And so THUNDERBIRDS was born.'

Gerry Anderson came into the world on Sunday 14 April 1929 in Hampstead, London. As part of a course in architecture at his local polytechnic, he studied fibrous plastering and found that he was very good at it, but his dreams of putting this skill to use producing mouldings for film sets were dashed when it was discovered that he was allergic to the lime in the plaster – he developed dermatitis, which took the skin off both arms up to his elbows. Instead, he went to work in a photographic portrait gallery in Regent Street, but he found the work boring and was increasingly attracted to the idea of working in the film industry. He applied for a job in the Colonial Film Unit, a branch of the Ministry of Information, and was taken on as a trainee, which gave him insight into every aspect of film production. It became clear that he had considerable talent as an editor and it was in this capacity that he was able to find work at Gainsborough Pictures, one of the country's leading independent film-makers.

Anderson made his film industry debut in 1946 as assistant editor for director Arthur Crabtree and producer Harold Huth on *Caravan*, a period romantic drama starring Stewart Granger and Jean Kent. He then worked on *Jassy* and *Snowbound* before he was called up in 1947 for National Service in the RAF, where he started as a radio telephone operator for air traffic control at RAF Manston. He ended his service as a direction finder on an airfield, and resumed his film career in 1949 at Pinewood Studios with work on *So Long at the Fair*, *The Clouded Yellow* and Anthony Havelock-Allen's *Never Take No for an Answer*.

More work followed on *South of Algiers*, *Appointment in London*, *They Who Dare* and *A Prize of Gold* before Anderson elected to leave Pinewood, first to join an independent television production company, Polytechnic Films (making his directorial debut on an unbroadcast documentary television series called YOU'VE NEVER SEEN THIS) and then, when Polytechnic folded early in 1957, to co-found a commercials company with his Polytechnic colleague, cameraman Arthur Provis. They were joined by three other members of the Polytechnic staff, designers Reg Hill and John Read, and secretary Sylvia Thamm.

Based at Islet Park in Maidenhead, the company was named AP Films after the initials of the two partners, but little work came their way and Anderson was forced to take on freelance directorial assignments for television. After six months in business, the company was on the verge of liquidation when the partners were approached by Associated-Rediffusion executive Suzanne Warner and children's author Roberta Leigh to produce a puppet series, THE ADVENTURES OF TWIZZLE, for newly formed Independent TeleVision. Desperate for the work, Anderson and Provis jumped at the contract, resolving to make the best puppet shows they could and hoping to prove that they could make even better live-action features given the chance. Fifty-two episodes of TWIZZLE were filmed between August 1957 and January 1958.

Leigh was delighted with the work and commissioned a second series, TORCHY THE BATTERY BOY, but after filming an initial series of twenty-six episodes, the partners decided to branch out and produce their own children's series, FOUR FEATHER FALLS. A fantasy Western series, it pioneered the use of a more sophisticated style of puppetry as Anderson and his team began to experiment with electronics to match dialogue to the puppets' mouth movements. The fibreglass head of each puppet was fitted with a solenoid connected to special tungsten wires on

GERRY ANDERSON
SCREENOGRAPHY
FILM

CARAVAN (1946)
  Assistant Editor

JASSY (1947)
  Assistant Editor

SNOWBOUND (1948)
  First Assistant Editor

SO LONG AT THE FAIR (1950)
  First Assistant Editor

THE CLOUDED YELLOW (1950)
  Dubbing Editor

NEVER TAKE NO FOR AN ANSWER (1952)
  Assembly Cutter and Dubbing Editor

SOUTH OF ALGIERS (1952)
  Assembly Cutter

APPOINTMENT IN LONDON (1953)
  Assembly Cutter and Dubbing Editor

ABDULLA THE GREAT (1954)
  Dubbing Editor

THEY WHO DARE (1954)
  Assembly Cutter and Dubbing Editor

A PRIZE OF GOLD (1955)
  Dubbing Editor

FURTHER UP THE CREEK (1958)
  Dubbing Editor

CROSSROADS TO CRIME (1960)
  Producer

THUNDERBIRDS ARE GO (1966)
  Executive Producer and Screenplay

THUNDERBIRD 6 (1967)
  Executive Producer and Screenplay

DOPPELGÄNGER (1968)
  Producer and Screenplay

Gerry and Sylvia Anderson pose for the press during the making of THUNDERBIRDS.

which the puppet was strung. Pulses could then be fed down the wires from a tape recorder running pre-recorded dialogue, and these pulses would trigger the solenoid to operate the puppet's mouth perfectly in sync. Over the next five years, this process was constantly refined into the technique that became known as Supermarionation.

A pilot episode of FOUR FEATHER FALLS was made at Islet Park, but when Anderson and Provis sold the series to Granada Television the company moved into new premises in Ipswich Road on the Slough Trading Estate to make a further thirty-eight episodes. FOUR FEATHER FALLS proved to be very popular so Anderson forged ahead with plans for a new series, SUPERCAR, but Granada refused to finance the show and APF was left on the verge of bankruptcy once again. Willing to accept any project to keep the company going, Anderson agreed to produce three television commercials for Blue Cars Travel in association with FOUR FEATHER FALLS voice artist Nicholas Parsons. One of the commercials, 'Martians', won the Grand Prix Award at the first British Television Commercials Awards in 1961.

At this point, Lew Grade, head of ATV, stepped in and put up the money for a full series of SUPERCAR, which followed the adventures of Mike Mercury and the crew of an amazing land, sea and air vehicle based at a secret laboratory in Nevada. An initial series of twenty-six episodes was sold to American television in 1960 and Grade immediately commissioned a second. Longing to move into the 'big league' with major live-action features, Anderson approached Anglo Amalgamated, who gave him £16,000 to produce and direct his first feature film, *Crossroads to Crime*, a live-action thriller, but the film's relative failure in comparison with

SUPERCAR resigned Anderson to the fact that his company's immediate future lay with Supermarionation.

Anderson married Sylvia Thamm in November 1960 during production of SUPERCAR's second season of thirteen episodes. Grade continued to finance subsequent APF series, each more elaborate and popular than the last. A new series, FIREBALL XL5, began production in 1961 and charted the interplanetary adventures of Colonel Steve Zodiac and the crew of a World Space Patrol spacecraft exploring Sector 25 of the galaxy in the year 2063. Grade sold the series to NBC in America and it became the first British television series to be networked on American television. He was so pleased with the series' performance, both at home and abroad, that he put up £3 million to buy AP Films, but insisted that Gerry Anderson should continue to run the company.

Grade also invested £75,000 to enable the company to move to larger, custom-built premises in Stirling Road, half a mile away on the other side of the Slough Trading Estate. Here, Reg Hill supervised the construction of three shooting stages, two for puppet filming and the other for special effects. Although small in comparison with live-action film studios such as those at Pinewood and Shepperton, the new AP Films Studios were ideal for Anderson's brand of film-making and became the company's home for the next eight years. The site incorporated production offices, property department, preview theatre and twelve cutting rooms, with additional offices for the art department in Edinburgh Avenue, just around the corner from Stirling Road.

All this activity was in anticipation of production on the company's first colour series, STINGRAY. Although a number of other British television series had already been filmed in colour, most notably the ITC series THE ADVENTURES OF SIR LANCELOT (1956) and MAN OF THE WORLD (1962), STINGRAY was the first children's series to be given the colour treatment and thirty-nine half-hour episodes were filmed over a ten-month period from early 1963. Essentially reworking the format of FIREBALL XL5 by relocating the heroes under the sea, STINGRAY followed the adventures of Captain Troy Tempest and the crew of the World Aquanaut Security Patrol super-submarine Stingray, patrolling the world's oceans in the year 2064. Massively successful in Britain, the series also netted over £3 million in overseas sales when the programme was syndicated in the United States.

But Lew Grade wasn't a man to rest on his laurels and neither was Gerry Anderson. Their next series had to be even bigger and better.

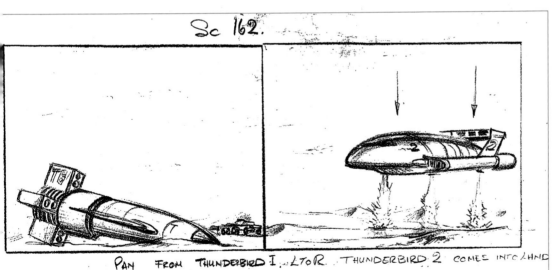

Sc 162.

PAN FROM THUNDERBIRD I. L TO R. THUNDERBIRD 2 COMES INTO LAND FROM THE TOP OF PICTURE. USE BIG THUNDERBIRD I, JEEP NO TO FAR AWAY FROM IT, THUNDERBIRD 2 CAN JUST BE IN PICTURE. ON THE WAY DOWN ON END OF PAN.

SPEED 72.
Nº 10946-1
AKE 1102 R+2+4

A storyboard by Derek Meddings for a visual effects sequence in The Uninvited.

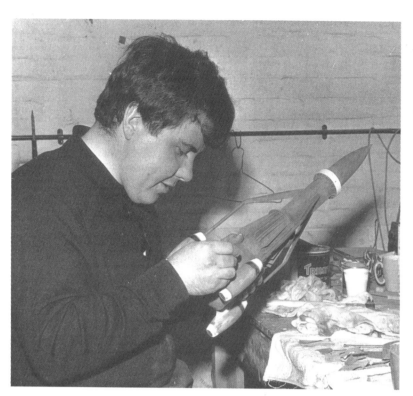

A model-maker puts the finishing touches to Thunderbird 3.

PRE-PRODUCTION

Having sold Lew Grade on the concept of INTERNATIONAL RESCUE (as the new series was initially entitled), Anderson was faced with the task of fleshing out his basic idea. At his holiday home in Albufeira in Portugal, he developed a series which would chronicle the amazing exploits of a team of heroes who could fly to anywhere in the world to rescue ordinary people trapped in extraordinary situations. However, whereas all AP Films' previous series had been aimed primarily at a juvenile audience, the decision was taken with INTERNATIONAL RESCUE to go for a more adult market. It would be transmitted in an early-evening time-slot, making the potential audience as much adult as children.

Dictating the opening script to his wife, Sylvia, in four sessions, Anderson set out the format for INTERNATIONAL RESCUE, describing a half-hour programme (twenty-five minutes plus commercials) in which the protagonists would carry out their rescue operations using a variety of incredible equipment. Acting in secrecy behind a façade of decadence from a luxurious island base somewhere in the Pacific Ocean, the members of International Rescue would be ever on the alert, with a vast manned space satellite monitoring radio messages for any situations that might require their very special talents and machinery.

A primary concern for the Andersons and their AP Films partners, Reg Hill and John Read, was that the series should appeal to American audiences. Throughout the production of SUPERCAR, FIREBALL XL5 and STINGRAY, the APF team had become very aware that the sheer cost of producing the various series could not be recouped in the UK alone, and so elements of each series (primarily locations and the characters' accents) had been tailored to take into account American requirements. This policy had proved successful with STINGRAY, where the entire regular cast of WASP heroes were American and only the villainous Titan spoke with a British accent.

So it was that the main characters in INTERNATIONAL RESCUE were the members of the American Tracy family, ex-astronaut Jeff and his five sons, Scott, Virgil, Alan, Gordon and John. However, in an effort to give the new series transatlantic appeal, the Andersons created the characters of Lady Penelope and Parker, British-based International Rescue agents who went on to become the series' most popular characters.

With their completed script in hand, the Andersons returned from Portugal to a wet and miserable Slough. In the shadow of the Mars chocolate factory, Gerry mobilized his hundred full-time staff to the development of the characters, craft and settings that would be required for the new show. Supervising every aspect of the production, he liaised with scriptwriters Alan Pattillo, Dennis Spooner and Alan Fennell on the story ideas, with art director Bob Bell on the set designs, with puppetry supervisors Christine Glanville and Mary Turner on the design of puppet characters, and with special effects supervisor Derek Meddings on the designs of the vehicles and craft.

Foremost among the International Rescue equipment were the five IR craft, each of which was to be particularly suited to a specific rescue task. On previous series, the task of creating the visual appearance of the featured craft had fallen to designer Reg Hill. This time the ambitious nature of the new series forced Hill to concentrate on the production side of the series, which explains why the job of designing the International Rescue vehicles was passed to Derek Meddings. Meddings was given a brief description of the function and purpose of each vehicle in the Andersons' original script for *Trapped in the Sky*, in which the five vehicles were to be featured in the series' title sequence:

RESCUE ONE, the 15,000-m.p.h. rocket piloted by Scott Tracy, comes out of the swimming pool, palm trees swaying and smoke billowing from its tail.

RESCUE TWO, transporter of heavy rescue equipment, is piloted by Virgil Tracy and housed in a hangar behind a cliff face. It is comparatively slow, travelling at a maximum speed of 2,000 m.p.h., and is the heavy-duty arm of the International Rescue fleet.

RESCUE THREE, the spacecraft, awaits pilot Alan Tracy down in the heart of Tracy Island. There is an eruption of sound as three giant engines kick into thunderous life. As they scream louder, the craft begins to shudder and then she is away, roaring through the Round House for the emptiness of space.

RESCUE FOUR, the underwater scout, is carried aboard Rescue Two and piloted by Gordon, who is also Virgil's co-pilot.

RESCUE FIVE, the super-satellite, appears. Its function is to orbit Earth and monitor global communications.

'When we moved on to do THUNDERBIRDS and it just became so huge, it became a whole way of life. We hardly ever left the studios and on many occasions you'd find people sleeping in the theatre at night.

'We had so much work to do. We were working late, we were starting early and there was no point in going home. But it was a wonderful atmosphere. It was like being at school really and we were playing. We were all roughly the same age and there was this wonderful feeling of it all happening.'

KEITH WILSON

After several abortive attempts, which included a blue Rescue Two and a Rescue Three with nose fins, Meddings presented his completed designs to Gerry Anderson and Reg Hill, who gave him immediate approval to start work on building the models. Meddings's team made up specification plans of each craft and these were then sent out to Master Models, a professional model-making company based at a factory on the Feltham Trading Estate in Middlesex, whom Meddings often employed to build the largest-scale models used in the Anderson series.

Just as construction work commenced, word came down from the production office that the title of the series was to change, along with the names of the five Rescue vehicles. During the Second World War, Anderson's older brother, Lionel, had trained as an RAF pilot in Misa, Arizona, learning to fly at Falcon Field. Anderson recalled his brother telling him that a neighbouring field being used by the USAF was called Thunderbird Field. The name excited him and remained at the back of his mind for over twenty years, until he realized that Thunderbird was the perfect name for the International Rescue vehicles. It also made a 'punchier' title for the series and so INTERNATIONAL RESCUE became THUNDERBIRDS.

Script editor Alan Pattillo remembers, 'I was told that the next series was going to be called INTERNATIONAL RESCUE and that there would be a family of sons controlling the craft. Soon afterwards, the name of the series changed to THUNDERBIRDS. I remember saying to Gerry, "Oh, fine," and thinking that it wouldn't catch on.'

Although it was originally envisaged that the 'star' of the show, as far as the hardware was concerned, would be the supersonic reconnaissance rocket Thunderbird 1, the most popular of the five vehicles with the writers and production staff (and, ultimately, the viewers) turned out to be Thunderbird 2, the heavy-duty transporter vehicle which was to carry rescue equipment to the danger zone in a detachable pod. Meddings found the vehicle a challenge to design, but eventually developed an aircraft with a pod that was part and parcel of the craft's fuselage. However, it was not until he turned the vehicle's stub wings to face forwards that he was entirely happy with it. Various sizes of the craft were constructed by Meddings's team, but the large-scale Thunderbird 2 was built entirely from balsa wood by Arthur 'Wag' Evans at Master Models.

The largest Thunderbird vehicle model built for the series was Thunderbird 3, International Rescue's space rocket. Based on a Russian Soyuz rocket, the biggest version of Thunderbird 3 stood 6 feet tall. However, the largest 'regular' model to appear in the series was Lady Penelope's FAB 1 Rolls-Royce. Built to a size that would accommodate the 2-feet-tall

The visual effects team film the Thunderbird 2 launch sequence.

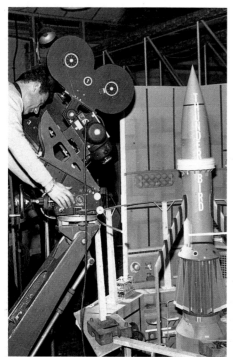

Derek Meddings supervises the filming of the Thunderbird 3 launch sequence.

puppets of Lady Penelope and Parker, the finished model was 7 feet long, built mainly from flat sheets of plywood, with solid wooden tops over each wing. The model cost £2,500, around 10 per cent of the budget for a whole episode. An equivalent model built today would cost in the region of £30,000.

While Thunderbirds 1 to 4 and FAB 1 were being constructed in Feltham, back in Slough Meddings set to work designing the miniature settings of Tracy Island that would be seen in each episode: the exterior sets of the various parts of the Tracy Villa and the hidden hangar bays beneath the island that housed Thunderbirds 1, 2 and 3. Meddings soon realized that his existing small team of experts – including effects director Brian Johncock (now known as Brian Johnson, visual effects supervisor on Anderson's later series SPACE: 1999) and model-makers Eric Backman and Ezra Deering – would be incapable of tackling this complex task in the time available to them, so he set about hiring additional staff to cope with the workload.

The main additions to Meddings's effects department at this time were Roger Dicken, who had been working in the visual effects department at the BBC, and Mike Trim, a designer fresh out of art college. Dicken's first job was to construct the three International Rescue hangars and these were then painted and dirtied down by Trim. The rest of the team built the three exterior Tracy Island settings: the Main House (with foldaway swimming pool), the Cliff House and Thunderbird 2 runway, and the Round House, through which Thunderbird 3 would be launched.

It was while the Round House was being built in the model workshop that Meddings realized that the design of the building was just right for Thunderbird 5, the IR space station. Unable to come up with a convincing design before now, this was the last of the five Thunderbird craft that he created. By adding aerials and transmitters to the Round House, he developed the series' most unusual and effective vehicle, although it was to play only a minor part in the finished programmes.

As the models were completed, Meddings began to film the launch sequences for the craft, as well as other stock shots of the island and the vehicles in flight. This footage would later be incorporated into episodes throughout the series, either as establishing shots or linking sequences between scenes, leaving the effects unit free to concentrate on shooting sequences that would appear only in individual episodes.

Meanwhile, at their office in Edinburgh Avenue, art director Bob Bell and his newly arrived assistants Grenville Nott and Keith Wilson were hard at work designing all the interiors of the craft and the Tracy Island buildings. With the responsibility to design and build (within budget and on time) all the sets that were required for the puppet 'actors' to appear in, Bell found his biggest problem lay in deciding upon the scale of his miniature sets: as the heads and hands of the characters were in a different proportion to the bodies, he had to decide whether to tailor the sets to the size of the heads or the size of the bodies. Through their experience with creating the sets for SUPERCAR, FIREBALL XL5 and STINGRAY, Bell was able effectively to 'mix and match' scales in a manner that allowed for furniture that suited the puppets' bodies and tableware that suited their hands.

Many of the more futuristic sets, such as the cockpits of the Thunderbird vehicles, could be dressed with toothpaste-tube tops, egg-timers and second-hand wireless parts, but the interior of Lady Penelope's stately home, Creighton-Ward Mansion, needed rather more attention to detail. Bell's team of miniature props specialists, Eddie Hunter, Arthur Cripps, Tony Dunsterville and Stewart Osborn, furnished the house with 1/3-scale period chairs based on Georgian and Regency furniture, a rug made from a piece of fur fabric cut in the shape of a polar bear, mock Tudor paintings and small plaster busts cast to the same size as the puppet heads. Eddie Hunter also designed the International Rescue logo which appeared on the Tracy brothers' costumes.

Bell's problem with scale was not as severe as it had been on the earlier AP Films Supermarionation series, because, as associate producer Reg Hill explained at the time, 'For this series the size of the puppet heads has been slightly reduced to give added realism and the figures are now perhaps more "human" and less a caricature.' Certainly, the heads and hands were still out of proportion to the bodies, but not to the extremes of the puppets in SUPERCAR, FIREBALL XL5 and STINGRAY.

Looking back now, many of the series' creators feel that the design of the puppet characters in THUNDERBIRDS was the pinnacle of the Andersons' achievements in Supermarionation: the earlier puppets were too exaggerated and 'cartoonish', and the later true-proportion puppets too stiff and featureless. Puppeteer Wanda Brown (formerly Wanda Webb) recalls, 'The puppets were easier to operate and more enjoyable because they had more character to them, especially Parker and Grandma. Even some of the more normal-looking faces, such as Scott and Jeff, for me had more character than the puppets in the series that came afterwards.'

The thirteen main puppets for THUNDERBIRDS were designed and sculpted by John F. Brown (Jeff Tracy, Virgil Tracy and the Hood), John Blundall (Parker, Kyrano and Grandma Tracy), Christine Glanville (Scott Tracy, Alan Tracy and Tin-Tin) and Mary Turner (Brains, John Tracy, Gordon Tracy and Lady Penelope). The team was given six months to create the characters, basing many of the faces on pictures of actors in *Spotlight*, the actors' directory: heroic lead character Scott Tracy was based on the young Sean Connery, then making his name as James

In the model workshop, Mike Trim completes the detailing on the Round House model.

Bond in *Dr No* (1962), *From Russia with Love* (1963) and *Goldfinger* (1964); IR head Jeff Tracy was modelled on American actor Lorne Greene, who could be seen at the time as the father of five sons in BONANZA; Brains resembled Anthony Perkins, star of *On the Beach* (1959) and *Psycho* (1960); and TB3 pilot Alan Tracy was based on lesser-known American actor Robert Reed – seen then in THE DEFENDERS with E. G. Marshall, he later co-starred in MANNIX.

Virgil Tracy was also indirectly based on Robert Reed. Although he had previously created the 'Phones' Sheridan puppet for STINGRAY, John Brown ran into difficulties in developing Virgil until Christine Glanville suggested that, as they were supposed to be brothers, he might try copying her puppet of Alan Tracy. Virgil emerged as John Brown's version of Alan, suitably different, but close enough to pass as Alan's brother.

Other characters had more eclectic origins: on Sylvia Anderson's suggestion, John Blundall based his most famous creation, Parker, on 1950s music hall comedian Ben Warris, half of Jewel and Warris from the Crazy Gang.

The construction of the puppets was revolutionized for the THUNDERBIRDS team by the development of Bondaglass, a fibreglass cloth and polyester resin, similar to that used to make custom-car bodies. The character's head would be originally sculpted in clay or Plasticine, roughly painted and wigged and then screen-tested for approval by the producers before being made permanent. A silicone rubber mould would be taken from the clay sculpture and this would then be laminated with layers of Bondaglass cloth, each one soaked in the resin. Completely dry within an hour, the beige-coloured fibreglass head shell could then be removed from the mould, sanded down, and fitted with spring-loaded eyeballs and flexible leather mouth parts. A track rod for the eye movement and a solenoid to activate the hinged lower lip were then inserted into the head shell, before it was finally painted and then wigged with mohair.

Furthering a technique pioneered on STINGRAY, each character was given four or five different interchangeable heads which could be altered between takes to simulate changed expressions. In addition to the 'normal'-expression head, there would be a smiling head and a frowning head, and then a special 'blinking' head in which the eye movement was engineered to move up and down (enabling the puppet to blink) rather than from side to side. Each puppet also required a duplicate set of heads as two episodes were to be filmed simultaneously by separate units on the two different puppet stages.

The heads were fitted to plastic bodies which, along with the feet and hands, were provided by an outside contractor. Three different styles of body were produced: a 'large male' for the leading male characters (Jeff, his five sons and the Hood), a 'small' male for the supporting male characters (Parker, Brains and Kyrano) and a 'small female' for Penelope, Tin-Tin and Grandma. The completed puppets weighed between 7 and 9 pounds and stood around 22 inches tall. 'Wired up' with eleven special steel wires drawn at a diameter of 0.005 inches by P. Ormiston & Sons Ltd, they would be tested from a 12-feet-high gantry before being passed to Elizabeth Coleman's wardrobe department for dressing.

Derek Meddings (left) and Brian Johnson (right) film the Thunderbird 2 launch sequence.

Taking into account the conflict betwen design and the practical requirements of the puppet operators, Betty Coleman and her staff of dressmakers avoided man-made fibres in the creation of the costumes, using only silk, cotton or wool, which allowed the puppets freedom of movement in a way that nylon and polyester did not. Just as there were duplicates of the puppet characters, so each costume had to be duplicated to dress them.

Towards the end of summer 1964, all of the pre-production design work was finally completed and the crew geared up to start shooting on THUNDERBIRDS' first episode, *Trapped in the Sky*. Only one job now remained before the cameras could roll: the casting and recording of the puppet characters' voices.

THE VOICE ARTISTS

Peter Dyneley.

The Andersons' brief to the casting agencies they approached was simple: actors and actresses were required who could perform convincing accents from both sides of the Atlantic in a variety of different vocal styles. The series' budget, while large by comparison with other shows being made at the time, simply would not allow for each character to be voiced by a different actor, nor was it necessary. Previous experience on FIREBALL XL5 and STINGRAY had shown that with the right cast of versatile artists, it would be possible to populate THUNDERBIRDS with fewer than ten actors. Australians proved to be extremely desirable, as they were more adept at American accents than their British counterparts, and better with British accents than most American actors.

Peter Dyneley, described by Sylvia Anderson as 'a real Hemingway lookalike, larger than life and great fun', was cast in the series' lead role as Jeff Tracy, head of International Rescue. Born on 13 April 1921 in Hastings, East Sussex, Dyneley was known to Gerry and Sylvia Anderson for his roles in *The Roman Spring of Mrs Stone* (1961), *House of Mystery* (1961) and *Call Me Bwana* (1963), but he had also appeared in numerous television series, including ONE STEP BEYOND, GHOST SQUAD, OUT OF THIS WORLD, MAN OF THE WORLD, CRANE and two episodes of ITC's THE SAINT (*The Careful Terrorist* and *The Bunco Artists*). After THUNDERBIRDS, he went on to guest-star in a third episode of THE SAINT, *To Kill a Saint*, with CAPTAIN SCARLET voice artist Francis Matthews.

Married to ex-Rank starlet Jane Hylton, Dyneley became a close friend of the Andersons, who later cast him in the role of David Poulson in their 1968 live-action feature film *Doppelgänger*. Unfortunately, rushes of Dyneley's scenes in the film with Patrick Wymark (playing Eurosec chief Jason Webb) showed too many similarities between the two actors, so Dyneley's footage was re-shot with Ed Bishop (later Commander Straker in UFO) as Poulson. He also lent his vocal talents to the title character in the Andersons' unscreened Supermarionation pilot THE INVESTIGATOR. One of Peter Dyneley's last roles was in an episode of THE SWEENEY (*Sweet Smell of Succession*). He died on 19 August 1976.

Toronto-born Shane Rimmer had previously appeared in DOCTOR WHO (*The Gunfighters*), Stanley Kubrick's *Dr Strangelove* (his first film role) and the BBC's COMPACT series, and it was his work in the latter that inspired Gerry and Sylvia Anderson to cast him as the voice of Scott Tracy. As he remembers, 'I was doing variety as a solo singer at the City Varieties in Leeds when my wife called me and said somebody called Sylvia Anderson had been on the phone and wanted to know if I wanted to test for a part in this television puppet series. Well, I didn't really

Shane Rimmer.

want to do it because it's a hell of a way down from Leeds and there was a show every night anyway. But I did come down, put a track down and didn't think any more about it. Then about two weeks later, I got a call saying, "Do you want the part of Scott Tracy?"'

STINGRAY cast members Ray Barrett and David Graham had proved their versatility in numerous roles during the run of the undersea adventure series and were the first voice artists hired for THUNDERBIRDS. Australian actor Ray Barrett was a former 1950s radio soap opera star who came to Britain in the 1960s. He had been seen in DOCTOR WHO (*The Rescue*), THE SAINT (*The Loving Brothers*), OUT OF THIS WORLD and THE MAN IN ROOM 17, and had a regular role as Peter Clarke in GS5, but it was Barrett's experience in radio, where he often had to play British and American characters, that had landed him the roles of Sam Shore and Titan in STINGRAY.

For THUNDERBIRDS, Barrett provided the voices for not only the regular characters John Tracy and the Hood, but also numerous 'guest' puppet characters. 'I remember times when I was playing three characters and they were all talking to one another. I said, "Just keep the tape going" and I changed voices as I went along, talking to myself! Some of the actors, mainly the English actors, weren't used to those quick radio days. Some of them had to stop and sort of change view for the different voice.'

Left: David Graham.
Right: Ray Barratt.

'Whether with children or with puppets, you have to act with a basic reality. It doesn't matter how extravagant or eccentric the characters are.

'The series were aimed at children but the adults enjoyed them as well. In fact, the whole genre seems to pass down from father to son and so on. It all has to be believable and you can't go over the top for the sake of it. Certainly that was Gerry's thought process, as well as that of the actors.'

DAVID GRAHAM

One English actor who had no trouble whatsoever with quick voice changes or American accents was David Graham, who first came into contact with Gerry Anderson in 1957 while filming an episode of MARTIN KANE, PRIVATE INVESTIGATOR which Anderson was directing at Elstree Studios. 'Although he happened to be directing this cops and robbers thing, his background was on the technical side of the business, and his mind was very set on puppet film-making,' Graham remembers. 'When I heard that, I pricked up my ears and told him that I wasn't bad on accents and voices. When he got under way on FOUR FEATHER FALLS, he was good enough to contact me and it all started.'

After FOUR FEATHER FALLS, Graham went on to voice characters in SUPERCAR, FIREBALL XL5 and STINGRAY. Concurrently, he provided voices for Daleks in DOCTOR WHO and made an on-screen appearance in the series as a barman in *The Gunfighters* with THUNDERBIRDS co-star Shane Rimmer.

Born in England but trained as an actor in New York, Graham used his vocal abilities to provide voices for no fewer than four of the THUNDERBIRDS regular characters: Brains, Parker, Gordon Tracy and Kyrano – two Americans, a Cockney and an Asian. 'When THUNDERBIRDS came along, I'd been with Gerry for so long that I think he already had me down for Parker and the others. Then, during the recordings, Ray and I would split up most of the villains between us.'

When it came to casting Lady Penelope Creighton-Ward, Gerry Anderson had only one actress in mind: Fenella Fielding, an Anglo-Romanian actress with a cool and sultry delivery who had made her name in William Castle's *The Old Dark House* (1963). However, Sylvia Anderson wanted to play the part herself, despite Gerry's concerns that a professional actress was needed. She had already voiced young Jimmy Gibson in SUPERCAR and Dr Venus in FIREBALL XL5, but it was Marina in STINGRAY that gave her the opportunity to play a refined English accent that was not far removed from her natural speaking voice. Although Marina was mute, she was voiced by Sylvia on two occasions: in the dream episode *Raptures of the Deep* and on the Century 21 mini-album 'Marina Speaks'. Both illustrate similarities with the voice she was later to use for Lady Penelope, which she described as a cross between Fenella Fielding and Joan Greenwood.

Sylvia Anderson shared all the additional guest female voices for THUNDERBIRDS with actress Christine Finn, who lent her vocal talents to the series as Tin-Tin Kyrano and Grandma Tracy. Christine was best known at the time for her role as Barbara Judd in the 1959 BBC serial QUATERMASS AND THE PIT and later guested in episodes of GIDEON'S WAY (*The 'V' Men*) and ADAM ADAMANT LIVES! (*Death by Appointment*).

The only American actor in the cast was David Holliday, who first came to London when he landed a role in the original European tour of *West Side Story*. Appearing extensively on the British stage in the early 1960s in productions of *Who's Afraid of Virginia Woolf?*, *The Rainmaker*, *The Wayward Way* and Noël Coward's *No Strings*, Holliday was spotted by Sylvia Anderson and cast as Thunderbird 2 pilot Virgil Tracy.

Canadian Matt Zimmerman joined the cast very late in the day, after recording had already been completed for the series' first episode, *Trapped in the Sky*. 'A friend of mine, David Holliday, had already been cast as Virgil and they were having great difficulty casting the part of Alan as they wanted a certain sound for him, being the youngest brother. David, who is a bit older than I am, told them that he had this friend, me, who would be great. At the time I was doing a show in the West End called *High Spirits*. David phoned me up and told me to contact Sylvia Anderson and I arranged an appointment. I went out to Slough, where the studios were, and when I walked in the model of Alan Tracy was on the table. Sylvia said, "Don't speak! Don't say a word! My God, you've got a dimple on your chin just like Alan! In fact, if you were blond and blue-eyed you would look very much like him!" So then she let me speak and she said, "That's his voice!" So I got the job.'

The final member of the cast for the first season of THUNDERBIRDS received no on-screen credit for his role. Born in 1914, John Tate was a well-known and highly respected personality among the acting fraternity both in England and in his native Australia. He was probably best known for his leading role in the 1950s Australian soap DYNASTY, but made a career for himself in England in the 1960s with appearances on television in series such as THE SAINT, DANGER MAN, MAN OF THE WORLD, THE BARON, THE AVENGERS, THE CHAMPIONS, DEPARTMENT S, STRANGE REPORT, THE TROUBLESHOOTERS and THE POWER GAME. He also appeared in the feature films *On the Beach* (1959), *The Day of the Triffids* (1962) and *It's All Happening* (1963).

Although Tate did not voice any of the regular characters in THUNDERBIRDS, he made an important contribution to the series as various guest characters such as Solarnaut Camp in *Sun Probe* and Blackmer in *Attack of the Alligators!*. His son Nick later starred for Gerry Anderson as Eagle pilot Alan Carter in SPACE: 1999 and Captain Harry Masters in THE DAY AFTER TOMORROW (*Into Infinity*). Tate died at his home on the Isle of Wight in March 1979.

The pre-recording of the dialogue for each episode of THUNDERBIRDS took place at AP Films' own small sound studio in Slough. As most of the actors involved were committed to theatre and television during the week, recording sessions were scheduled for Sundays, with the cast performing as many as three half-hour episodes at any one session.

Matt Zimmerman recalls, 'Originally we used a studio in Slough which was located in Gerry and Sylvia's offices. It was like a living room with couches in and the microphones were hung above them. It was a very small area. We all had to double up and do lots of other voices, and we had to change our voices as much as we could. I remember Ray Barrett had to play a duchess in *The Duchess Assignment*. He would always find something funny and get the giggles during the recordings and he was at his worst during that episode. I played Ned Cook in *Terror in New York City*, a lovely character who was the host of a television show. He had a really thick accent and it was great fun to do. I also loved doing *Move – and You're Dead*, stuck up on that bridge with Grandma, talking into my watch.

'The other one that sticks in my mind for some reason is *The Uninvited*, where I'm playing a crook or a gangster and I'm caught in a pyramid and go crazy. I had to yell and scream, "Hahaha! You won't take me alive, Tracy!" We had a lot of fun doing that one. We also had to make crowd noises and provide screaming and yelling. We laughed an awful lot. Sometimes we had to stop and pull ourselves together because we were getting hysterical.

Matt Zimmerman.

The late David Holliday, who provided the voice of Virgil Tracy for the first twenty-six episodes.

Jeremy Wilkin, the voice of Virgil Tracy in the last six episodes and the two feature films.

'We would read the scripts through on the Sunday morning and allocate the parts so that we didn't end up talking to ourselves too much. Obviously, we all had our main characters to play as well. Then, after lunch, we would begin the recordings in the afternoon, just reading from the scripts. There was never any necessity to memorize anything.

'The sessions were supervised by Gerry and Alan Pattillo, and Sylvia had a lot to do with it as well. I always felt that Gerry was like a rock. He used to smoke a cigar a lot in those days and he would sit in with us on read-throughs. Then, when it was time to record he would disappear into the control room. I can still picture him sat with his big cigar behind the mixing desk.'

Once the dialogue was recorded, it had to be edited to remove any pauses (primarily where one actor was playing two different characters in a scene) and to insert re-takes to cover mistakes. This was done at the Gate Recording Theatre by C. H. W. Productions, who would cut the dialogue track down to a suitable length for filming and return it to the studios on 1/4-inch master sound tape. A special duplicate of this tape would be played back during filming, and through a resistance-capacity network pulses would be taken off the tape to operate the solenoids in the head of each puppet figure, controlling the lip mechanism so that the lips moved in perfect sync with the recorded sound.

As previously mentioned, this was Supermarionation, a system devised by Anderson and his technical team for FOUR FEATHER FALLS and developed for AP Films by two Midlands concerns long experienced in recording and electronic work. Technical help was given by R. T. C. Wright and Company Ltd of Perry Barr and the Hollick and Taylor Recording Company Ltd of Handsworth Wood, Birmingham. Hollick and Taylor built the prototype of a control system to Anderson's specifications and R. T. C. Wright gave invaluable aid in subsequent lip-sync development.

During filming on THUNDERBIRDS, the control dupe tape was played back in the studios on modified EMI TR-90s, the circuitry being completed through what was known around the studio as a 'natterer', a device that acted as an electronic relay for the pulses taken from the tape, providing varying currents to operate the solenoids in the puppets' heads. Each replay-head winding was connected to a network with diodes operating relays which put a 50-volt DC supply on to parallel copper wires running along the puppeteers' gantry.

By this method, up to four figures could be made to talk at once, all from the same tape. Sound engineers Maurice Askew and John Taylor had experimented with automatic control tracks to pinpoint each individual figure and also used ultrasonic switching with some success, but it was found that the most practical system was to route the correct 'natter' pulses to the appropriate character by means of four quick-action switches on the lip-sync console.

Christine Finn.

Since the original development of the Supermarionation lip-sync system, Askew had furthered the development of a retention scheme, adding more realism to the puppets' lip movements by means of a third resistance-capacity network fed off the tape's sensitivity level, so that the lower-jaw solenoid opened only a little way for the narrow sounds (such as 'he' and 'me') but much wider for the open, long-sustained vowels (like 'oh' and 'ah').

Originally, all the lip-sync equipment was housed in a booth behind a sound-proof screen overlooking the main stages, but for THUNDERBIRDS it was decided to move each 'natterer' out on to the floor, giving the director more immediate control over dialogue replay.

With the dialogue recorded and edited for the first episode, *Trapped in the Sky*, everything was set to begin filming on the puppet stages at the AP Films Studios. Little did the production team know, however, that just around the corner was looming a problem of nightmare proportions. The successful solution to this problem was to earn THUNDERBIRDS a place in television history.

THE HALF-HOUR EPISODES

Derek Meddings had completed work on stock shots of the Thunderbird vehicles and main settings over the summer of 1964, and as summer turned to autumn he and his crew turned to shooting effects specifically for the series' opening episode, *Trapped in the Sky*. The concept for the rescue in this first episode was inspired by Gerry Anderson's early experiences as a radio telephone operator for air traffic control at RAF Manston.

'I remember seeing an aircraft coming in to land with its wheels still up. Luckily it was warned off just as it was about to touch down. I will also never forget seeing a Mosquito aircraft that was giving an aerobatics display crashing and blowing up. Years later, when we were working on pre-production for THUNDERBIRDS, I recalled those two incidents and together they helped me form the basic idea for the first episode.'

Trapped in the Sky involved a plot by the evil Hood to draw International Rescue to the scene of a disaster that he had engineered himself, enabling him to photograph the Thunderbird vehicles as they arrived on the scene. To this end, the Hood attached a bomb to the undercarriage of the atomic-powered Fireflash aircraft on its maiden flight from London to

Thunderbird 2 is flown in front of the 'rolling sky'.

'Derek Meddings was a great friend of mine and, because he didn't live far from me, he used to bring me to work and we were late every single day, but I was the one who used to get into trouble. Reg Hill was always taking me into the office and telling me off for being late, but it was never my fault!

'I happen to think that Derek was one of the greatest special effects influences not only in this country, but around the world. If you look at his career, he did things that had never been done before. He made miniature special effects legitimate. When he got his Oscar for Superman: The Movie that was really something. I was so happy, I cannot tell you. A friend of mine had actually got an Oscar for his work on Superman.

'He saved the film industry to a degree. Derek actually made it OK for people to think about doing shots with models. When you look at his work on the Bond films, you never know which shots are models and which shots are real, he was so good at it. He really was the best.'

KEITH WILSON

Left to right: Mobile Elevator Cars are dispatched from Thunderbird 2 Pod 3 in Trapped in the Sky.

Tokyo, forcing the plane to return to London Airport, where it would be assisted in its landing by International Rescue using a trio of High-speed Mobile Elevator Cars.

Meddings realized that to shoot the climax of the episode with the landing of the Fireflash at London Airport he was faced with the problem of building a runway set long enough to accommodate the sequence in the limited amount of studio space available. His solution was a pioneering technique: three loops of canvas running around rollers powered by electric motors, each loop dressed to represent a different element in the shot: foreground, runway and background.

Meddings had already developed a 'rolling sky' for STINGRAY, used for shooting sequences of vehicles in flight. This was a similar loop of canvas painted with a sky backdrop running around two rollers so that a model hung in front of it would create the illusion that it was moving through the sky, while remaining stationary in front of the camera. The 'rolling sky' was positioned behind the 'rolling road' apparatus and all four rollers would then be run at different relative speeds to create the effect of the static camera moving at high speed along an infinitely long road. By adjusting the angle of the foreground roller and the relative positions of the 'rolling sky' and the camera, Meddings was able to film a variety of shots from different angles.

The Mobile Elevator Cars in this sequence were radio-controlled models placed on the 4-feet-wide 'rolling road' section. A happy accident with one of the cars added unexpected tension to the completed episode when, during filming of the Fireflash about to land on the three Elevator Cars, the car beneath the model craft's port wing suddenly went out of control and shot off the side of the set. Viewing the rushes the next day, Meddings was so taken with the 'spoilt' footage that he encouraged Anderson to write the scene into the sequence and filmed spectacular additional footage of the Elevator Car crashing into a stationary aircraft at the side of the runway.

Meanwhile, over on the puppet shooting stages, principal photography began using Arriflex cameras with 35mm Eastman Kodak stock. On the miniature sets, the biggest problem for director of photography John Read was achieving depth of focus.

'Our biggest sets were no more than 10 feet deep and with standard lenses this brought depth-of-focus troubles, so the only solution was to stop down and illuminate at high level. As is well known in camera work, the closer one has to get, the greater the depth of focus you need to hold for a certain distance. Our cameras were usually worked close down to the floor for the small stages and the average point of focus was around 5 feet 6 inches. Zoom lenses were of no material help, although we did continually experiment with zooms.'

Filming that first episode became a gruelling and monumental task for the production team under the guidance of director Alan Pattillo. He remembers, 'Making that first episode was not easy. There were lots of technical problems and it took ages to shoot the various scenes showing how the pilots reach their craft. We got very weary with it but in the end, when we all saw the finished film, the way Gerry had planned and edited it with the editors, we all agreed it was well worth it.'

During filming, the puppets were controlled from a bridge walkway 3 feet wide and 30 feet long, supported some 12 feet above the set on a gantry that could be easily moved about on the smooth concrete floors of the studio. From here, the puppeteers were able to watch their puppets' performance on a 23-inch CCTV monitor which displayed the image seen through the viewfinder of the film camera via an all-transistor Pye Lynx camera coupled to it. This image was also displayed on other monitors around the studio floor and in the producer's offices, enabling everyone to see each scene as it was filmed. As the puppeteers were used to practising their actions in a mirror, they were more accustomed to piloting themselves from reversed

Filming Scott's return from Thunderbird 3 in **The Uninvited.**

action, so the gantry monitor was switched to scan-reversal to give them a mirror effect on the TV screen.

Reg Hill explained at the time how important CCTV was in the studios. 'Use of CCTV monitoring has proved essential. The lighting cameraman can see what part of the set is being shot without needing to get down and monopolize the viewfinder. Further, he can light without the need to look through the camera. Apart from mirror work, the puppeteers could see only the tops of the characters' heads were it not for CCTV. The eye movements are so important and viewing on a 23-inch monitor helps to produce a sympathetic and artistic result.'

A normal puppet unit would include the director, camera crew, assistant director, lip-sync operator, three set artists for dressing the sets, three electricians, two bridge puppeteers operating the puppets from the gantry and a floor puppeteer. It was the floor puppeteer's job to check continuity, adjust the angle of the puppets to camera, spray the puppet wires to make them invisible to camera by matching the background colours with powder paint in a puffer and, if necessary, to steady the puppet from out of shot.

From the start of filming on FIREBALL XL5, the Anderson productions had employed two self-contained puppet units working simultaneously on separate episodes. In the small studio at Ipswich Road, it had been possible for the team to utilize only two puppet gantries – one large, one small – on a single soundstage, with episode production staggered so that at the end of any given week, one episode was being completed while the other was half-way through. The move to the larger premises at Stirling Road, with two soundstages for the puppet units, enabled both units to shoot separate episodes simultaneously right from the start of filming on STINGRAY, and this practice was carried through on to THUNDERBIRDS. In this way, it was possible for principal photography on two episodes to be completed in two working weeks of five and a half days (Monday to Friday plus Saturday morning), the equivalent of one episode per week in the can.

With duplicate puppets of each of the thirteen regular characters, each crew could work with their own cast of puppets entirely independently of the other. Unfortunately, it was virtually impossible for the sculptors to create truly identical sets of puppets and there were minor differences between the characters on each soundstage. Puppeteer Wanda Brown recalls, 'There

A floor puppeteer prepares Lady Penelope for a scene in Trapped in the Sky.

'The first one I directed came along at the time my wife was due to have our first baby. I knew that the episode was looming and the baby was too. I was dreading the birth coming at the same time and, of course, that is exactly what happened.

'I remember that she went into labour and we were at the hospital and it was getting close to 8.00 a.m. I was due on the stage at about 8.30 a.m. and I was saying to her, "Come on, get on with it! I've got my first episode to direct. Please get on with it!"

'In the end, I had to go to the studio, and it didn't go down too well with the wife.'

DAVID LANE

were variations in the faces between unit one and unit two. They always used the best heads on the first episode, so whichever unit got the first film got the best puppets for picture three, picture five, picture seven and so on.'

Director of photography John Read split his time between the episodes in a supervisory capacity, but left the on-set decisions to his two lighting cameramen, former STINGRAY camera operators Paddy Seale and Julien Lugrin. Seale's team comprised camera operator Alan Perry and a trio of puppeteers supervised by Christine Glanville, while Julien Lugrin's group included camera operator Geoff Meldrum and a puppetry team supervised by Mary Turner. Directors were assigned to each unit on a rotational basis, with Alan Pattillo and David Elliott handling the first pair of episodes (*Trapped in the Sky* and *Terror in New York City*), while David Lane and Desmond Saunders prepared the next pair (*End of the Road* and *Pit of Peril*).

Three of the four directors were old hands with the techniques of Supermarionation: Alan Pattillo and David Elliott were the most experienced, having previously directed episodes of FOUR FEATHER FALLS, SUPERCAR, FIREBALL XL5 and STINGRAY, while Des Saunders had joined the AP Films team as a director on the last of these. Former editor David Lane, however, made his directorial debut on THUNDERBIRDS and, at twenty-four, was the youngest director working for the studio. He quickly proved his ability and was later entrusted to direct both THUNDERBIRDS feature films.

Writers Alan Fennell and Dennis Spooner were invited to prepare scripts for the series based on the format outlined in Gerry and Sylvia Anderson's script of *Trapped in the Sky*. Fennell and Spooner were reliable Supermarionation writers who had previously written for FIREBALL XL5 and STINGRAY. Between them, they had scripted thirty-six of the thirty-nine episodes of STINGRAY, so they immediately grasped the dynamics of the new series and quickly turned in two episodes apiece.

Terror in New York City (filmed with the working title *Terror of New York*) was inspired by a story that Anderson had seen in a newspaper. 'I read that a large store in Japan was in the way of a big road-widening scheme, but because of its huge value as a going concern it was not demolished but jacked up and moved inch by inch to a new site. The movement of the store was so slow that customers continued to shop there throughout the operation.' In Fennell's script, the store became the Empire State Building in New York, being moved to allow for redevelopment of the site and ultimately causing the collapse of the surrounding area.

Both writers embraced the theme of incredible technology in a developing world as a springboard to disaster. Spooner's first script for the series, *End of the Road*, featured Eddie Houseman, an engineer for a road construction firm, trapped on a crumbling mountain ledge in a truck full of explosives. His second, *Day of Disaster*, told of a manned probe rocket proving too heavy to be transported across a suspension bridge and subsequently falling into a river, entombing the astronauts on the river bed. Similarly, Fennell's second episode, *Pit of Peril*, featured a massive US Army Sidewinder vehicle collapsing into disused mine-workings, trapping the three-man crew in a blazing pit.

As the scripts for these episodes arrived on Derek Meddings's desk, he realized that the amount of effects work was more than he could cope with on his own, so he decided to set up a second visual effects unit with its own riggers, electricians and camera crew, led by the new second unit lighting cameraman Harry Oakes, all under the control of Brian Johnson. This unit enabled Meddings's assistants (including Shaun Whittacker-Cooke and Ian Scoones, who had both come to AP Films via Hammer effects supremo Les Bowie) to take a more active role and responsibility for their effects, as well as easing the pressure on the main effects unit.

With the introduction of the new unit, Meddings found himself with less time to devote to the creation of new vehicles and craft so Mike Trim took it upon himself to design two Recovery Vehicles that were required for *Pit of Peril*. Meddings was so impressed with the work that Trim was entrusted with designing the bulk of the rescue vehicles and guest aircraft in the later episodes, including the Domo vehicle for *The Duchess Assignment* and the Skythrust for *Alias Mr. Hackenbacker*.

Pit of Peril also introduced the most popular pod vehicle of all, the Mole, a collaborative design by Meddings and Ray Brown, a model-maker who had joined the team from Master Models. As the model unit didn't have a lathe, Brown had to create the Mole's drill bit by turning a piece of wood by hand and then adding a metal screw thread. A motor fitted inside the model turned the bit, but the tracks on the vehicle were left loose so that it could be simply pulled across the model sets. This was standard practice for many of the pod vehicles such as the aforementioned Recovery Vehicles. If wheel-spin was required, a power drill was connected to one of the axles with a flexible link. For added effect, Meddings wanted the vehicles to give off a lot of smoke and dust, and at first he experimented with titanium tetrachloride (TTC), a chemical solution which turns to smoke on contact with the air. Unfortunately, this solution tended to corrode the metal and plastic attachments on the models, so he introduced Jetex pellets, small chemical tablets which produced a powerful jet of air. One of these pellets attached to the underside of a vehicle being pulled across a set covered in a layer of cement powder created the convincing effect of the vehicle throwing up a dust trail.

The other main vehicle to appear in *Pit of Peril* was the Sidewinder itself, a US Army all-terrain vehicle that was seen falling into the remains of an open-cast mine that had been used as a military equipment dump after the Second World War. A four-legged vehicle with crab-like arms, the design was the suggestion of episode director Desmond Saunders and became a nightmare for Meddings to film. With the model suspended on wires, the legs were moved from beneath the model set by an elaborate scissor mechanism. Constructed from wood and card, each of the vehicle's arms was created by threading together fourteen small cake tins.

As filming progressed through October, director Alan Pattillo took on an additional role as the series' script editor. This new position at AP Films was created to ease the burden on producer Anderson, who had previously taken on all the responsibilities for hiring writers, developing plots and re-writing scripts where necessary. As script editor, Pattillo worked very closely with Gerry Anderson, who had overall script supervision, but the day-to-day commissioning and development of scripts were down to him. He recalls, 'Everything mushroomed for Gerry so much that he wanted someone to take charge of all the scripts and deal with the other writers too. So, about two months after we filmed the pilot, I became the series script editor. I would discuss storylines with Gerry and the required special effects with Derek Meddings.'

After a series of straightforward rescue stories, Pattillo was keen to develop the regular characters and set the ball rolling with a script of his own. *The Perils of Penelope* greatly expanded on the role of International Rescue's London agent, Lady Penelope Creighton-Ward, who had been seen only briefly at the end of *Trapped in the Sky*. 'In a way, the male characters were so dull. All they had to do was pilot the craft and say, "Left, left three degrees," or "Opening Pod 3." Penelope was much more flexible. You felt that she lived a life apart from International Rescue. She wasn't living on this island in this practically all-male society. We tended to develop her more. The story of *The Perils of Penelope* was a take-off of the silent movie *The Perils of*

Gerry and Sylvia Anderson with Lady Penelope.

Puppeteers working on a gantry above the Tracy Lounge set.

Pauline, starring Pearl White, who specialized in making films where she was always in danger.'

Filming continued throughout November while editing was completed on *Trapped in the Sky* and, on 8 December, music maestro Barry Gray recorded the theme and incidentals for the episode with a thirty-piece orchestra at the Olympic Studio in Barnes. With Christmas just around the corner, the finished pilot episode was shown to Lew Grade.

Gerry Anderson remembers, 'Shooting a filmed television series is a huge operation and by the time we had completed the first episode, edited it and struck a print we were already starting episode nine back in the studio, with ten other scripts lined up. We arranged a screening of the first episode, *Trapped in the Sky*, for Lew in London. I rushed down to town and sat there quaking in my boots while Lew watched the show, and at the end he jumped up shouting, "Fantastic, absolutely fantastic! This isn't a television series – this is a feature film! You've got to make this as an hour!"

'So I had to go back to the studio and somehow turn a series of half-hour shows into hour-long episodes. Everything had been geared towards the twenty-five-minute format and we had to continue shooting half-hour episodes until we could introduce the new regime and start producing hour-long episodes. We then went back and shot extra footage which we added to the half-hour shows to convert them to run fifty minutes. It was a terrifying ordeal, but I'm glad we did it, because it made the series much bigger and much more important. But it was still a very, very difficult job.'

The news came as something of an unpleasant surprise to the production personnel over the Christmas break. Alan Pattillo recalls, 'I was staying with my parents in Scotland over Christmas 1964 when Gerry telephoned and said, "Guess what? We're going to make them into an hour or so, so while you're up there keep thinking how you're going to enlarge the scripts to make them longer."'

New writer Tony Barwick was brought in to help Anderson and Pattillo to write the extra scenes. In an interview completed in 1986, he spoke about his work on the series: 'My job, at first, was to edit and expand quite a lot of the stories, although the original writers' names stayed on the credits. Because most of the films had already been shot, I just supplied new material to pad them out. The format was already there, obviously, so usually it would mean sitting around and watching the films and then working out some kind of subplot. Often you'd find that they had an extra ten minutes here and there anyway, because they'd over-shot, so you'd then have to work that into the story, somehow.

'Each case was different. I can't really remember any specific plots but, for example, five guys are trapped down the deepest coal mine and International Rescue have to dig down and get them out. Now that is really your half-hour story. You then have to go away and invent a sub-story – like, on the way there, something happens and it's now a race against time, or you could put in another hurdle. For instance, in the half-hour story they could dig down, find rock, burrow through that and they're there. In the hour-long story they dig down, burrow through the rock and they suddenly realize it's flooding. That sort of thing.'

For the pilot episode, a sequence was added which showed an attempt to winch a man into the landing gear of the Fireflash from a TX 204 Target-carrying Aircraft. Scenes with Thunderbird 1 chasing NTBS reporter Ned Cook after a dramatic rescue at an oil refinery were added to the start of *Terror in New York City*, and *Pit of Peril* was filled out with the Army's attempts to attach a line to the Sidewinder. In the main, however, the extra time in these episodes was made up with character development via additional dialogue between the main characters and the supporting cast, fleshing out the puppets with genuine personalities. This proved very effective in episodes such as *End of the Road*, where it was now possible to establish Eddie Houseman as an old flame of Tin-Tin.

Anderson recalls, 'I used to write bits and pieces and Tony Barwick used to write stuff. We worked very much as a team. The irony, though, was that the episodes were bumped up into one-hour shows and then after we'd shot the thirty-two episodes we were asked to slice them down again into sixty-four half-hours!'

'The characters were developed as the series progressed and in turn the voices became more refined. It was a learning curve for all of us. Brains's stutter came into being because it seems that with clever people the mind works faster than the mouth can speak.'

DAVID GRAHAM

SEASON ONE

The early months of 1965 proved to be a period of organized chaos for the AP Films team. Additional filming was now required to turn the already completed twenty-five-minute episodes into fifty-minute programmes, while new episodes, already prepared as half-hour shows, began shooting. New material had to be written, not only for the completed episodes but also for the new ones in production and some dozen or so additional scripts already prepared in the half-hour format.

As luck would have it, one of the new episodes, *Operation Crash-Dive*, had been conceived as a sequel to the pilot episode and involved many of the same guest characters and sets, so it therefore made sense to shoot the new footage for *Trapped in the Sky* while *Operation Crash-Dive* was in production. Similarly, new footage for *The Perils of Penelope* could be filmed back-to-back with *Sun Probe*, enabling the post-production processes to begin in earnest so as to complete *Trapped in the Sky* and *The Perils of Penelope* as the first two episodes.

A page from the script of **Operation Crash-Dive,** *written by Martin Crump.*

Over the coming months, the crew worked steadily through the additional sequences required for the remaining half-hour shows, fitting in sequences where they could alongside shots for the new episodes. Gerry Anderson credits the ultimate success of this organizational nightmare to the production skills of Reg Hill, the series' associate producer and deputy managing director of AP Films.

An artist who worked in advertising at Odhams Press before wartime service in the RAF, Hill was encouraged to join the film industry after the war by a friend from his time at Odhams. For twelve years, he worked on films for the Army at National Interest Picture Productions, instructional films that required a large amount of model work and animation, and it was here that he met cameraman John Read. Their subsequent association with Gerry Anderson and Arthur Provis at Polytechnic Films led both men to join AP Films after the collapse of Polytechnic. Initially, Hill was responsible purely for design and art direction, but by the time filming began on THUNDERBIRDS he had moved on to the executive side of production.

Gerry Anderson recalls, 'As the years rolled by, Reg was at the forefront of all the development work we undertook. He played a key part in the development of the sophisticated puppets that were used when we introduced Supermarionation. He designed the aquariums and model sets that enabled us to film STINGRAY under the sea without the models ever getting wet. He also designed the water tanks that were used for shots where Stingray was to travel on the surface. These tanks had to be strong enough to contain a huge amount of water, and light enough to be wheeled on and off the stages quickly. Whenever there was a technical problem to be solved, Reg was always there with the answer. He was a perfectionist and whatever he did, he did brilliantly.

'In the early days, the special effects department had to repaint the entire scenic backing every time they changed from a scene that required a night sky to one that required a day sky, and vice versa. Reg

A Carrier Aircraft on show at the London Air Display in **The Duchess Assignment.**

Brian Johnson (right) and the visual effects crew filming a scene for **The Man from MI.5.**

overcame this problem by building a tower above the studio roof which allowed the special effects technicians to fly all the backings overhead and then lower whichever one they wanted to use in a matter of minutes instead of the hours it used to take them to repaint the backings. Multiply these examples by a hundred and you will begin to have some idea of Reg's talents and the huge contribution he made to our films.

'This very unusual combination of engineer, artist, art director, model-maker and photographer enabled him to support our production line in many ways. Although it isn't widely known, Reg played an important part in the setting up and running of our special effects department, which was headed by Derek Meddings. An outstanding artist, Reg was able to paint with photo-realism. His storyboards were the finest I have ever seen. One would have to write a book to list all the things Reg did for the company. Unfortunately, his invaluable contribution was mainly made behind the scenes and he never received the recognition he deserved.

'Reg and I were firm friends and it was a matter of great regret when he told me towards the end of the second series of SPACE: 1999 that he was going to resign from the company. I tried to get him to stay on, but once Reg made up his mind about something, nothing would change it. He said to me as he was leaving, and I remember it so well, "I'm very happy with Lilly [his wife] and I'm going to live as long as possible to be with her as long as possible." And that's exactly what he did.

'I am sure there are many, many people in the industry – and especially those who worked for AP Films and Century 21 – who would wish to join me when I say that Reg was a true gentleman who made a huge contribution to all the films we made together.'

Lew Grade expanded the series' budget to £40,000 per episode, and the extra money enabled Derek Meddings and his crew to create more elaborate effects sequences than ever before. Even two model units proved insufficient to handle the programme's effects requirements, however, so Meddings set up a third unit to handle the flying sequences, under the supervision of Peter Wragg. This unit was based in a separate building on the Slough Trading Estate because space in the studio was at a premium.

As Peter Wragg recalls, 'It was basically a flying unit, for all the straight flying shots that didn't require sets and landscapes – the air-to-air flying shots. That was all down to a timescale in order to get the episodes finished so that they could be dubbed and meet their transmission dates. One effects unit would be working on one episode, another effects unit would be working on another episode and I would be doing straight flying shots for both episodes. Gerry used to expect five shots a day, so you knew what you were trying to achieve, but sometimes that was totally impossible. If you had a landscape with one shot and then you had to build a totally new landscape for the next sequence, you might only get one shot in that day.

'Flying a model convincingly on wires was a devil of a job. You're standing on the edge of a plank, hovering over the edge of a set, holding something out at arm's length. There was quite a sense of balance that you had to have and it was a case of shifting your weight from one foot to another without going up and down, while keeping your hand and body on the same plane. If you got a slight twitch in the hand, it was accentuated on the model below, so you got an enormous lurch of the model. We used to fire the rockets by putting current down the tungsten wires, so you could actually fly the model in, and then at a given point the rockets would start. You had to know that the rockets were going to start, because otherwise the shock and crack of the rockets starting might make you jump and the model would do a horrendous lurch.'

Revamping the half-hour episodes into hour-long episodes ultimately took over seven months and spring had turned to summer before the newly edited episodes were handed over to composer Barry Gray for scoring. Reg Hill explained to *Television Mail* at the time why editing

'There was a really awful time when we were re-doing bits to fill out the half-hour episodes as well as shooting the new hour-long ones, and I was just in the studios constantly. I did, I think, three episodes without a break and I was feeling a bit rough. I was just whacked. It was good groundwork for me in the industry but, nonetheless, I was preparing one episode, shooting another, looking over the "filler" stuff, and in the end I was exhausted. I was tearing about from stage to stage, going over to the cutting rooms and it was just manic.

'I was intent on all the "padding" looking all right and matching up to the original half-hour stuff. When I'd finished this particularly stressful period I was just hanging in pieces.

'Gerry called me in to see him and said, "We really appreciate all the extra work you've done and I'm sending you on a holiday." It was a lovely gesture and Gerry paid for my wife and myself to go on a cruise to Africa.'
DAVID LANE

the puppet series took longer than with a conventional live-action series, even with six cutting rooms in full-time use at the AP Films Studios: 'We must do three or four times the amount of cutting as in live action. This is made necessary, for instance, by the fact that you cannot hold the interest of a scene for more than a few seconds since a puppet's facial expression cannot be altered – except by cutting, of course, to a different strip, shot when the puppet is fitted with a different head. In live action, you can hold a scene for an appreciable time, getting continuity of dramatic effect by an actor's changing expression, or perhaps by moving from a mid-shot to a close-up of the actor's hand. With puppets this can also be done, but it involves cutting – cutting, in many cases, from a close-up of the puppet's head to a live-action shot of a hand.'

Eventually, filming on THUNDERBIRDS settled back into a routine of sorts, with just two hour-long episodes being shot simultaneously, but as the crew was now shooting twice as much footage per episode, it was unreasonable to expect each pair of episodes to complete principal photography within the two-week turnaround previously allotted for the half-hour episodes, so the schedule was expanded to allow four weeks of shooting on each pair of episodes – meaning two completed episodes per month.

This in itself created further pressures for the production team, as filming and post-production work on each episode came perilously closer and closer to the scheduled broadcast premiere date: Thursday 30 September 1965. Early in August, Barry Gray recorded 'Flying High', a song performed by Gary Miller, for THUNDERBIRDS' end-title sequence, but he was unhappy with the session and re-recorded it twice early in September. 'Flying High' was to have followed the tradition set by FIREBALL XL5 and STINGRAY where each episode ended with a song that would act as an alternative theme tune to the one used on the series' opening titles. Gerry Anderson ultimately decided that having a song (and, in particular, this song) playing over the end titles no longer suited the format of the series, so 'Flying High' was scrapped and replaced by the 'Thunderbirds March' just a fortnight before the first episode was transmitted.

Throughout the autumn, the later episodes were still being filmed while the earliest episodes were being unveiled to the viewing public for the first time. Popular reaction to the series boosted the enthusiasm of the production team, and on at least one occasion assisted in smoothing over a potentially difficult situation.

Anderson explains, 'I don't remember much about the shooting of the actual shows, but one that does come to mind is *Attack of the Alligators!*. I decided that we would use real alligators, but not full-size ones, as a 13-foot alligator would dwarf a 13-inch puppet. We got a couple of baby crocodiles in and we had all these tanks that were properly heated to the correct temperature for the crocodiles when they arrived. We started filming and then I got a call from the operator to say that an RSPCA man had turned up. I invited him in and he said, "It's been reported that you've got crocodiles," and I said, "Yes." He said, "It's been reported that your boys are giving them electric shocks," and I said, "Well, I didn't know that, but let's go on to the stage and have a look." So we went on to the stage and he was very, very grave and terribly concerned, but then he saw one of the puppets and he said, "You're not filming THUNDERBIRDS, are you? Oh, God, that's my favourite programme."

'After about half an hour talking about the show, he got around to the purpose of his visit. Derek Meddings explained that his team were laying the crocodiles down and they weren't doing anything. They were just lying there. The RSPCA man said, well, they would, because of the warmth of the lamps. So Derek said, "We've been giving them a touch with an electrode just to make them move." The guy asked what voltage they were using and Derek said that it was about 20 volts, and the guy said, "Oh, they've got terribly thick skins, you know. If you want them to move, you'll have to pump it up to about 60!" He ended up taking his annual leave and coming to the studio to work for us, and he was personally giving the crocodiles electric shocks. It was quite amusing the way it turned out.'

Attack of the Alligators! was a memorable episode for many other members of the production team. Bob Bell recalls, 'We had great trouble trying to motivate the crocodiles, which

'I can't tell you how wonderful those days were. To this day I don't think I've ever worked with a better bunch of people than that lot. They were, without doubt, some of the best days of my life in terms of working camaraderie. It was fantastic. Most of us were pretty young. We were keen as mustard and excited by it all.'

KEN TURNER

'In THUNDERBIRDS, the characters were very much caricatures. You could tell that these were puppets and that they could appear to do most things that a human could, but with more eccentric imagery. This made them more lovable and appealing. I still look on them with great affection. There was a naïve quality about them and nothing too complex. They all had their slight weaknesses and could make mistakes, and that was all part of their success.'

SHANE RIMMER

Filming a scene in The Cham-Cham *on one of the puppet soundstages.*

John Brown (in white coat) and Keith Wilson (standing) create a tail for Attack of the Alligators!.

'One of the things we loved about THUNDERBIRDS was that one minute we were building the interior of THUNDERBIRD 2 and next we were doing Lady Penelope's mansion or a sort of everyday house. We did some Egyptian stuff as I recall and that variety was always great fun for us and very challenging. It kept us on our toes.'

KEN TURNER

'One of the main problems I found with the puppets was in fight situations. These were action programmes but the characters couldn't have a realistic punch-up. A couple of times they tried it, but it just looked phoney and silly.

'I remember once saying, "Look, just cut all the wires and we'll throw the character across the set at the other puppet." It wasn't that much better really, but it illustrates how everyone was always prepared to look at things from other angles and that is why things were always worked out in the end.'

DAVID LANE

tended to just sit and look at us. We couldn't get anything dramatic to happen. I remember Lew Grade came to see us that day with his bevy of henchmen and we were faced with the terrible smell being given off by the crocodiles! Unperturbed by the creatures, he thought the filming was all wonderful.'

Derek Meddings was the man who had to work the most closely with the creatures. In an interview completed in 1984, he remembered, 'We got the alligators from some place up north and had them shipped down by some private little zoo. They were actually 3-foot crocodiles and we also had a 5-foot crocodile that we could never get out of the basket because he was so vicious. We had one crocodile that was so docile that it used to lie on the studio floor and we used to cover it with wet sacks and put a couple of 10-K lights on it. It used to stay there all day long. We used to step over this thing and it wouldn't blink an eye.'

For a shot of one of the alligators chasing a boat, Derek climbed into the tank holding on to a rope that was tied to the crocodile. 'I was pulling this rope from under the water at an angle, towards the camera from a corner of the tank. The reason I was doing it was that I thought I knew the sort of speed I wanted to pull it. The crocodile had to snap the back off the boat but it wouldn't open its mouth as we wanted it to, to make the scene look more frightening.

'Nothing happened for six takes. I told the crew that we would have one more attempt to get the shot and I pulled the rope to feel the tension, but there was nothing. I tugged and tugged to feel the weight of the crocodile but there was no response – the crocodile had disentangled itself from the rope and was swimming free in the tank! As soon as I realized that it was free, I leapt over the high edge of the tank, clearing it very quickly and leaving my waders in the water. I don't think the crew had ever seen me move as fast!'

During the *Attack of the Alligators!* shoot, publicity photos were taken of Lady Penelope (who did not actually appear in the episode) with a couple of the crocodiles. Christine Glanville remembered that one crocodile took a fancy to Penelope's leg. 'We had terrible trouble trying to retrieve her leg from the crocodile's mouth! It probably had a sore mouth afterwards because it just refused to let go of her. The crocodiles must have had an awful time of it, lying in the studio tank, which was filled with all sorts of dirty paint water, oil and soapy water to make it look swampy.'

Filming on the first season drew to a close with *The Cham-Cham*, and it was decided to end the series (as far as the crew were concerned at that time) on a high note with an episode that would be the Supermarionation equivalent of a Hollywood musical, a show-business special set in the Alpine resort of Paradise Peaks.

Gerry Anderson has fond memories of this episode. '*The Cham-Cham* gave our art and design departments a chance to show what they could really do, and they didn't let us down. Bob Bell turned in some spectacular settings, the ski sequences were quite stunning and the puppets skied superbly. I dreamt up the idea of ski-thrusters, which were small jets that would propel the puppets uphill without having to make too many difficult manoeuvres, and I thought it worked perfectly.'

Unfortunately, many of the elaborate sequences in the episode turned out to be extremely time-consuming and *The Cham-Cham* went over schedule by nearly a week. Alan Pattillo was both writer and director of the episode. 'We tried to do things in that picture that we hadn't done before, such as Penelope dancing a slow foxtrot. It was an experimental production, but was great fun to do.'

As an in-joke, Pattillo named Lady Penelope's *alter ego* Wanda Lamour after puppeteer Wanda Brown. She recalls, 'Penelope had to start right at one end of the set and walk the whole length of it singing and waltzing around. I was lying on the floor, just out of shot of the camera. I was just able to hold her by the bottom of her legs, but it was extremely awkward. Penelope's legs were stiffened a bit so there wasn't too much bend in them. Christine Glanville was up on the gantry holding the strings so that she could still be doing head and arm movements.'

Both *Attack of the Alligators!* and *The Cham-Cham* went seriously over-budget, so to compensate Alan Pattillo turned in a script that could be shot in half the time at half the cost of a standard episode: *Security Hazard*. The only new shots required were framing scenes which allowed edited highlights from four early episodes (*Trapped in the Sky*, *End of the Road*, *Day of Disaster* and *Sun Probe*) to act as 'flashback' sequences. These episodes were specifically chosen as, having originally been filmed as half-hour episodes, Pattillo knew that the stories could be more easily condensed down to around ten minutes each.

With filming completed on the first twenty-six episodes, post-production work on the series progressed during December so as to enable the remaining episodes to be broadcast in the New Year. Public response to the series was phenomenal. The programme had netted ITC over £350,000 in advance sales to overseas markets before it had even been screened, and it was seen in some thirty different countries as diverse as Ghana, Holland, Saudi Arabia and Japan. AP Films' licensing subsidiary, AP Merchandising, sold around 120 licences for toys, which sold in their millions in the early part of 1966. There was no doubt in Gerry Anderson's mind that more episodes would be required, but perhaps the concept could go even further.

While discussing plans to shoot a second series of THUNDERBIRDS, Anderson suggested to Lew Grade that the logical progression was to do a feature film based on the series. Grade agreed and the budget was set at £250,000. Alan Pattillo was invited to direct the film, but he turned it down. 'I had had enough,' he says. 'Working with puppets is so limiting and I found that it was not creative enough. Everything was a compromise. I also wondered whether it would really work on a big screen because it was such a cosy show, with nice little characters appearing on the small screen. I felt that the intimacy would be gone.'

The job went instead to David Lane, who had directed seven complete episodes of the series (including *Attack of the Alligators!*) and part of *Terror in New York City*. Gerry and Sylvia Anderson set to work on the script for *Thunderbirds Are Go* and, at the studios, three months of pre-production work began as 1965 drew to a close. Plans were set in motion for the first four of the new television episodes (*Atlantic Inferno*, *Path of Destruction*, *Alias Mr. Hackenbacker* and *Lord Parker's 'Oliday*) to be filmed alongside the movie on a sixteen-week shooting schedule, and the puppet crew was split accordingly: the 'A' team, led by lighting cameraman Paddy Seale, was assigned to shoot the movie, while the 'B' team, under Julien Lugrin, filmed the television episodes.

On the special effects stages, Derek Meddings acted in a supervisory capacity on both projects, although he would concentrate mainly on the effects for the movie and entrust responsibility for the episodes' effects to former camera operator Jimmy Elliott. The company purchased two additional buildings on the Slough Trading Estate, one of which incorporated a massive soundstage custom-built to the requirements of the effects crew, enabling Meddings to build and shoot models for the movie on a much larger scale than had previously been possible for the television series.

Towards the end of February 1966, as the production team geared up to start shooting again, the atmosphere at the studios was electric. THUNDERBIRDS was a hit and the staff at AP Films had high hopes that *Thunderbirds Are Go* would finally break the company out of television and launch it into the 'major league' of feature film production. Speaking about the film late in 1965, Anderson told *Television Mail*, 'I can't tell you anything about it yet, but I can say this: it will be bigger and better than anything we have ever done before.' And it was.

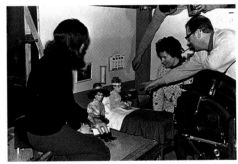

Filming The Duchess Assignment.

SEASON TWO AND THE FIRST FEATURE FILM

Extensive pre-production work was required to prepare both puppets and models for their first big-screen appearance. Everyone involved was very much aware that many of the flaws that could be overlooked on the television screen simply wouldn't hold up to the rigorous examination of a cinema audience watching their puppet heroes expanded to a picture size some twenty times larger.

Bigger, more detailed models of all the International Rescue vehicles had to be constructed, as did larger model sets for them to appear in, while in the puppets workshop the puppeteers went to great pains to ensure that the characters would look their best on the cinema screen. Puppeteer Wanda Brown recalls, 'The best puppets were selected for the feature film and given a clean-up, a re-paint, wigs freshened up and possibly new costumes. So much would be showing on the big screen that you wouldn't see on the small screen.'

Wanda's husband, John Brown, supervised the construction of the puppets. He explains, 'We had to make sure that we were attacking it right, to see whether the sets, the lighting and the figures were right. It gave them the opportunity to say, "Well, we can hold a close-up," or "We're going to have to move back a bit." We held our breath, because we shot some film and then we sent it to one of the cinemas in Slough to show it, to see how it would stand up on the big screen. We've got a puppet face that we've been used to seeing on television and then, suddenly, there's a close-up on a big cinema screen.'

Some of the regular THUNDERBIRDS characters were re-created as entirely new puppets for the feature film (most noticeably, Scott Tracy), and further duplicate puppets were made for the simultaneous filming of the second-season episodes. The puppet cast was expanded with the creation of the new featured characters required for *Thunderbirds Are Go*, primarily the five-man crew of the space exploration vehicle Zero X, and also five puppet replicas of real-life personalities Cliff Richard, Hank Marvin, Brian Bennett, Bruce Welch and John Rostill, who were to appear in a dream fantasy sequence. Gerry Anderson explains, 'Using Cliff Richard and The Shadows was my idea. At the time I had a house in Portugal and there were only about ten houses nearby occupied by people from outside Portugal. My next-door-but-one neighbour was Cliff Richard. One day we got talking and I asked if he would be interested in doing the film.'

Although the puppet sculptors were used to using the facial features of real people on which to base their puppet characters, actually creating puppets that resembled recognized personalities was a new departure for the team. John Brown was responsible for creating the Cliff Richard puppet, while Christine Glanville made the Brian Bennett puppet. Both used numerous photographs as reference. As Shadows drummer Bennett recalls, 'We all posed for lots of photos from different angles and great attention was given to how we moved and even to the grip of my sticks. They seemed such a happy bunch of people, but they took the puppets so seriously. I remember the lighting men treating the puppets like real actors, with a great deal of time spent on each shot. The puppet of me was brilliant and the first thing I did was to ask if I could keep him when filming was finished, but apparently he was to be turned into another character after the film had been finished.'

Cliff Richard remembers, 'When the idea was put forward that The Shadows and I were to be "puppeted", we were quite thrilled really. THUNDERBIRDS was a very famous TV series and kids loved it, so we were happy to do it. It was quite a hoot to see our puppets for the first time. I was never really sure whether I looked like my puppet or it looked like me! I thought Hank Marvin's puppet was really good, but then he always looked like a puppet anyway!'

Hank Marvin was sculpted by Terry Curtis, who had joined the art department during the making of The Uninvited but later moved into the puppet workshop. He echoes Cliff Richard's appraisal of the Hank Marvin puppet. 'I have to be honest and say that I think that Hank was probably the best in terms of likeness to the real person. I was allocated the job as I was the next senior sculptor behind John Brown, who did Cliff.'

Curtis also created the three primary new puppet characters for the film, Zero X crew-members Paul Travers and Greg Martin, and the Glenn Field Assembly Controller. 'With Paul, I tried to make him look like Sean Connery. It was something I wanted to do as I liked the look of Connery. As I had become a bit more senior in the team, I got to do more important characters, so I did the Glenn Field Controller, Paul and the blond-haired co-pilot, whom I kind of based on myself. I did that again later on with Captain Blue in CAPTAIN SCARLET AND THE MYSTERONS. Some people would say that all my characters were a version of Sean Connery or myself. It was a style that worked at the time.' Curtis's Paul Travers puppet made an interesting comparison with Christine Glanville's Scott Tracy. Although both were based on the features of Sean Connery, the two puppets were quite unalike. Curtis's skill at re-creating Connery's face on a puppet was quite remarkable and his Paul Travers puppet was an uncanny likeness of the James Bond actor.

John Blundall left the puppet workshop before work began on the feature film, disagreeing with the direction in which Gerry and Sylvia Anderson were taking the puppets, making them look more realistic and less caricatured. New staff were taken on and John Brown and Terry Curtis were joined by Tim Cooksey, Peter Hayward and Mike Richardson.

Before filming could begin anew on the puppet soundstages, all of the dialogue for the film and the initial second-season episodes had to be recorded. The original THUNDERBIRDS voice cast was reassembled, but with one notable exception. Since the completion of the dialogue recordings for the series' first season, David Holliday, who had provided the voice for Virgil Tracy on the initial twenty-six episodes, had relocated in his native America and was, therefore, unavailable to continue his role. He was replaced by Canadian actor Jeremy Wilkin.

Born in Byfleet, Surrey, Wilkin had trained as a doctor before switching to the stage and studying at the Royal Academy of Dramatic Art. He emigrated to Canada, settling in Toronto, where he became established as a leading performer, appearing in over a hundred television programmes. Returning to London in the mid-1960s, he guested in episodes of COURT MARTIAL and MAN IN A SUITCASE, and took the starring role as Drewe Heriot in UNDERMIND, before being cast as the voice of Virgil.

This was the start of a working relationship with the Andersons that continued for the next seven years as Wilkin subsequently voiced Captain Ochre in CAPTAIN SCARLET AND THE MYSTERONS, appeared as a launch control technician in Doppelgänger, voiced the Bishop in THE SECRET SERVICE and had a regular role as Lt. Gordon Maxwell in UFO. He also contributed various voices to JOE 90 and later appeared as Inspector Lars Bergen in THE PROTECTORS episode Route 27. He has since

'I really got on well with Gerry and he had maybe seen something in me and kind of nurtured it, I guess. He must have had a lot of faith in me and he liked what I had done with all the programmes I had been involved with, particularly THUNDERBIRDS. He just called me in to see him one time and asked me if I would like to direct a THUNDERBIRDS feature film. I remember I had a huge rise, £15 a week.

'Obviously, I was delighted to have been asked. I had to go off and have these meetings with United Artists. All that sort of stuff was pretty new to me.

'I remember one particular meeting when Gerry was showing the United Artists people a series of poster proposals. One of them, which Gerry was especially keen on, was a sort of James Bond-type thing with a silhouette of a woman – Lady Penelope, I guess. It was sort of sexy and I remember United Artists said to Gerry that he had to realize that it was ultimately a kids' film regardless of what he personally hoped for.'

DAVID LANE

been seen in DOCTOR WHO, THE NEW AVENGERS (twice), BLAKE'S 7 and the James Bond film *The Spy Who Loved Me* (1977).

Two new actors joining the regular voice cast at this point to play guest roles in both *Thunderbirds Are Go* and the second-season episodes were Charles Tingwell and Paul Maxwell, neither of whom was credited for his work on the television series. Maxwell provided the voices for Captain Paul Travers in *Thunderbirds Are Go* and Captain Ashton in the second-season episode *Alias Mr. Hackenbacker*. He had previously provided the voice for Colonel Steve Zodiac in FIREBALL XL5 and went on to voice Captain Grey and the World President (among others) in the first twelve episodes of CAPTAIN SCARLET AND THE MYSTERONS, as well as making a guest appearance as Lt. Jim Lewis in the UFO episode *Sub-Smash*.

An international stage and screen actor whose long and varied career included television roles in DANGER MAN, THE SAINT, THE BARON, THE CHAMPIONS, RANDALL AND HOPKIRK DECEASED, THE ADVENTURER and CORONATION STREET, as well as the feature films *Aliens* (1986) and *Indiana Jones and the Last Crusade* (1989), Paul Maxwell continued working until his death at the end of 1991.

Australian actor Charles Tingwell was best known for his role as Alan Dawson in the 1957 series EMERGENCY WARD 10. He had a prolific career in British films and television during the 1960s, with appearances in *Murder She Said* (1963), *The Secret of Blood Island* (1965) and *Dracula, Prince of Darkness* (1965), and guest roles in episodes of DANGER MAN, THE AVENGERS, CRANE, THE MAN IN ROOM 17, ADAM ADAMANT LIVES! and OUT OF THE UNKNOWN. Tingwell provided the voice for Dr Tony Grant in *Thunderbirds Are Go* and a number of guest characters in the television episodes, most notably the waiter Bruno in *Lord Parker's 'Oliday* and Dr Lang in *Give or Take a Million*. He later voiced Dr Fawn, Captain Brown and numerous guest characters in the first twelve episodes of CAPTAIN SCARLET AND THE MYSTERONS.

Art director Bob Bell and designer John Lageu examine the Crablogger One model built for Path of Destruction.

Following a regular role as Mr Bennett in CATWEAZLE and a guest appearance as Captain Beaver James in the UFO episode *Mindbender*, Tingwell returned to Australia, where he has enjoyed a prolific career with a starring role as Inspector Lawson in the mid-1970s series HOMICIDE and appearances in many feature films, including *Summerfield* (1977), *Breaker Morant* (1980), *A Cry in the Dark* (1988) and *The Castle* (1997).

In isolated roles as members of the Zero X crew in *Thunderbirds Are Go* were Bob Monkhouse (Brad Newman), Alexander Davion (Greg Martin) and Neil McCallum (Dr Ray Pierce). Comedian, actor, writer and presenter Bob Monkhouse had previously been seen in *Carry on Sergeant* (1958) and *Dentist in the Chair* (1960), the television series MAD MOVIES and THE BIG NOISE, and as compere of SUNDAY NIGHT AT THE LONDON PALLADIUM and CANDID CAMERA. Shortly after recording his THUNDERBIRDS role, he replaced Jackie Rae on THE GOLDEN SHOT and turned the failing series into a teatime hit. He went on to chair CELEBRITY SQUARES, FAMILY FORTUNES, BOB SAYS OPPORTUNITY

KNOCKS and THE $64,000 QUESTION, becoming Britain's most popular (and highest-paid) game-show host.

Monkhouse recalls how his role in *Thunderbirds Are Go* came about. 'I had gone to the studios to seek Gerry's permission to have Stingray jump out of Des O'Connor's bathwater between his knees in a sketch I had written and, after he had agreed in a rather preoccupied way, he explained that the actor he had hired to play one or two roles in the film, the late Alfred Marks, had pulled out due to a disagreement about the fee. Then he looked at me shrewdly and said, "How much would you charge for the job?" I said, "Gerry, I'd do it for nothing." And that was the first time I ever heard the phrase, "The price is right."'

French-born Alexander Davion was best known for his role as Chief Inspector David Keen in the 1965 ITC series GIDEON'S WAY, which had resulted from several notable guest appearances in THE SAINT. After *Thunderbirds Are Go*, Davion was again employed by the Andersons as the Executive in UFO's *The Psychobombs* episode.

Canadian actor Neil McCallum made one of his earliest screen appearances as Sam Scroop the cook in the 1956 BBC children's series SPACE SCHOOL. In the early 1960s, he made feature film appearances in *The Inspector* (1962), *The Longest Day* (1962), *The War Lover* (1963) and *Witchcraft* (1964), and also guested in several episodes of THE SAINT. Shortly after recording his role in *Thunderbirds Are Go*, he appeared in episodes of DEPARTMENT S and RANDALL AND HOPKIRK DECEASED, and went on to make two further Anderson series contributions: as film producer Carl Mason in the UFO episode *Court Martial* and as Bennett in the *One and One Makes One* episode of THE PROTECTORS. He died in April 1976.

While preparations to start shooting the puppet footage were being completed, on the new special effects soundstage, Derek Meddings and his team began filming their sequences for the feature film. Meddings wanted to ensure that his team created the most spectacular effects scenes possible and everyone worked around the clock to shoot all the sequences that the film needed. These included new wide-screen footage of the Thunderbird craft being launched, the Zero X launch, a dream sequence set in a nightclub in outer space, a car chase involving FAB 1, an attack on the Zero X MEV by Martian Rock Snakes and the Zero X crash-landing that formed the film's finale.

Completion of the effects material for *Thunderbirds Are Go* took five and a half months. During this time, Meddings was in charge of twenty-eight visual effects technicians working on three stages to shoot effects footage for both the film and the TV series. Under the supervision of director Jimmy Elliott, the team working on the television episodes produced many of the series' most spectacular and memorable sequences, including the destruction of the Seascape drilling rig in *Atlantic Inferno* and that of Crablogger One in *Path of Destruction*.

In the art department, Bob Bell and Keith Wilson split their production design duties between the film and the television episodes, with Bell acting in a supervisory capacity but mainly concentrating his efforts on the many spectacular sets required for *Thunderbirds Are Go*, while Wilson designed the sets for the television series. He was joined by John Lageu, formerly an engineering draughtsman in the aerospace industry, who applied his talents to creating more realistic vehicle interiors, such as the cabin of Crablogger One in *Path of Destruction* and the cockpit of Skythrust in *Alias Mr. Hackenbacker*, leaving Wilson to develop what were described as 'aesthetic design' (as opposed to 'technical design') sets: Lady Penelope's farm at Bonga Bonga in *Atlantic Inferno* and the interiors of the Monte Bianco hotel in *Alias Mr. Hackenbacker*, among many others.

For *Thunderbirds Are Go*, Bell created the Glenn Field Control Tower and Press Conference Room interiors, both the real and fantasy Swinging Star nightclub sets, and larger, more detailed

'When we started to do THUNDERBIRDS features as well, as you can imagine, it was a beehive. The place was swarming with people. There were models, sets and puppets everywhere and it was an amazing atmosphere.

'The programmes were immensely popular and we could see what Gerry was thinking. He was thinking of another Disneyland and you could see the whole future laid out. Every building nearby had been taken over by Gerry as we got bigger and bigger and bigger.

'All of a sudden, we had an empire: we had workshops, we had studios, we had where they were doing the comic, we had four special effects stages and it was just getting massive. You could imagine the gates going up with "Andersonland" over the top of them. That's the way it looked and everyone thought that it could really happen.'

KEITH WILSON

The Crablogger One model is prepared for a scene in **Path of Destruction.**

sets of various locations on Tracy Island. Perhaps the film's most stunning set, however, was the duotone Enquiry Room at the Space Exploration Center.

Sylvia Anderson, the film's producer, had very definite ideas for this particular set and asked Bob Bell to design it using only two colours, tangerine and black. This, she felt, would offer a pleasing contrast to the blue uniforms of the puppets in this particular scene. During the construction of the set, Sylvia was frustrated to discover that every time she walked on to the puppet stage, one of the members of the art department had dressed the set with props that broke away from the duotone scheme. As was her right as producer, she put her foot down, insisting that everything should conform to the tangerine and black design, and the boldness of her vision resulted in the most visually arresting example of production design seen in any of the Supermarionation productions.

Thunderbirds Are Go was the first feature film to be shot using the Livingston Electronic Viewfinder Unit, also known as Add-a-Vision. This was a major development of the prototype CCTV system that the AP Films team had been using up to that point. It basically consisted of an electronic viewfinder which could be used in conjunction with a Mitchell BNC Camera to take a high-definition television picture directly from the camera. This system enabled the camera operator and director of photography more accurately to determine the precise exposure of any scene (without reference to light meters and conversion tables) and balance the lighting on back-projection sequences. The monitored pictures could also be recorded on tape and played back to the director to check that a take was satisfactory. For the puppeteers on the gantry, it gave them a much clearer picture of what was going on on the set below them.

Filming began on the puppet stages on Thursday 3 March 1966. With one puppet crew occupied full-time on the feature film, progress on the television episodes was slow. Instead of two hour-long episodes being shot within a four-week period, as had been possible on the first season, now only one episode could be completed each month. It was the end of June before filming on *Thunderbirds Are Go* was finished and the film's puppet and effects crews returned to the television side of the operation, once again taking up their duties to shoot *Ricochet*, while the 'B' team completed work on the Christmas episode *Give or Take a Million*. As with a number of previous episodes, the plot of *Ricochet* was inspired by current news events.

Gerry Anderson remembers, 'At that time, Radio Caroline was often in the news. The BBC had a complete monopoly on radio broadcasting, but many people were looking for something different and Caroline fulfilled that need by broadcasting pop music from their ship in the North Sea. There was always something exciting about Caroline – after all, they were actual pirates, except, of course, they weren't doing anyone any real harm.

'At the time it was also the early days of space travel, so it seemed inevitable that we would eventually come up with the idea for a show that would feature a pirate radio station in space. Whenever we used guns in a sequence, our sound editor, John Peverill, would introduce lots of ricochets which always met with my approval. It was such an exciting sound that it seemed like a good name for a disc jockey: Rick O'Shea, the voice in space!'

That summer, it seemed that nothing could go wrong for the marionation mini-Hollywood on the Slough Trading Estate. The first season of Thunderbirds had completed its initial broadcast on ATV Midlands at the end of March and proved immensely popular with both children and adults. A repeat run of the series was scheduled to begin screening at the end of September and this would incorporate five of the new second-season episodes, building up to a Christmas Day premiere for the broadcast of *Give or Take a Million*, and the cinema opening of *Thunderbirds Are Go* in mid-December.

Merchandisers lined up for licences to produce Thunderbirds-related toys, games and books to have them ready in time for the 'Thunderbirds Christmas', and in recognition of Thunderbirds' financial and artistic success, Gerry Anderson was awarded the silver medal for Outstanding Artistic Achievement by the Royal Television Society. Further recognition for his contributions to TV came when he was also made an Honorary Fellow of the British Kinematograph Sound and Television Society.

So it was that, with everything set to continue filming second-season Thunderbirds episodes for the next ten months, the AP Films team was dealt a savage blow when Anderson was called to a meeting with ITC financier Lew Grade.

Alan Perry films the new Thunderbird 3 launch sequence for Thunderbirds Are Go.

'All our planning was geared towards a second series of Thunderbirds and that it would continue for a long time. It was only when I went to see Lew Grade during filming of those last six episodes that he shook me by saying that he really wanted something else. This came as a serious blow to the organization. I was absolutely shattered. We had two studios, a weekly comic, a record company and a whole merchandising operation. We had just opened an office in Hong Kong and ordered a million pounds' worth of machine tools, all based on the success of Thunderbirds – and the series was cancelled. When the trade heard that we were not going to be making any more Thunderbirds, people started cancelling orders and the whole thing went down the drain.

'What happened was that Lew couldn't get a sale for the series in America. I have never been involved in the sale of the programmes and, therefore, I don't know the whole story, but Lew went to America and came back with two of the three networks having made an offer for it. When he got back to London Airport, he was tannoyed and when he went to the telephone it was the other network saying that they wanted to bid for it as well. Unfortunately, the deal fell through and I can only speculate why: whether Lew asked too much or whether the network had second thoughts, I don't know the reason. But when that one network dropped out of the bidding, panic set in with the other two and they began asking, "I wonder why they've dropped out?" and so on. It was tragic. We couldn't get an American sale with Thunderbirds, so it was cancelled and we had to do something new.'

That 'something new' was Captain Scarlet and the Mysterons.

THUNDERBIRD 6

'Thunderbirds Are Go *was done like an episode but on a bigger scale. Whereas we would think that it might be nice to do a particular shot on the series but couldn't afford to, with* Thunderbirds Are Go *we just did it because we had the money.*

'There was a scene at the start of the film with all these military characters in the black and orange room. In the series we might have had half a dozen puppets or something but in that scene we had about twenty.

'It was a big project for us. The premiere was a huge affair. It was at the London Pavilion in Piccadilly, just off Leicester Square. There were the puppets, all the models, The Shadows and the Royal Marines military band.

'To be honest, I do think that the film was a little disappointing – it was a bit flat. It got off to a very good start and kind of fizzled away, although the stuff that Derek did at the end with the crash was wonderful. The stuff with Cliff was quite good fun, but it was made up of good "moments" and not a complete film, if you know what I mean. It was very much like that first episode of THUNDERBIRDS with the Fireflash.

'Maybe the problem with the other film, Thunderbird 6, was that it tried to be too different to an episode and went too far the other way.'

DAVID LANE

As the summer of 1966 drew to a close, the production team at AP Films became resigned to the fact that THUNDERBIRDS' life as a television series had come to an end and it was time to move on to start work on the company's next television production, which, it was hoped, would prove to be even bigger and better than THUNDERBIRDS.

The technicians in the puppet workshops at Slough had not been idle during the filming of THUNDERBIRDS' second season and the feature film, and had continued to work on developing the technology of Supermarionation. They had discovered that it was now possible to re-locate the solenoids that controlled the puppets' mouth movement from the head to the chest of the puppet, the movements of the solenoids being transmitted through the puppet's neck by cable to activate the mouth movement in the head. This development meant that the size of the head could be reduced for the first time to be in correct proportion to the body, resulting in the next generation of Supermarionation puppets, more believable, easier to model and easier to dress.

The team recognized that, having already established the style of the show with the disproportionate characters, it would not have been possible to introduce this new type of puppet as long as THUNDERBIRDS was still in production. But now that THUNDERBIRDS had been cancelled by Lew Grade, the creation of a new series was the ideal opportunity to begin using the more advanced marionettes.

So it was that the new Gerry Anderson series, then entitled THE MYSTERONS, went into pre-production with the construction of correctly proportioned puppets, together with costumes, sets and vehicles all designed to match, in what would be a more realistic representation of a twenty-first-century world than had previously been possible. As the construction of the new style of puppet was extremely complicated, the crew realized that it would not be so easy to re-vamp puppets and create new characters from episode to episode, so Anderson decided that a large repertory company of puppets would be constructed, comprising an extensive range of characters, both male and female. These would then be cast from episode to episode in much the same way as living actors in live-action productions.

This development in Supermarionation represented the biggest single advance in the puppetry techniques on the Anderson productions since the development of the synchronized mouth movement seven years earlier. As a reflection of this great leap forward, the company directors decided that it was finally time to discard the old AP Films name for the film and television production arm of the business (Arthur Provis had left the company some years before and the AP had since become an acronym for Animated Pictures) in favour of a name which more accurately described the studio's output: Century 21 Productions. The company name was formally changed on Saturday 3 December 1966.

The first production to carry the Century 21 name was *Thunderbirds Are Go*, which moved into post-production in the autumn so as to be ready for a Christmas opening. Once veteran Supermarionation cutter Len Walter had finished editing the picture, composer Barry Gray assembled a seventy-piece orchestra, the largest to be used on any Anderson production, to perform the epic score for the film. This was recorded over six sessions (two each day) on 9, 10 and 11 October at the Anvil Studios near Denham, engineered by Gray's old friend Eric Tomlinson.

With the film nearing completion, Lew Grade closed a deal with United Artists to distribute it and the Rank Organization agreed to act as exhibitors. Sound editing, dubbing and final process work took another three weeks and the film was finally submitted for British Film Catalogue classification in November 1966. A special screening was arranged for the United Artists executives and Gerry Anderson remembers, 'Lew had commissioned *Thunderbirds Are Go* on spec but United Artists saw it and picked it up immediately. They were so impressed with the picture that an executive named David Picker turned to me when the lights came up and said, "Whatever subject you want to make, Mr Anderson, it's yours."'

The film premiered at the London Pavilion cinema in Piccadilly on Monday 12 December 1966 at a charity gala evening to benefit Dr Barnado's. The puppet stars and their vehicles were on display in the foyer and the event was also attended by the voice artists and members of the production crew, among them Gerry and Sylvia Anderson, Peter Dyneley with his wife, Jane Hylton, Charles Tingwell, Cliff Richard with his sister Donella, the four members of The Shadows, David Lane and Lew Grade.

A hundred boys from Dr Barnado's were also invited and the Band of the Royal Marines performed the 'Thunderbirds March' in the theatre both before and after the performance. Puppeteer and wardrobe assistant Zena Relph has fond memories of the premiere. 'It was wonderful to see Lady Penelope on the cinema screen. The premiere was a wonderful night and it was unbelievable to think of puppets 1 foot 8 inches high in Cinemascope. It was incredible.'

Gerry Anderson also recalls the event, and its aftermath. 'When the film went out for its premiere, Piccadilly was blocked. It was a wonderful premiere and it was absolutely packed. Everybody cheered and I remember leaving the cinema and the manager said, "You get a picture like this and they start queuing up at four o'clock in the morning." We went back to the Hilton for a fabulous party, where they had made all the vehicles in ice. The head of United Artists said to me, "I don't know whether it's going to make

more money than Bond or not, I can't decide." I was sitting there thinking that I was a millionaire. I mean, all these experienced people, how could they be wrong? The next day, the Dominion at Tottenham Court Road had about ten people in it.

'It was an absolutely unmitigated disaster. I went on a whistle-stop tour across the country for publicity and went to local cinemas to see how *Thunderbirds Are Go* was doing and it was playing to houses with fifteen people. United Artists were so shocked by the result that they couldn't believe what had happened any more than I could. They said, "Look, we know something went wrong, but make another one." So we made *Thunderbird 6*.'

The budget for the second THUNDERBIRDS feature film was set at £300,000, and Gerry and Sylvia Anderson immediately began work on writing the script, which was completed over a period of three months. Just as the first feature film had drawn on elements of the television episode *Operation Crash-Dive*, so the second re-vamped ideas from the episode *Alias Mr. Hackenbacker* to create a plot in which the maiden voyage of the airship Skyship One, designed by Brains, is hijacked by crooks in the employ of the Hood to lure International Rescue into a trap.

All the dialogue for the film was recorded over an intensive six-day period and reunited the THUNDERBIRDS cast for one last time. Once again, however, one of the key players was unavailable to take part: Ray Barrett had returned home to Australia. He was replaced by two newcomers who were to become regular performers in Anderson productions over the next three years: Keith Alexander and Gary Files.

Another Australian by birth, Keith Alexander emigrated to the UK in 1965 after studying engineering and law at Adelaide University, where he took part in university revues and was bitten by the acting bug. With a reputation for his imitations of statesmen and celebrities, Alexander was often called upon to do voice-over work and he found international acclaim as the voice of the lovable puppet mouse Topo Gigio. For *Thunderbird 6*, Alexander provided the voice of John Tracy and also recorded the film's short opening narration. He was to return to the Anderson fold as the voice of Sam Loover in JOE 90, the Eurosec Flight Director in *Doppelgänger*, and the voice of Agent Blake (and numerous guest voices) in THE SECRET SERVICE, but he is probably best known for his regular role as Lt. Keith Ford in UFO. Alexander continues to work in film and television, but in recent years he has moved behind the scenes into research, production and direction back in Australia.

Gary Files voiced only three small roles in *Thunderbird 6* (the Hood, the real Captain Foster and the steward impostor Lane), but at the same time he was also providing the voice for Captain Magenta and other guest characters in CAPTAIN SCARLET AND THE MYSTERONS. He went on to voice guest characters in JOE 90 and Matthew Harding in THE SECRET SERVICE, and later made a brief on-screen appearance as Phil Wade in UFO's opening episode *Identified*. Files, too, has now returned to his native Australia, where he appeared in a regular role as Tom Ramsey in NEIGHBOURS.

Jeremy Wilkin once again took on the part of Virgil Tracy in the absence of David Holliday,

'I think if the chemistry works and the characters are interesting and charming, then the series lasts. It had such a charm about it. There was violence, but never in an angry way that you see so much of today. It never frightened the kids watching it, which is very important.

'It was a kind of technological Shangri-La where people had this wonderful existence, flying around the world doing good wherever they went. Everything worked for them and they were never defeated.

'At the time, we never knew how successful they would be. Whenever you get other work and you tell people what you have done, their face lights up. It's great because actors like to be praised and to know what pleasure they may have given.'

DAVID GRAHAM

Vehicle construction in the model workshop.

and also provided the voice for Hogarth, another of the bogus stewards. The third steward, Carter, was performed by Matt Zimmerman, doubling up on his regular role as Alan Tracy.

The primary guest voices in *Thunderbird 6* were provided by two established British character actors, John Carson and Geoffrey Keen, both of whom were known to the Andersons for their starring roles in the BBC drama series THE TROUBLESHOOTERS.

As the villainous impostor of Skyship One's Captain Foster, Carson fooled many viewers into believing that the Andersons had managed to persuade James Mason to take on the role, such was the similarity of his delivery. He had established himself as a regular player in British film and television in the 1960s, with guest roles in series such as THE SAINT (four times), MAN IN A SUITCASE, THE BARON, THE CHAMPIONS, PUBLIC EYE and DEPARTMENT S, and a big-screen appearance in *The Plague of the Zombies* (1967). He later found a niche in horror films with roles in *The Man Who Haunted Himself* (1970), *Taste the Blood of Dracula* (1970) and *Captain Kronos Vampire Hunter* (1972), but also continued to be seen on television throughout the 1970s in ADAM ADAMANT LIVES!, OUT OF THE UNKNOWN, CRIBB, THE NEW AVENGERS and THE PROFESSIONALS.

An incisive character actor, the son of actor Malcolm Keen, Geoffrey Keen has made appearances in more than a hundred films and also has numerous television and stage credits to his name. Prior to recording his *Thunderbird 6* role as the President of New World Aircraft, he had been seen in *Genevieve* (1953), *The Heroes of Telemark* (1965), *Dr Zhivago* (1965) and *Born Free* (1966), and on television in episodes of DANGER MAN and THE SAINT. He has continued to work extensively in film and television, with roles in *Taste the Blood of Dracula* (1970), *Living Free* (1971) and *Doomwatch* (1972), and for a period of ten years made regular appearances as Frederick Gray in the James Bond films *The Spy Who Loved Me* (1977), *Moonraker* (1979), *For Your Eyes Only* (1981), *Octopussy* (1983), *A View to a Kill* (1985) and *The Living Daylights* (1987).

After five months of pre-production work, principal photography began on CAPTAIN SCARLET AND THE MYSTERONS on Monday 2 January 1967. Once again, two self-contained camera and puppet crews worked simultaneously on separate episodes with duplicate sets of the main character marionettes, completing two half-hour episodes every two weeks. Nearly half of the episodes of CAPTAIN SCARLET were in the can before pre-production work on *Thunderbird 6* was completed. One of the camera and puppet crews was reassigned to the feature film and filming began on *Thunderbird 6* on Monday 1 May 1967. The remaining episodes of CAPTAIN SCARLET were shot back-to-back with *Thunderbird 6* over the next four months.

Faced with the choice of retaining the original proportions of the THUNDERBIRDS characters for *Thunderbird 6* or substituting the new proportionally correct style of puppets, Anderson's team reached a compromise and new puppets were created that featured 'half-way house' proportions: the heads and hands were still disproportionate to the dimensions of the bodies, but less so than in the television series and the first feature film. These new puppet proportions made designer Bob Bell's job somewhat less complicated, as he could more easily reconcile the scale of the sets and properties without worrying whether the characters were sitting or standing.

As a result, he was able to concentrate on setting himself new challenges, and his creations for *Thunderbird 6* remain those of which he is most proud. Bell cites the interior of the Whistle Stop Inn, visited by Lady Penelope, Alan, Tin-Tin and the false Captain Foster while in Switzerland, as his favourite design. 'The setting was a restaurant designed as a railway station, with food being brought to the tables by toy trains. This was a real challenge and took a lot of working out, as we had the puppets in one scale and the trains in another scale and it all had to have precise timing.'

Bell also furnished the interior of Skyship One with a variety of amazing sets. Each of the rooms on the airship was designed with a particular theme in mind, so the Ballroom featured spherical or circular fixtures and fittings, the Games Room was decked out like a chess board, with huge dice as tables and chairs, and everything in the Bottle Room was shaped like a bottle, even down to the dining table which doubled as an unusual aquarium. Keith Wilson took time out from his duties as designer on CAPTAIN SCARLET to create Lady Penelope's bedroom, the airship's Pink Room, which, as its name suggested, was decorated and furnished entirely in a shocking pink that matched the colour of FAB 1.

One of the earliest ideas for *Thunderbird 6* was the notion of integrating a full-size Tiger Moth biplane into the proceedings. Initially, all of the biplane sequences were going to be shot on location using this full-size vehicle, but it was soon realized that model shots would also be necessary for sequences of the plane leaving Tracy Island, flying over Lady Penelope's stately home and rescuing the passengers of Skyship One from the deck of the airship. Nonetheless, the dramatic climax of the film, as Lady Penelope attempts to land the biplane on the M104 motorway, was to be shot entirely on location on the real-life M40 motorway, which had just been completed and was not yet open to traffic.

Unfortunately, filming of this sequence landed members of the crew in court when a shot involving stunt-flying by ace pilot Joan Hughes contravened the instructions of an official from the Department of Transport. The scene, towards the end of the film, called for the Tiger Moth to fly under a motorway bridge at Lane End near High Wycombe, Buckinghamshire, between junctions 4 and 5 of the M40. The Department of Transport official, on-site to ensure that the Department's regulations were adhered to during the performance of the stunt, insisted that the biplane could pass under the bridge only if the wheels were in contact with the road, a stipulation that made the stunt significantly less exciting but significantly more difficult for Hughes to accomplish successfully.

After several passes under the bridge in which she controlled her plane exactly as the official had stipulated (none of which had any visual impact), Hughes decided to make one last attempt at the manoeuvre. But as she approached the bridge, a breeze sprang up and a sudden crosswind prevented her from landing the plane. She was forced to fly under the bridge without touching down, or risk losing control of the Tiger Moth. Hughes squeezed under the bridge with only 9 feet to spare and later admitted, 'It was the only time that I have ever been scared.' The official was furious, the Department of Transport prosecuted Hughes and production manager Norman Foster, who was supervising the shoot, and a hearing was scheduled before the Aylesbury quarter sessions jury for the following March.

In the meantime, filming on *Thunderbird 6* had to go on, but the company was refused permission to film any more scenes on the M40, so Derek Meddings's special effects crew built an entire section of the motorway in miniature on the studio backlot to complete the necessary shots. In the finished film, the miniature work was indistinguishable from the material shot on location.

Finally, on Wednesday 20 March 1968, Hughes was acquitted of seven charges of dangerous flying and Foster was acquitted of three charges of aiding and abetting. The jury at Aylesbury had deliberated for two and a half days before coming to their decision and were entertained with a film show of the actual flight so as to enable them to make up their minds. With a track record of thirty-two years as a pilot and more than 9,500 hours in the air without a single accident, Hughes was delighted by the outcome of the hearing. 'It's a terrific relief to know that my flying history remains unblemished,' she said.

Although the film was completed and submitted for classification by the British Film Catalogue in January 1968, it was perhaps indicative of United Artists' loss of faith in THUNDERBIRDS following the termination of the television series and resulting drop in popularity that *Thunderbird 6* sat on the shelf for six months before finally receiving its premiere at the Odeon Cinema in Leicester Square, London, on the afternoon of Monday 29 July 1968. As with its predecessor, box-office returns on *Thunderbird 6* were disappointing and sealed the fate on any further THUNDERBIRDS productions.

Over the last thirty years, however, THUNDERBIRDS has proved its continuing popularity time and time again as screenings around the world entertain new generations of viewers and legions of long-time fans who remember the show from the original 1960s screenings. Recognizing that it had been a terrible mistake on Lew Grade's part to cancel the series at the height of its popularity, Gerry Anderson is philosophical about the series that he will probably always be remembered for.

'Nothing was as successful as THUNDERBIRDS,' he says. 'CAPTAIN SCARLET AND THE MYSTERONS was very successful, but once you've had a smash hit, everything tends to look less successful in comparison.'

Construction of the M104 motorway model for **Thunderbird 6.**

'I think to have been involved in THUNDERBIRDS is, for me, the thing that I am most proud of. I think that it was really the ultimate Gerry Anderson programme.

'The whole thing started with Gerry's FOUR FEATHER FALLS and as it grew the technique developed. By the time we got to THUNDERBIRDS, the whole team had got it just right. Gerry, Alan Fennell, Dennis Spooner and Alan Pattillo came up with some great stories, Barry Gray's music for the show was outstanding and Christine Glanville and her team created the most wonderful characters I have ever worked with. We had a genius in Derek Meddings, great sculptors and model-makers and a superb post-production team.

'I made friends with people that, to this day, I remain in contact with. I really do love that programme and all the people involved in it.'

DAVID LANE

THE WORLD OF THUNDERBIRDS 2

DATELINE: 2065

The world of 2065 is one that thrives on remarkable engineering projects and technological innovation, yet is increasingly reliant on the discovery of new resources of food and fuel. Population increases have depleted many natural resources to a critical level, so projects that can reverse this downward spiral have become of paramount importance.

In the Australian Outback and the Sahara Desert, irrigation stations are being constructed that will use atomic reactors to pump sea water into the desert, enabling those areas to be reclaimed for farming. In South America, scientists experimenting with the drug theramine hope to provide a solution for the world food shortage by stimulating the growth of livestock, which could increase meat output tenfold. In Europe, experiments with cyclonic generators promise to be able to process solar radiation into electricity, solving the problem of storing electricity on a commercial scale by using cyclonic batteries to concentrate sunlight into a beam of intense heat and thereby generate power.

Population growth has also meant that builders and architects need to look at more economic use of land for housing, with one solution being multi-level accommodation. The newly completed Thompson Tower on America's west coast is a completely self-contained city, with every single commercial item produced throughout the entire world available on its 350 floors. A person could live for a whole year without moving from one of the rooms of the twelve hotels housed in the Tower, which is half a mile wide and 2 miles deep. Beneath the structure is a massive sub-basement that has parking for 10,000 cars and is linked to the store by a monorail 4 miles long.

The city of New York, on the other hand, has embarked on a long-term programme of urban renewal which involves an expensive and ingenious scheme to preserve the Empire State Building by moving it 200 yards to a new site. Ten years of planning and two years of construction have gone into the operation, all to enable the surrounding area to be completely redeveloped.

Over the last fifty years, saturation road usage has been resolved by the development of more economic and efficient public transport. Many cities around the world, including London, Paris and New York, have replaced their old subway systems with overhead monorails, and monorail is also the transport service of choice for many transcontinental services, such as the coast-to-coast Pacific–Atlantic monorail which crosses the United States, and the Paris–Anderbad monorail through the Alps.

Motorways and autobahns have largely been replaced by multi-lane superhighways such as the Great North–South Superhighway constructed in Britain in the early 2020s, and the more recent M104, still under construction. Roads such as these can now be completed at incredible speed using massive Road Construction Vehicles which flatten the ground in the path of the road, lay tarmac and paint lane markings all in a single pass. Similar vehicles are used to clear heavily forested regions for urban development or road construction. The Crablogger felling vehicle uses forward-mounted grabs on telescopic arms to cut down trees and feed them into a pulping machine. Powered by

An Air Terrainean Fireflash passenger aircraft arrives at New York Central Airport (The Duchess Assignment).

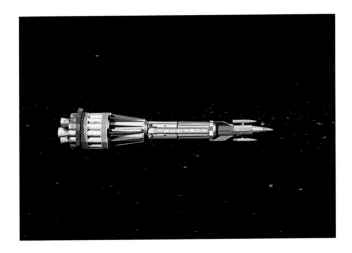

a Superon-fuelled atomic reactor, the Crablogger processes the wood pulp and packs it into barrels, producing up to sixty barrels of wood pulp every thirty minutes.

Air travel has become more efficient and extensive, principally through the introduction of Air Terrainean's fleet of Fireflash atomic-powered passenger aircraft. Capable of flying at six times the speed of sound, the Fireflash carries 600 passengers at a height of 150,000 feet to destinations around the globe, including Tokyo, San Francisco, New York and Nice. The most aerodynamic vehicle yet created, the Fireflash's pencil-slim design relocates the pilot's cockpit to the rear tailfin, which is mounted by an elevated tailplane housing six atomic engines. These engines will, in principle, enable the craft to stay in the air for up to six months at a time, although the anti-radiation shielding on the reactor requires regular servicing.

Civil and military aviation is monitored and directed by International Space Control, which operates a network of orbiting space observatory platforms and maintains complete records of the positions of all authorized satellites. Space exploration continues to be high on the agenda in the search for new resources, as projects to investigate other planetary bodies in the solar system will, it is hoped, have a beneficial impact back on Earth. The most costly project yet devised by man is the Space Exploration Center's plan for the first manned landing on Mars. This will utilize the incredible Zero X modular spacecraft, assembled from five component parts – the main body, two lifting bodies, a specialized Martian Excursion Vehicle and heat-resistant nose cone – and launched from Glenn Field in Nevada to convey a five-man scientific team to the red planet. Should this mission fail, an alternative plan will launch two astronauts aboard a Martian Space Probe rocket from a suitable launch site in Britain ahead of the next Zero X launch window in two years' time.

Equally important is the Operation Sun Probe project, a manned mission to capture matter from the Sun by sending a probe capsule into a solar prominence. The launch of the Sun Probe rocket will rely on a new process which converts sea water into rocket fuel capable of exerting 20 million pounds of thrust.

Rocket launches of this kind are now almost entirely computer-controlled and automated, and advances in computer technology have encouraged an increasing reliance on automation at every level of society. Gazelle Automation Incorporated in New York leads the world in robotic and automatic devices, such as automated secretaries, elevators, cigarette and drinks dispensers, and even window blinds, while Robotics International in England specializes in larger-scale technology, such as the aforementioned Crablogger.

Even with such levels of automation, human error and outside interference can still have a disastrous effect and when this occurs, given the scale of many of the projects in operation around the globe, the results can be devastating. For in one area the world of 2065 is sorely lacking, and that is in the development by the authorities of suitable rescue machines and equipment to cope with the kind of disasters that are now possible. This imbalance has been redressed by the formation of an independent privately funded organization: International Rescue.

Left: The Sun Probe rocket on its historic manned mission to the Sun (Sun Probe).

Right: The revolutionary Skythrust aircraft designed by Hiram K. Hackenbacker (Alias Mr. Hackenbacker).

The atomic-powered Fireflash shortly after take-off from London Airport.

INTERNATIONAL RESCUE

The Tracy Villa, luxury home of Jeff Tracy and his family.

Thunderbird 3 lifts off from Tracy Island.

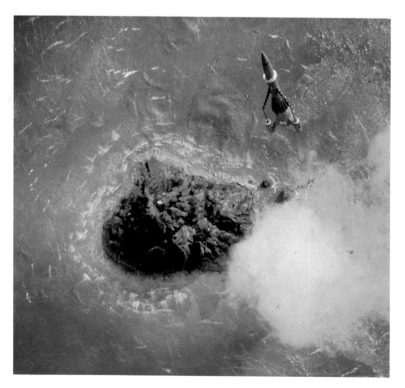

The top-secret International Rescue organization is based on Tracy Island, which is located near the island of Moyla in the Southern Pacific and owned by multi-millionaire Jeff Tracy. Hidden away beneath Jeff Tracy's elaborate two-storey villa are the secret hangars and storage facilities for the numerous incredible aircraft, machinery and vehicles that the operatives of International Rescue can call upon in an emergency.

The Tracy Villa itself is set in a prime location with beautiful views of the island and a staircase connecting it to a full-sized swimming pool outside. This is the home in which Jeff Tracy lives with his five sons and their extended family. As well as accommodation for the ten permanent residents, the Tracy Villa contains guest rooms, a lounge, library, dining room, laboratory, games room, shooting range, music room, workshop and cinema, as well as a kitchen that is equipped with a nuclear-powered cooker.

From the lounge, the Tracy brothers can access International Rescue's Thunderbird craft, which are positioned at various locations around the island, while Jeff directs operations from his desk. Jeff maintains constant contact with each of his sons during rescue operations via an aerial beacon set on a promontory of the island. Portraits of the brothers on the wall of the lounge double as monitor screens which enable Jeff to see and speak directly to all five men at once, if necessary. A sixth portrait puts him in touch with International Rescue's London agent, Lady Penelope Creighton-Ward.

In order to operate freely, but covertly, in the outside world, International Rescue maintains a network of agents, all trusted individuals known personally to Jeff for their loyalty and integrity. Among these are Sir Jeremy Hodge, the British scientist who helped Thunderbirds designer Brains to get certain components for the Thunderbirds vehicles manufactured secretly in Europe, and Jeremiah Tuttle, a hillbilly known to Jeff from his Space Agency days. All agents are issued with specialized equipment to assist them in any International Rescue assignment, including an Intercall miniature video transceiver disguised as a watch and a personal edible transmitter that can be swallowed in an emergency to act as a homing device. One of the most vital services that agents perform concerns the supply and delivery of replacement parts for the International Rescue machines, as spares are ordered from different aircraft corporations, none of which knows what the individual components are for.

International Rescue's function is to act on any emergency call to assist in situations where conventional rescue methods have proved inadequate. At times, the organization may also choose to involve itself in operations which will ultimately save life by the prevention of disaster situations before they arise. The motto of International Rescue is 'Not to give up at any cost' and each of the organization's agents must be prepared to sacrifice his or her own life if to do so would mean saving the lives of others.

THE VEHICLES

THUNDERBIRD 1

Thunderbird 1 is the spearhead craft of International Rescue. Sleek and fast, with a top speed of 15,000 m.p.h., it is 115 feet long and has a wing span of 80 feet. It is housed in a hangar adjacent to the Tracy Villa and accessed by its pilot, Scott Tracy, from a revolving panel in the lounge. This ferries him on a moving gantry directly to a hatch in the vehicle's nose section. The craft is then transported on a trolley down a ramp beneath the villa to its launch site below the swimming pool. The entire pool slides back under the patio and Thunderbird 1 is launched through the opening that is revealed.

Thunderbird 1 is equipped for take-off and landing with four booster rockets, but after switching to horizontal flight control, ram-jet thrusters and a centrally mounted high-performance sustainer rocket come into play. Each of a pair of folding wings contains a landing leg with interchangeable feet (wheels or skids) which enable the craft to effect a horizontal landing at the danger zone. The vehicle is powered by rocket propellant, turbo-jet fuel and an atomic pile in a protective sandwich shielding.

In the cockpit, the pilot's seat is mounted on a swing to keep the pilot upright during the change from vertical to horizontal flight. A control panel in front of him features a central multi-purpose television monitor on which can be projected route maps, touchdown viewing and normal communications. All of the vehicle's systems are automated where possible to simplify the pilot's task at high velocity.

The principal role of Thunderbird 1 is to get to the danger zone as soon as possible so that Scott can assess the situation, advise on specialist equipment required and direct the rescue operation. He can then oversee the rescue either from the cockpit of Thunderbird 1 or from a Mobile Control Console which forms an essential part of his equipment. The craft is also equipped with an ultra-high-frequency guidance system, an automatic camera detector, a remote camera specially constructed to withstand extreme heat, an electronic beam for wiping magnetic film, sonar sounding equipment consisting of sonar spheres attached to a flotation device, a retractable destructor cannon (normally used for demolition of dangerous wreckage) and steel spears.

Thunderbird 1 touches down on Seascape (Atlantic Inferno).

THUNDERBIRD 2

Thunderbird 2 is International Rescue's heavy-duty freighter which carries the organization's auxiliary rescue equipment to the danger zone. 250 feet long, with a wing span of 180 feet and standing 60 feet high, it is housed in a hangar beneath the Cliff House, which overlooks the island's runway. Pilot Virgil Tracy gains access to his vehicle via a tilting picture in the lounge of the villa. This tips him on to a padded slide which glides down a chute. The chute levels out and the slide comes to a stop on a turntable which revolves so that Virgil is facing feet first as he continues his journey down the chute and directly into his seat in the cockpit of Thunderbird 2.

The central section of the craft carries one of a selection of six interchangeable pods, each housing different auxiliary vehicles. Virgil selects the appropriate pod as it passes on a conveyor belt beneath and hydraulic legs drop the main fuselage into place over the pod. A steel door disguised as a section of the cliff wall then moves down into a trench at the hangar end of the runway and a second 'drawbridge door' swings down to cover the trench and provide smooth access to the runway. As an airstrip that would accommodate the full width of Thunderbird 2's wing span would draw attention to itself, the runway is lined with movable palm trees which fall back to allow Thunderbird 2 passage to a concealed launch ramp.

Powered by an atomic pile in lightweight shielding, Thunderbird 2 is capable of speeds of up to 5,000 m.p.h. Four tailplane-mounted turbo-jets provide power at cruising speed (2,000 m.p.h.) and fore and aft VTOL rockets enable the vehicle to effect take-off and landing without the aid of a launch ramp. On arrival at the danger zone, Thunderbird 2 lands and then lifts clear of the pod on its hydraulic legs to enable unloading operations. Pod 4 is fitted with flotation equipment which enables it to be released over water.

Thunderbird 2 contains living accommodation with foldaway bunks, an 'armoury' of cutting tools, drills, lasers and thermic lances, a variety of magnetic grabs on high-tensile winch cables, and an astrodome with a roof hatch for air-to-air rescue operations. The craft is also equipped with missiles for heavy-duty demolition.

THUNDERBIRD 3

Thunderbird 3 is International Rescue's massive orange space rocket. Standing 287 feet high, the spacecraft is housed in a deep silo concealed beneath the Round House, some distance from the Tracy Villa. Here, it rests on three immense columns which absorb the blast during take-off. Pilot Alan Tracy is ferried to his craft by sitting on the settee in the lounge in the Tracy Villa. This is lowered into an underground chamber and replaced by a duplicate piece of furniture while the settee is transported on a motorized bogie through an access tunnel to the Thunderbird 3 launch bay. There it is lifted through the base of the spacecraft into the Thunderbird 3 lounge, from where Alan can enter a lift which will carry him to the cockpit.

The rocket is launched on chemical rockets fed by helium-pressurized rocket propellant and rises through the centre of the Round House, quickly accelerating to escape velocity (25,200 m.p.h.). Once escape velocity is achieved, three particle accelerators powered by atomic generators provide a steady, continuous acceleration by means of an exhaust stream of atomic particles. Course is controlled by a flywheel rotor assemblage, although the rocket is also equipped with pitch-and-yaw correction jets. The craft houses the lounge, cockpit and rudimentary sleeping accommodation within a twin-walled hull which provides additional meteor protection, and the nose cone contains the craft's sensors, accelerometers and other flight instruments.

The primary function of Thunderbird 3 is to act as a regular link to the Thunderbird 5 satellite for servicing and personnel transfer, but the spacecraft doubles as a rescue vehicle on the rare occasions when it is required for operations in Earth orbit and outer space. The basic crew complement is two, which usually means that Scott will accompany Alan on each space mission.

Thunderbird 4 leaves Pod 4 towing a Sealing Device (Atlantic Inferno).

THUNDERBIRD 4

Thunderbird 4 is a small underwater and sea surface rescue craft piloted by Gordon Tracy. Just 30 feet long, the submarine is usually carried to and from the danger zone by Thunderbird 2 aboard Pod 4, although the craft is fitted with hover jets which enable it to travel short distances across land to reach the water under its own power. Highly manoeuvrable, Thunderbird 4 is one of the fastest-known craft on or under the sea, rivalling even the capabilities of the super-subs operated by the World Aquanaut Security Patrol.

A pair of main turbo drives and six drive turbos powered by twin atomic generators propel the submarine when submerged, while small jet engines at port and starboard, powered by a 'mini-pile', are used for surface cruising. A forward-mounted lighting trough provides subsurface illumination and a quartet of tubes in the nose house an array of auxiliary equipment: port and starboard hydraulic rams, a central ram with interchangeable tool heads, and a missile launcher for underwater demolition. The craft is also equipped with a laser cutter, electromagnet, soundcsan and paralyser.

Thunderbird 4 recovers the Seascape Diving Bell (Atlantic Inferno).

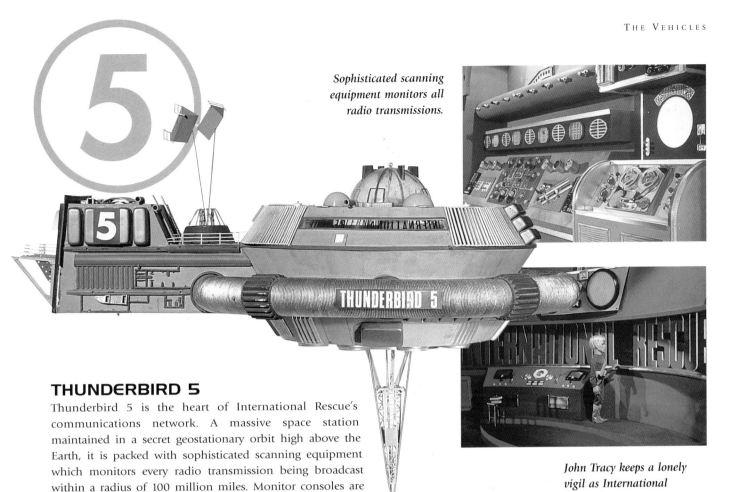

Sophisticated scanning equipment monitors all radio transmissions.

THUNDERBIRD 5

Thunderbird 5 is the heart of International Rescue's communications network. A massive space station maintained in a secret geostationary orbit high above the Earth, it is packed with sophisticated scanning equipment which monitors every radio transmission being broadcast within a radius of 100 million miles. Monitor consoles are fitted with special filters attuned to messages of distress in any language. John Tracy and his younger brother Alan take turns to man Thunderbird 5, staying aboard for duty tours of one month at a time. Contact with International Rescue headquarters on Tracy Island and the organization's agents around the globe is maintained via special-frequency antennae.

John Tracy keeps a lonely vigil as International Rescue's space monitor.

The station's monitoring and life-support equipment is powered by atomic batteries and piles in a main generating room which occupies the entire first floor of the three-storey complex.

Accommodation and living quarters are on the second floor, while the monitoring rooms occupy the top floor. Above this level is an astrodome housing a high-resolution telescope which can be used manually or coupled to a TV screen in a monitor room. The whole is contained by double walls filled with coagulant compound to seal micro-meteorite punctures and surrounded by a plasma-cored localized field meteor deflector. A pylon extends beneath the satellite to hold the main antenna clear of distortion caused by the anti-meteor device.

FAB 1

FAB 1, Lady Penelope's striking pink Rolls-Royce, has the outward appearance of a powerful, sophisticated vehicle suitable for a lady of leisure, but the highly polished exterior hides a complete armoury of gadgets, weapons and specialized equipment. At 21 feet long and capable of speeds in excess of 200 m.p.h., FAB 1 requires two additional wheels at the front of the vehicle to support the weight of the power unit. All six wheels are fitted with retractable studs for driving on snow and ice, tyre slashers which extend from the hubcap motif, and a rotating axle which allows the car to drive sideways over short distances.

Access to the completely air-conditioned car is via a gull-wing canopy and down-and-under doors. Inside the bullet-proof cabin, the driver sits beneath a laminated, anti-glare bullet-proof canopy in front of a centrally positioned steering wheel which incorporates radar-assisted steering. There is no driving mirror as the driver relies on a small television monitor screen on the dashboard. This receives images from a camera hidden in the boot, which also conceals a hydraulic platform with fold-down safety rails. Centre pull-down armrests on the back seat are fitted with retractable handcuffs and a restraining chest band. The silver lady on the bonnet doubles as a directional signal locator.

The car's weaponry includes heavy machine guns mounted at the front and rear, a swivel laser beam set into the rear wings, and jets which expel smoke and oil from the rear bumper. For use at sea, FAB 1 is equipped with hydrofoils which extend below the level of the wheels to lift the whole car clear of the water at speed, minimizing resistance. The rear hydrofoil has a centrally fitted vortex-aquajet powerpack. For extreme snow conditions, the car is also fitted with skis.

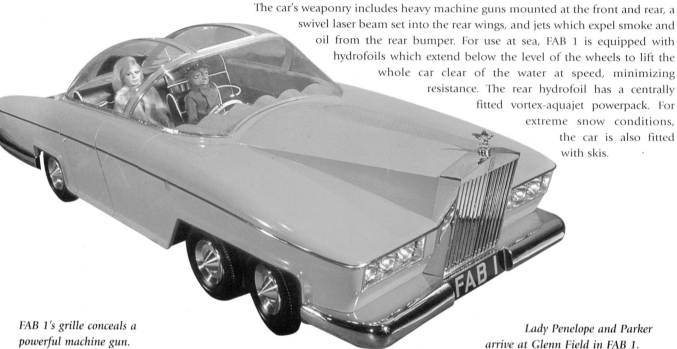

FAB 1's grille conceals a powerful machine gun.

Lady Penelope and Parker arrive at Glenn Field in FAB 1.

THE POD VEHICLES

A variety of specialized auxiliary vehicles are transported to the sites of rescue operations inside the six Thunderbird 2 pods.

The **Mole** is a 30-ton jet-propelled boring machine powered by a nuclear reactor and fitted with a Formula C30/1 drill bit which can cut through any known metal. A tracked trolley carries the Mole to the drill site, where it is tilted for vertical drilling. Caterpillar tracks on the side of the Mole enable it to return to the surface when the rescue is complete.

The **Firefly** is the principal vehicle in International Rescue's fleet of fire-fighting machines. A tracked vehicle with a Cahelium Extract X heat-resistant shield, it travels to the heart of a blaze and snuffs out the fire at its source by means of nitro-glycerine shells, which are fired from a nozzle in the protective plate.

The **High-speed Elevator Cars** incorporate a master control car with two radio-controlled subsidiaries. Each twelve-wheeled car supports a flat landing pad with cushioned suspension which can be positioned beneath the hull and wings of an aircraft landing at speed, becoming a substitute for the aircraft's disabled landing gear.

The **Recovery Vehicles** are a pair of tracked units fitted with magnetic lines, powerful electromagnets on high-tensile cables which can be projected at a target up to 300 feet away. Successfully attached, the lines are winched back in, drawing the target towards the vehicles. One of the vehicles is a master control car, while the other is a radio-controlled subsidiary.

The **Transmitter Truck** is a tracked vehicle equipped with a powerful rear-mounted transmitter dish capable of directing and projecting a control beam more than 90 million miles into space.

The **Neutraliser Tractor** is a single-seater tracked vehicle with a front-mounted sonic dish which projects sonic waves at a specific frequency to match and neutralize sonic waves being generated by third-party equipment.

The **Jet Air Transporter** is a small vehicle carrying a powerful jet engine which emits a cushion of air capable of supporting a mass of more than 170 pounds, enabling it to be used as a mobile 'safety net'.

The **Excavator** is a tracked drilling and crushing machine fitted with an excavator shovel with the ability to break down rock and other debris into dust and pebbles, which it ejects from the rear. This enables the vehicle to clear a path through heavy rubble.

The **Monobrake** is a low-slung tracked search and recovery vehicle specifically designed for use on monorail lines. A front-mounted telescopic arm can be attached to the overhead monorail, giving the vehicle greater speed.

The **Booster Mortar** is a small tracked vehicle with a front-mounted mortar cannon used to project auxiliary rescue equipment, such as low-altitude escape harnesses, sealed inside missile capsules to a height of up to 500 feet.

The **Laser Beam Equipment** incorporates a powerful laser cutter mounted on a small tracked vehicle, similar in appearance to the Booster Mortar, with powerful air blast jets for removing obstructions once the laser has cut them free.

The **Domo** is a restraining vehicle used in demolition work. A tracked vehicle similar in appearance to the Excavator, the Domo is fitted with three powerful suction pads on the end of jointed arms.

The **Mobile Crane** is a six-wheeled truck with a telescopic arm which raises a maintenance platform to a height of about 50 feet.

The Mole returns to Pod 5 after completing another successful rescue mission.

The Domo restrains a collapsing house wall which threatens an underground rescue operation (The Duchess Assignment).

THE CHARACTERS

JEFF TRACY

The patriarch of the Tracy family and founder of International Rescue, Jeff Tracy was born on 2 January 2009, the son of a Kansas wheat farmer. A colonel in the US Air Force before transferring to the Space Agency, Jeff counts himself among the first astronauts to land on the Moon during the early days of colonization. He abandoned his space career to raise his five sons after the tragic early death of his wife.

Entrepreneurial, spirited and adventurous, Jeff's genius for civil and construction engineering soon made him one of the richest men in the world, giving him the ability to finance International Rescue. He was inspired to form the organization after reading a report of a tragic air crash in which eighty people died, largely owing to inadequate rescue equipment and craft. Within two years, he had transformed his dream into reality.

Intelligent, kindly and with a sense of humour, Jeff also exhibits the ability to be decisive and stern when the situation demands. Now fifty-six, Jeff is absolutely dedicated to the goals of International Rescue and rarely allows himself the luxury of time off from his duties.

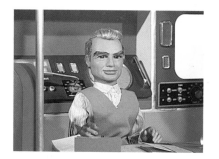

Jeff Tracy enjoys a rare holiday at Lady Penelope's sheep farm in Bonga Bonga (Atlantic Inferno).

SCOTT TRACY

The eldest of Jeff Tracy's sons, Scott was born on 4 April 2039 and is now twenty-six years old. Named after the pioneer astronaut Scott Malcolm Carpenter and educated at Yale and Oxford Universities, Scott was decorated for valour during his service with the US Air Force, before joining International Rescue.

As the pilot of Thunderbird 1, Scott is always the first to arrive at the danger zone, where he assesses the situation and quickly determines which special rescue equipment will be required for the task at hand. His complete lack of arrogance enables him to assist his brothers in even the most menial of tasks. In addition to his Thunderbird 1 duties, Scott often co-pilots Thunderbird 3 with his brother Alan, and has even been known to take occasional spells of duty aboard Thunderbird 5. Whenever his father, Jeff, is absent, Scott's seniority places him in command of the island headquarters.

Fast-talking and quick-thinking, with brains, brawn, daring and drive, Scott has the confidence to make instant decisions, backed by a fierce determination and unfaltering bravery.

Scott pilots Thunderbird 1 on another rescue mission.

Below left: Scott at the controls of Thunderbird 1, with automatic camera detector behind.
Below right: Scott co-pilots Thunderbird 3 (Ricochet).

VIRGIL TRACY

The most serious of the Tracy brothers, Virgil was born on 15 August 2041 and is now twenty-four years old. Named after astronaut Virgil Grissom, he is an accomplished graduate of the Denver School of Advanced Technology. This gives him the experience and mechanical dexterity necessary to make him the ideal pilot of Thunderbird 2 and its various complex auxiliary rescue vehicles.

Like his brothers, Virgil never places technology above human needs, even if it means placing his own life in danger. As a result, he is always on hand, taking part in virtually every daring situation in which International Rescue is involved. Possessing a demeanour and maturity well beyond his years, Virgil is a complex young man who combines a physical strength and fearless bravery with a gentler side as a gifted artist and pianist.

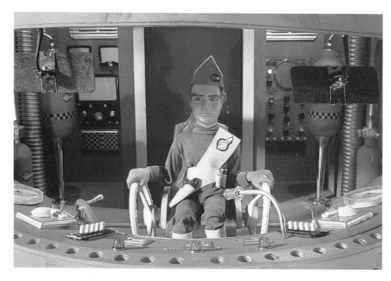

Above: At the controls of the Master Elevator Car (Trapped in the Sky).
Below: Virgil and Brains prepare to intercept the KLA pirate television satellite (Ricochet).

ALAN TRACY

Named after astronaut Alan B. Shephard, Alan Tracy was born on 12 March 2044 and is now twenty-one years old. Caring and deeply romantic, he has a love of motor-racing and was a champion racing-car driver prior to becoming the pilot of Thunderbird 3. The blond-haired, baby-faced astronaut is utterly dedicated to International Rescue, meeting his great responsibilities with a maturity that belies his years. Yet there are times when his father still sees him as the college student whose rocket experiments went haywire, and accordingly treats him as a wayward schoolboy.

Educated at Colorado University, Alan is a great sportsman and practical joker. However, he is not without his quiet side and likes nothing better than to explore the rocks and potholes located in the more inaccessible points of Tracy Island. Apart from piloting Thunderbird 3, Alan also assists his brother John by taking turns at manning the space station, Thunderbird 5. He jealously guards his romantic relationship with Tin-Tin Kyrano, although he secretly harbours a passion for London agent Lady Penelope Creighton-Ward.

*Above left: Alan leaves Thunderbird 3 to rescue O'Shea and Loman (*Ricochet*).*

*Left: Alan takes a tour of duty on Thunderbird 5 (*Danger at Ocean Deep*).*

*Left: Alan flies Thunderbird 1 to the danger zone (*Atlantic Inferno*).*

GORDON TRACY

Born on 14 February 2043, Gordon Tracy is a twenty-two-year-old who revels in all aquatic sports, from skin-diving to water-skiing. Named after astronaut Leroy Gordon Cooper, he is a highly trained aquanaut, with stints in the Submarine Service and the World Aquanaut Security Patrol under his belt. During his time with the WASPs, Gordon commanded a deep-sea bathyscaphe and spent a year beneath the ocean investigating marine farming methods. An expert oceanographer, he is also the designer of a unique underwater breathing apparatus, which he has modified and improved for International Rescue.

Shortly before International Rescue began operating, Gordon was involved in a hydrofoil speedboat crash when his vessel capsized at 400 knots. The craft was completely shattered and Gordon spent four months in a hospital bed. Now, as the pilot of Thunderbird 4, he commands the world's most advanced and versatile one-man submarine. Good-natured and high-spirited, he possesses a strength and tenacity that make him a respected leader and commander. He is also one of the world's fastest freestyle swimmers and is a past Olympic champion at the butterfly stroke.

Gordon at the controls of Thunderbird 4.

Gordon searches for Ned Cook and his cameraman (Terror in New York City).

JOHN TRACY

Born on 8 October 2040, twenty-five-year-old John Tracy was educated at Harvard and followed in his father's footsteps to become an astronaut prior to his involvement with International Rescue. Named after astronaut John Glenn, he is an electronics expert with a degree in laser communication. John is the quietest and most intellectual of the Tracy brothers, slighter in build than his siblings and tremendously lithe and graceful.

As space monitor for International Rescue stationed aboard Thunderbird 5, John has ample time on his hands to indulge his favourite pastime, astronomy. Four astronomy and outer space textbooks have been published bearing his name, and his incessant space searching led to the discovery of the Tracy quasar system. His duties aboard Thunderbird 5 nonetheless leave him feeling frustrated that he is unable to take part in as many rescue missions as his siblings.

Top: John responds to a distress call from Seascape (Atlantic Inferno).

Middle: John relaxes by the pool (Danger at Ocean Deep).

Bottom: John intercepts a messages from Fireflash (Trapped in the Sky).

BRAINS

Born on 14 November 2040, Brains was orphaned when a hurricane struck his Michigan home. He was adopted at the age of twelve by a Cambridge University professor who recognized the boy's genius and encouraged his phenomenal learning abilities. During a worldwide search for a brilliant scientist who could help him accomplish his plans for International Rescue, Jeff Tracy discovered Brains nervously delivering a lecture at a cultural hall in Paris. Brains recognized in Jeff Tracy a philanthropic entrepreneur striving to save mankind and accepted his challenge without hesitation.

As the inventor of all of International Rescue's dazzling machines, Brains is an esteemed and valuable part of the secret organization. An incurable perfectionist, the twenty-five-year-old is never satisfied with his creations and is often to be found endlessly modifying and tinkering with his machines. His idea of off-duty relaxation includes studying trigonometry and thermodynamics, while designing new ways of improving Braman, a robot that he hopes will one day defeat him at chess.

To protect his identity in the outside world while developing incredible new machines and aircraft for business and industry (such as Skythrust and Skyship One), Brains goes by the alias of Hiram K. Hackenbacker. His real name is unknown.

Brains teaching Braman to play chess (Sun Probe) *and, below, wishing he was on Skyship One's maiden voyage* (Thunderbird 6).

LADY PENELOPE CREIGHTON-WARD

Born on 24 December 2039, Lady Penelope Creighton-Ward is the twenty-six-year-old daughter of aristocrat Sir Hugh Creighton-Ward and his wife, Amelia. Lady Penelope inherited her father's spirit and determination, craving danger, action and intrigue, so after completing her education at Rowden and a finishing school in Switzerland, she rejected the aristocracy's endless round of social engagements and became a secret agent. It was while working as the chief operative of the Federal Agents Bureau that Lady Penelope first met Jeff Tracy, and she immediately accepted his invitation to become International Rescue's London agent, a key part of the organization's network of undercover agents.

Stylish and fashionable in every aspect of her life, Lady Penelope owns FAB 1, an incredible six-wheeled Rolls-Royce, as well as Seabird, a 40-foot ocean-going cruiser, FAB 2, a sleek private yacht, and FAB 3, a prize-winning racehorse. Her clothes are specially created for her by top fashion designers Elaine Wickfen and François Lemaire, and she wears an exclusive perfume, Soupçon de Péril, mixed for her in Paris by Jacques Verre.

Working from Creighton-Ward Mansion, her eighteenth-century stately home at Foxleyheath in southern England, Lady Penelope appears to those ignorant of her secret life to be just another member of the English landed gentry. But with her poise and nerves of steel, she has proved time and again to be an invaluable addition to the International Rescue team.

Far left: Lady Penelope visits the Century 21 Film Studios for TV Century 21 *magazine.*

Left: Lady Penelope prepares for a holiday in Monte Bianco (Lord Parker's 'Oliday).

ALOYSIUS PARKER

Born on 30 May, 2013, Aloysius Parker is the last of a long line of faithful Cockney retainers who have served the English aristocracy for centuries. However, unable to follow in the family tradition and find employment as a butler, he fell in with various villains in the London underworld who taught him the tricks of the trade. Known to his new friends as 'Nosey', Parker soon gained a reputation for himself as one of the world's finest safe-crackers and cat burglars, a reputation that also landed him in Parkmoor Scrubs prison for a spell.

After his release, he attempted to make an honest living, but he soon fell back into his old ways and was caught by Lady Penelope Creighton-Ward while he was helping himself to the contents of an oil tycoon's safe. Penelope had heard of Parker's superior talents and offered him a working partnership in her espionage activities, employing him as both butler at Creighton-Ward Mansion and chauffeur of her Rolls-Royce, FAB 1.

Now fifty-two years old, he remains a loyal and indispensable assistant to Lady Penelope during her many dangerous assignments for International Rescue.

Parker takes the wheel of FAB 1.

KYRANO

The son of a wealthy Malayan plantation owner, Kyrano turned his back on material gain after his rightful inheritance was usurped by his evil half-brother, the Hood. Becoming an expert botanist, he spent a number of years at Kew Gardens advising on Asian orchids, before being invited to Kennedy Space Center to help in a project to produce synthetic food from plants. It was here that Kyrano first met Jeff Tracy and the two became firm friends.

Later, Kyrano moved to Paris and became head chef at the Paris Hilton, but he was happy to abandon this prestigious position when he was contacted by Jeff Tracy to help with the Tracy Island domestic arrangements. A vital part of the smooth running of the secret island base, Kyrano has only one failing: his susceptibility to the evil influence of his half-brother. He is often used as an unwitting pawn in the Hood's attempts to learn the secrets of International Rescue. His exact age is unknown as his birth certificate was lost in Malaya.

TIN-TIN KYRANO

Born on 20 June 2043, Tin-Tin Kyrano is the daughter of the Tracys' faithful family retainer, and the unlikely half-niece of their arch-enemy the Hood. Her education in America and Europe was paid for by Jeff Tracy as a token of his gratitude for her father's loyal services, and she graduated with degrees in higher mathematics, advanced technical theory and engineering. She joined International Rescue directly after completing her education, assisting Brains and organizing the maintenance of all of the Thunderbirds vehicles.

Also a qualified pilot, Tin-Tin's main interests outside her work include pop music, water-skiing, swimming and designing her own clothes. She enjoys a playful relationship with Alan, whom she adores. Her name comes from the Malaysian word for 'sweet'.

GRANDMA TRACY

Very little is known about Jeff Tracy's mother, other than that she was born in the late 1980s and can clearly remember her grandmother telling her about the old subway systems in London, Paris and New York, before they were replaced by overhead monorail. Prior to formally joining International Rescue in 2065 and going to live on Tracy Island, Grandma maintained a home near the western seaboard of the United States, not far from Parola Sands and San Miguel. Brave, fiercely loyal and protective of her family, Grandma is an excellent cook and assists Kyrano with the domestic chores at the Tracy Villa.

THE HOOD

Feared as the world's foremost villain, the Hood (so named because of his many disguises) is the half-brother of Kyrano and wields an uncanny, supernatural power over him. Unlike his brother, the Hood is massive in stature and his main aim in life is the acquisition of wealth regardless of justice and ethics. His primary target is International Rescue, as the plans of their incredible vehicles and machines could make him rich beyond his wildest imaginings.

Operating from a strange temple hidden deep in the Malaysian jungle, the Hood has successfully eluded capture by the world's security forces for a great many years. Ruthless and calculating beyond comprehension, he uses mystical powers, steeped in voodoo and black magic, to deadly effect, allowing nothing to stand in the way of his evil objectives.

His criminal record indicates that he was born on 17 July 2018.

The Hood uses his strange powers to contact Kyrano (Trapped in the Sky).

Middle right: The Hood makes his escape in a stolen aircraft (Martian Invasion).

Right: The Hood at his temple in the Malaysian jungle.

SCREEN ADVENTURES 3

REGULAR VOICE CAST

Jeff Tracy	Peter Dyneley
Scott Tracy	Shane Rimmer
Lady Penelope Creighton-Ward	Sylvia Anderson
Virgil Tracy	David Holliday
	Jeremy Wilkin
Alan Tracy	Matt Zimmerman
Brains	David Graham
Aloysius Parker	David Graham
Tin-Tin Kyrano	Christine Finn
Gordon Tracy	David Graham
John Tracy	Ray Barrett
Kyrano	David Graham
Grandma Tracy	Christine Finn
The Hood	Ray Barrett

CREDITS: FIRST SEASON (1964)

Producer	Gerry Anderson
Associate Producer	Reg Hill
Director of Photography	John Read
Character Visualization	Sylvia Anderson
Art Director	Bob Bell
Supervising Special Effects Director	Derek Meddings
Puppetry Supervision	Christine Glanville
	Mary Turner
Script Supervision	Gerry and Sylvia Anderson
Script Editor	Alan Pattillo
Music Composed and Directed by	Barry Gray
Lighting Cameraman	Paddy Seale
	Julian Lugrin
	Michael Wilson
Special Effects Lighting Cameraman	Len Walter
Supervising Editor	
Editors	
Harry MacDonald	Harry Ledger
Peter Elliott	David Lane
Camera Operators	
Jimmy Elliott	Alan Perry
Geoff Meldrum	Noel Rowland
Puppet Operators	
Wanda Webb	Carolyn Turner
Judith Shutt	Ernest Shutt
	Yvonne Hunter
Sculptors	John Brown
	John Blundell
Wardrobe	Elizabeth Coleman
Assistant Art Director	Grenville Nott
Supervising Sound Editor	John Peverill
Special Effects 2nd Unit Director	Brian Johncock
	Ian Scoones
	Shaun Whittacker-Cooke
Special Effects 2nd Unit Lighting Cameraman	Harry Oakes

Special Effects 2nd Unit Camera Operator	John Foley
	Gary Coxall
Sound Editor	Brian Hickin
	John Beaton
	Tony Lenny
Dialogue Editor	Roy Lafbery
Property Master	Arthur Cripps
Puppet Properties	Eddie Hunter
Sound	Maurice Askew
	John Taylor

CREDITS: SECOND SEASON (1966)

Executive Producer	Gerry Anderson
Producer	Reg Hill
Associate Producer	John Read
Characters Created by	Sylvia Anderson
Supervising Art Director	Bob Bell
Supervising Special Effects Director	Derek Meddings
Puppetry Supervision	Christine Glanville
	Mary Turner
Script Supervision	Gerry and Sylvia Anderson
Music Composed and Directed by	Barry Gray
Lighting Cameraman	Julian Lugrin
	Paddy Seale
Special Effects Lighting Cameraman	Michael Wilson
	Harry Oakes
Supervising Editor	Len Walter
Editors	Harry MacDonald
	Harry Ledger
Camera Operators	
Noel Rowland	Gary Coxall
Alan Perry	Ted Cutlack
Puppet Operators	Judith Shutt
	Wanda Webb
Sculpting Supervision	John F. Brown
Wardrobe	Elizabeth Coleman
Art Director	Grenville Nott
Designer	Keith Wilson
Special Effects Director	Jimmy Elliott
	Shaun Whittacker-Cooke
Supervising Sound Editor	John Peverill
Sound Editor	Norman Cole
	Peter Pennell
Dialogue Editor	Roy Lafbery
Property Master	Arthur Cripps
Sound	Maurice Askew
	Ken Scrivener

The episodes that follow are listed in the official ITC recommended broadcast order.

First Season (1964)

1. TRAPPED IN THE SKY

Written by **Gerry and Sylvia Anderson**
Directed by **Alan Pattillo**

'OK, boys. That's the brief. It's our first assignment, so make it look good.'

Through his psychic rapport with his half-brother, Kyrano, the Hood learns that International Rescue is ready to begin operations. Plotting to lure the International Rescue craft, he straps a bomb to the landing gear of the atomic-powered airliner Fireflash on its maiden flight from London to Tokyo. If the crew attempts a landing by conventional means, the bomb will detonate. The situation is desperate. Although its atomic motors will enable the Fireflash to stay in the air for six months, the passengers and crew will receive fatal doses of radiation after two hours and ten minutes, when the anti-radiation shield on the reactor fails. On board is Kyrano's daughter, Tin-Tin, *en route* to Tracy Island to join International Rescue.

The Fireflash crew attempt to dislodge the bomb with aerobatics, without success. Then an attempt is made to winch a man to the landing gear from a TX 204 Target-carrying Aircraft, but this also fails. Jeff Tracy dispatches his sons Scott and Virgil in Thunderbirds 1 and 2, and International Rescue are in business!

Thunderbird 1 arrives at London Airport and Scott assesses the situation. The plan is to bring the Fireflash, with its landing gear up, down on to High-speed Mobile Elevator Cars – two radio-controlled vehicles operated by Virgil in a third master control car. While the Tracys are organizing the rescue, the Hood, disguised as a police officer, takes photographs of Thunderbird 1. Spotted by the automatic camera detector in Thunderbird 1, he flees with the police in hot pursuit, but they lose him on the M1. Scott calls in International Rescue's London

agent, Lady Penelope Creighton-Ward.

The Fireflash makes its approach to London Airport, but one of the radio-controlled Elevator Cars suddenly develops a fault and the landing has to be aborted at the last second. With a replacement car in position, the Fireflash makes a second approach as the radiation safety factor on the anti-radiation shield expires. The Fireflash lands on the Elevator Cars without detonating the bomb, but when Virgil applies maximum brakes his master control vehicle goes out of control and crashes. Supported by only a subsidiary vehicle under each wing, the Fireflash finally slides to a halt with only yards of runway to spare.

Meanwhile, on the M1 heading for Birmingham, Lady

In his single, short line of dialogue, Alan Tracy's voice is completely different from the one heard in the rest of the series. For this episode only, Alan is voiced by Ray Barrett, as Matt Zimmerman had not been employed when voice recording commenced (although he is credited on the end titles).

In several shots from beneath Thunderbird 1, seen while the Hood takes photographs at London Airport, the vehicle's markings show the 'T' of Thunderbird painted on the red nose cone. All other shots of the craft show the nose cone free of markings.

At the end of the episode, a doctor visits Tracy Island to examine Kyrano and 'Operation Cover-up' disguises all evidence of the International Rescue organization in the lounge, with the portraits of the brothers in uniform replaced by pictures of them in civilian clothing. But when the doctor enters the room, the in-uniform portraits are still clearly visible in shots of Scott, Gordon and Jeff.

Penelope and her chauffeur, Parker, pursue the Hood in her Rolls-Royce, FAB 1. Coming to a quiet stretch of motorway, FAB 1's grille-mounted machine gun blows the Hood's car off the road and his pictures are ruined as the car crashes down an embankment. The villain vows that International Rescue has not heard the last of him.

The passengers and crew on board the Fireflash are saved, Virgil is unhurt and, with the security of the organization intact, International Rescue's first mission is a complete success.

Notes

The arrangement of the title music on the opening and closing credits of this episode differs from that used on all the other episodes. Uniquely, sound effects (such as Kyrano's scream) are also heard in the episode montage during the opening titles and the standard picture of the Mole is absent from the closing titles.

A short piece of Barry Gray's 'Formula Five' track, composed and recorded for FIREBALL XL5, can be heard on the monitors in Thunderbird 5. Air Terrainean's Lt. Meddings is named after THUNDERBIRDS visual effects supervisor Derek Meddings.

Fireflash is the only non-International Rescue vehicle to appear in the series' end titles. The airliner is seen again in *Operation Crash-Dive*, *The Impostors*, *The Man from MI.5*, *The Duchess Assignment* and *Security Hazard*.

Commander Norman makes further appearances in *Operation Crash-Dive*, *Edge of Impact*, *Security Hazard* and *Alias Mr. Hackenbacker*, while Captain Hanson is seen again in *Operation Crash-Dive*, *The Impostors*, *The Duchess Assignment* and *Security Hazard*.

Trapped in the Sky was adapted for audio on the Century 21 mini-album 'Thunderbird 1' (MA 108), narrated by Shane Rimmer as Scott Tracy.

Original UK Broadcast:
7.00 p.m., Thursday 30 September 1965
(ATV Midlands)

Original Broadcast Episode Number: 1

First UK Network Broadcast:
6.00 p.m., Friday 20 September 1991 (BBC2)

Regular Cast:
Jeff, Scott, Lady Penelope, Virgil, Alan, Brains, Parker, Tin-Tin, Gordon, John, Kyrano, the Hood

Major Equipment:
TB1, TB2 (Pod 3), TB5, FAB 1, Fireflash, Elevator Cars, TX 204 Target-carrying Aircraft

Guest Voice Cast

Commander Norman	**Peter Dyneley**
Captain Hanson	**David Graham**
Fireflash Co-pilot	**Ray Barrett**
Assistant Controller	**Ray Barrett**
Lt. Bob Meddings	**David Graham**
Harris	**Ray Barrett**
TX 204 Pilot (Target One)	**Ray Barrett**
TX 204 Co-pilot	**Shane Rimmer**
Interceptor One	**Peter Dyneley**
Air Terrainean Guide	**Sylvia Anderson**
Doctor	**David Graham**
Fireflash Passenger	**David Graham**

2. PIT OF PERIL

Written by **Alan Fennell**
Directed by **Desmond Saunders**

'Two brave men have been badly injured in that pit. I don't know if I should risk another life.'

In the African jungle, the US Army is testing a new all-terrain Sidewinder vehicle when the ground gives way beneath it and it falls into a blazing pit with a three-man crew trapped inside – 300 feet below ground. Lt. Mead, a member of the relief crew, is lowered into the pit from a helijet to assess the situation; he is badly burned but able to report on the condition of the vehicle. A second man, Sgt. Reynolds, is lowered into the pit to attach a line to one of the Sidewinder's legs to haul it upright, but he too is badly burned and the line slips off during the rescue attempt.

General Peters calls in International Rescue and Scott, Virgil and Brains are soon speeding to the scene in Thunderbirds 1 and 2. Thunderbird 1's remote camera reveals that the pit was once an open-cast mine which had been used as a military equipment dump after the Second World War. A crust of earth has formed over the top and spontaneous combustion has caused the wreckage in the pit to burn up. They must remove the remainder of the crust before the 500-ton Sidewinder can be dragged up the side of the pit.

Virgil is lowered into the pit in protective clothing to lay explosive charges, while Scott uses the Mole to drill through the side of the crater to recover Virgil. Brains detonates the charges and the explosions successfully clear the crust over the pit. Virgil takes control of two Recovery Vehicles equipped with magnetic lines – powerful electromagnets attached to winch cables. The electromagnets are fired at the Sidewinder and the Recovery Vehicles begin to haul it up the side of the pit. One of the electromagnets fails and becomes detached from the Sidewinder, so Virgil has to winch it in and fire again. This time, the magnet holds firm and on the second attempt the Recovery Vehicles finally manage to pull the Sidewinder up to the surface.

When the Mole returns to the surface with Scott and Virgil aboard, dust and sand can be seen pouring up from the ground on to the Mole's tracks – footage of the Mole tunnelling into the ground has simply been reversed.

Notes

As not a single female character appears in the episode, voice artists Sylvia Anderson and Christine Finn do not take part, although they are credited on the end titles. Indeed, *Pit of Peril* features the smallest number of regular characters seen in any THUNDERBIRDS episode – just five.

This episode introduces the Mole, which appears again in *City of Fire*, *Cry Wolf* and *The Duchess Assignment*. Thunderbird 1's remote camera is also used in *Edge of Impact*.

Colonel Sweeney previously appeared as Fireflash pilot Captain Hanson in *Trapped in the Sky*. Sweeney's subordinate was also seen as the Fireflash co-pilot in the same episode.

Pit of Peril was adapted as a comic strip by Steve Kyte and Alan Fennell for *Thunderbirds: The Comic* (issues 4–5, 1991).

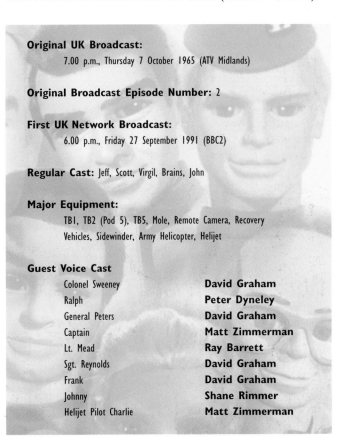

Original UK Broadcast:
7.00 p.m., Thursday 7 October 1965 (ATV Midlands)

Original Broadcast Episode Number: 2

First UK Network Broadcast:
6.00 p.m., Friday 27 September 1991 (BBC2)

Regular Cast: Jeff, Scott, Virgil, Brains, John

Major Equipment:
TB1, TB2 (Pod 5), TB5, Mole, Remote Camera, Recovery Vehicles, Sidewinder, Army Helicopter, Helijet

Guest Voice Cast

Colonel Sweeney	**David Graham**
Ralph	**Peter Dyneley**
General Peters	**David Graham**
Captain	**Matt Zimmerman**
Lt. Mead	**Ray Barrett**
Sgt. Reynolds	**David Graham**
Frank	**David Graham**
Johnny	**Shane Rimmer**
Helijet Pilot Charlie	**Matt Zimmerman**

3. CITY OF FIRE

Written by **Alan Fennell**
Directed by **David Elliott**

'I guess she had that coming. People like that cause accidents. They're a menace.'

A car crash in the underground parking lot of the newly opened Thompson Tower maxi-mall causes a raging inferno which soon consumes the building when the sprinkler system fails. Unseen by the security cameras, the Carter family – Joe, Blanche and their son, Tommy – is trapped by sealed fire doors in the access corridors beneath the Tower. By the time that they are spotted, it is too late to effect a rescue by normal means.

The Tower Controller calls International Rescue and Scott and Virgil race to the scene in Thunderbirds 1 and 2, in spite of having only just recovered from the side-effects of experiments

with new cutting equipment fuelled by oxyhydnite gas. As Thunderbird 1 arrives, the Tower collapses, raising doubts as to how long it will be before the ceiling of the underground corridor caves in. Scott and Virgil realize that the only way to reach the Carters in time is to cut through the fire doors with the oxyhydnite equipment, whatever the risks from the side-effects.

Virgil uses the Firefly to clear the burning remains of the Thompson Tower from the area. He then joins Scott in the Mole as they tunnel into the corridor system half a mile from the trapped family. The Tracys quickly cut their way through the numerous fire doors, with no ill-effects from the oxyhydnite gas, and manage to rescue the Carters just as the corridor roof caves in. The underground corridors collapse, but the Tracys and the Carters escape to the surface in the Mole, to the relief of the Tower Controller.

Back on Tracy Island, Brains realizes that the extreme heat in the underground corridors negated the side-effects of the oxyhydnite gas. With electrically heated tanks in place, the equipment will be safe to use in any conditions on future rescue operations.

Notes

This episode introduces the Firefly, seen again in *Terror in New York City* and *Cry Wolf*. For the first time, the Tracy brothers are seen using their hoverjets, vehicles which later come in handy in *Vault of Death*, *Martian Invasion*, *Cry Wolf* and *Attack of the Alligators!*.

A poster for the film *Volcano* is seen on one wall of the underground corridors: a retrospective screening of the 1997 disaster movie perhaps, or a twenty-first-century remake?

City of Fire was adapted as a comic strip by Keith Watson and Alan Fennell for *Thunderbirds: The Comic* (issues 15–17, 1992), and collected in the graphic album *Thunderbirds: Shock Wave* (Ravette Books, 1992).

Original UK Broadcast:
 7.00 p.m., Thursday 6 January 1966 (ATV Midlands)
Original Broadcast Episode Number: 15
First UK Network Broadcast:
 6.00 p.m., Friday 4 October 1991 (BBC2)
Regular Cast:
 Jeff, Scott, Virgil, Alan, John, Brains, Tin-Tin
Major Equipment:
 TB1, TB2 (Pod 3), TB5, Mole, Firefly, Hoverjets, Helijet
Guest Voice Cast

Joe Carter	**Ray Barrett**
Blanche Carter	**Sylvia Anderson**
Tommy Carter	**Sylvia Anderson**
Tower Controller	**Matt Zimmerman**
Tower Control Assistant	**David Graham**
WTV Reporter	**Matt Zimmerman**
Woman Driver	**Christine Finn**
Woman Driver's Husband	**David Graham**
Fire Chief	**Peter Dyneley**

Although the Thompson Tower is clearly situated in the United States, a sign on the wall uses the British spelling 'Control Centre' instead of the American 'Center'.

4. SUN PROBE

Written by **Alan Fennell**
Directed by **David Lane**

'Oh no, Virgil! We've brought the wrong box!'

The Sun Probe, a rocket designed to take three solarnauts to the Sun and return with a piece of solar matter, is launched from Cape Kennedy and within a week has arrived at its destination. The mission goes according to plan at first, with the Probe Module released into a solar prominence and returning to the Probe Rocket with its acquisition. But as the solarnauts prepare to return to Earth, high radiation levels prevent the Probe's control systems from firing the retro rockets. Cape Kennedy's systems are also powerless, and the Sun Probe is on a collision course with the Sun!

Brains realizes that a powerful radio beam is needed to fire the Probe's retros and Jeff decides to mount a two-pronged rescue: Thunderbird 3, with Alan, Scott and Tin-Tin on board, is launched into space, while Virgil and Brains head for Mount Arkan in Thunderbird 2 with a powerful mobile transmitter. Sixty-five hours later, Alan's first attempt to reach the Probe with the safety beam fails and he and Scott realize that Thunderbird 3 must go much closer to the Sun than originally planned.

A second attempt at closer range also fails, as does an attempt by Virgil and Brains from the Transmitter Truck at Mount Arkan.

Closer still, Alan makes a third attempt, with Tin-Tin boosting the signal from her console. This beam succeeds in activating the Probe's retros and enables it to move away from the Sun, but Thunderbird 3's retros now fail – Tin-Tin has collapsed in the extreme heat, leaving the signal booster turned on, sapping the ship of power. Brains realizes that he can jam Thunderbird 3's safety beam signal with the mobile transmitter, but this requires a complex calculation on the mobile computer in Thunderbird 2. Unfortunately, Brains's prototype robot Braman has been packed by mistake. However, Braman is able to complete the necessary calculations and the realigned transmitter beam successfully jams Thunderbird 3's safety beam. The retros fire and Thunderbird 3 returns safely to Earth.

Notes

Jeff states that this is Tin-Tin's first mission. This episode also marks the first appearance of Brains's robot Braman, which is later seen in *Edge of Impact* and *The Cham-Cham*. Although we do not see Grandma, Jeff tells Virgil that she will organize auxiliary clothing for the trip to Mount Arkan, implying that his mother is already living on Tracy Island (see *Move – and You're Dead*).

Sun Probe was adapted for audio on the Century 21 mini-album 'Thunderbird 3' (MA 112), narrated by Matt Zimmerman as Alan Tracy. The episode was also adapted as a comic strip by Malcolm Stokes and Alan Fennell for *Thunderbirds: The Comic* (issues 6–8, 1991–2).

Original UK Broadcast:
7.00 p.m., Thursday 9 December 1965 (ATV Midlands)

Original Broadcast Episode Number: 11

First UK Network Broadcast:
6.00 p.m., Friday 11 October 1991 (BBC2)

Regular Cast:
Jeff, Scott, Virgil, Alan, Gordon, Brains, Tin-Tin, Kyrano

Major Equipment:
TB2 (Pod 6), TB3, Transmitter Truck, Braman, Sun Probe

Guest Voice Cast

Colonel Harris	Ray Barrett
Solarnaut Asher	David Graham
Solarnaut Camp	John Tate
Colonel Benson	Ray Barrett
Professor Heinz Bodman	Peter Dyneley
TV Reporter	Matt Zimmerman
Braman	David Graham

During the television report about the Sun Probe, a diagram shows the solarnauts' control cabin within the Probe Module. But we later see that the control cabin is within the body of the Probe Rocket when the Module is fired into the solar prominence.

When Alan, Tin-Tin and Scott set off for Thunderbird 3 on the sofa, Alan is on the left, with Tin-Tin between him and Scott. As the sofa descends into the launch bay and ferries the trio to Thunderbird 3, Alan and Scott have swapped seats, but by the time the sofa arrives on board the spacecraft they are in their original positions again.

When Thunderbird 2 leaves the hangar, it appears that Pod 3 has been selected, as Pod 2 is visible to the right of Thunderbird 2. Yet when Virgil and Brains arrive at Mount Arkan, the Transmitter Truck emerges from Pod 6. This error occurs again in *Vault of Death*, *Move – and You're Dead*, *Martian Invasion*, *The Perils of Penelope* and *Day of Disaster*.

5. THE UNINVITED

Written by **Alan Fennell**
Directed by **Desmond Saunders**

'Garanga kabuko otulo. Nik nik tarassa!'

As Scott returns from the scene of a fire in Tokyo, Thunderbird 1 is shot down in the Sahara Desert by three unidentified fighter planes. Scott cracks his head as Thunderbird 1 crashes into the sand dunes, but he is found by two explorers, Wilson and Lindsey, who administer first aid. They radio International Rescue and Virgil, Brains and Tin-Tin soon arrive in Thunderbird 2. The explorers explain that they are searching for the legendary lost pyramid of Khamandides, and they continue their search as the International Rescue group return to Tracy Island, the origin of the fighter planes still a mystery.

The next day Wilson drives the explorers' Jeep too fast, causing their supplies trailer, containing food, water and fuel, to break loose. It overturns, slides down a sand dune and explodes. The pair are stranded without water, but their SOS call to International Rescue is picked up by Alan on Thunderbird 5 and Scott is soon on his way in Thunderbird 1. Wilson and Lindsey make their way to a nearby oasis, but discover that it has long since dried up. However, Lindsey spots a pyramid in the distance on the far side of the oasis and the pair realize that their search is at an end – they have found the lost pyramid of Khamandides!

They drive to the pyramid, but there is no apparent access. A door mysteriously swings opens in the side of the pyramid and they enter, but it then closes behind them, trapping the pair inside. Exploring the pyramid, Wilson and Lindsey discover an eternal fountain surrounded by treasure, but heat and dehydration is taking its toll on Lindsey and he starts to go mad. Outside, Scott spots the explorers' Jeep and lands Thunderbird 1 near the pyramid. As he approaches on foot, the door opens and

he follows the explorers' trail inside. The sound of voices leads him to Wilson and Lindsey, but Lindsey has cracked and, in the belief that Scott has come to steal their treasure, tries to shoot him. A gun battle ensues, ending only when Lindsey is stunned by two strangers bearing the same insignia as the mysterious fighter planes that brought down Thunderbird 1 the previous day. Scott, Wilson and the unconscious Lindsey are taken prisoner and travel by monorail deeper into the pyramid, where they find an advanced civilization of Zombites hidden for centuries beneath the desert.

Investigating Scott's disappearance, Virgil and Gordon arrive near the pyramid in Thunderbird 2. Scott, Wilson and Lindsey are brought before the Zombite Leader in their control room and Scott realizes that they are preparing to fire missiles at the International Rescue craft. He and Wilson overpower their guards and fight their way out, setting off back to the entrance with Lindsey in the monorail. *En route*, they exchange gunfire with a Zombite worker, accidentally detonating gas produced by an industrial plant beneath the pyramid. The trio emerge from the pyramid entrance and Scott radios Virgil to warn him to get clear. Then he and the explorers escape in Thunderbird 1 as the lost pyramid of Khamandides finally explodes in a huge fireball.

Notes

For the mission to rescue Scott, Tin-Tin wears the same blue uniform that she was seen in on board Thunderbird 3 in *Sun Probe* – presumably the female equivalent of the Tracy brothers' uniforms. John's dialogue indicates that Scott occasionally takes turns at manning Thunderbird 5.

The Zombites' jet fighters are adapted and re-sprayed WASP aircraft from STINGRAY.

The Uninvited was adapted as a comic strip by Steve Kyte and Alan Fennell for *Thunderbirds: The Comic* (issues 12–14, 1992) and collected in the graphic album *Thunderbirds: Shock Wave* (Ravette Books, 1992).

At some point between arriving on board Thunderbird 3 and climbing into the elevator to travel up to the control room, Alan completely changes his civilian clothes – from a purple suit to the green-checked shirt and beige trousers he wore in Sun Probe. Similarly, Scott returns from Thunderbird 3 wearing different civilian clothes from those he left in, swapping a yellow suit and orange shirt for his usual blue roll-neck and checked jacket.

It doesn't really make sense for the Zombite symbols on the walls of their control room to be the complete reverse of the symbol on their helmets.

Original UK Broadcast:
   7.00 p.m., Thursday 2 December 1965 (ATV Midlands)

Original Broadcast Episode Number: 10

First UK Network Broadcast:
   6.00 p.m., Friday 18 October 1991 (BBC2)

Regular Cast:
   Jeff, Scott, Virgil, Alan, Gordon, John, Brains, Tin-Tin, Grandma

Major Equipment:
   TB1, TB2 (Pod 6), TB3, TB5, Desert Jeep

Guest Voice Cast

Wilson	**Ray Barrett**
Lindsey	**Matt Zimmerman**
Zombite Leader	**David Graham**
Zombite Controller	**Matt Zimmerman**
Zombite Guard	**Ray Barrett**
Zombite Flight Leader	**David Graham**

6. THE MIGHTY ATOM

Written by **Dennis Spooner**
Directed by **David Lane**

'I fail to see why you're still laughing, Virgil. I just don't like mice, that's all.

Attempting to film the secrets of an atomic irrigation plant in eastern Australia, the Hood is caught up in a gun battle. A stray bullet causes a fire which eventually results in the explosion of the nuclear reactor. The resulting atomic cloud drifts towards Melbourne, but a strong wind fortunately blows the cloud away.

One year later, a second station is opened in the Sahara Desert. The Hood steals an amazing surveillance device from a research unit: 'The Mighty Atom'. Looking to all intents and purposes like a small mouse, this device can penetrate installations undetected and photograph control systems by focusing on the technicians' faces as they monitor the control panels. The Hood uses the device to photograph the control room of the new plant, and then sets off a fire in the manner of the one at the Australian plant. He plans to lure International Rescue and use the Mighty Atom to photograph the control cabins of the International Rescue craft.

Having previously witnessed the disaster at the Australian plant, Reactor Controller Wade recognizes the nature of the fire and immediately calls International Rescue. Scott sets off in Thunderbird 1 and Lady Penelope, holidaying on Tracy Island, begs Jeff to let her go along on the mission. She joins Virgil and Gordon in Thunderbird 2. With only twenty minutes before the reactor goes critical, Virgil drops Gordon in Thunderbird 4. He must block the sea water intake at precisely the right moment or the reactor will explode. Virgil leaves Lady Penelope in Thunderbird 2 as he and Scott don protective suits and enter the control room to push the reactor rods back into place. Gordon destroys the sea water intake with Thunderbird 4's missiles and the reactor shuts down safely.

The Mighty Atom is programmed only to photograph the profiles of human faces, yet we see it taking photographs of the control panels at the Saharan plant when no one is in the room.

The newspaper seen in the episode is dated Friday 24 December 1964. This same date is also seen on the newspapers in Edge of Impact, The Impostors, Cry Wolf and Path of Destruction and was clearly not intended to be visible to television viewers. (Oddly, 24 December 1964 was a Thursday!)

Meanwhile, the Hood has sent the Mighty Atom into Thunderbird 2 to photograph the controls, but he is furious when he later discovers that the robotic mouse has instead taken pictures of Lady Penelope screaming at it! In anger, the Hood destroys the device.

Notes

This episode features Lady Penelope's first visit to Tracy Island since International Rescue began operations, and also her first rescue mission. It is stated that International Rescue were not operating when the Australian plant exploded twelve months ago.

The teletype printout gives the date on which the atomic cloud is blown away from Melbourne as 6 October and it is then stated that the explosion at the plant took place the previous Monday. If this is 2064, the explosion therefore occurred on 29 September.

The rescue plane that evacuates the personnel of the Australian plant is the TX 204 Target-carrying Aircraft previously seen in *Trapped in the Sky*.

Incredibly, this is the only episode to feature the entire regular cast and all five Thunderbird craft.

Original UK Broadcast:
7.00 p.m., Thursday 30 December 1965 (ATV Midlands)

Original Broadcast Episode Number: 14

First UK Network Broadcast:
6.00 p.m., Friday 25 October 1991 (BBC2)

Regular Cast:
Jeff, Scott, Virgil, Alan, Gordon, John, Brains, Lady Penelope, Parker, Tin-Tin, Kyrano, Grandma, the Hood

Major Equipment:
TB1, TB2 (Pod 4), TB3, TB4, TB5, Desert Jeep, TX 204

Guest Voice Cast

Reactor Controller Wade	**Ray Barrett**
Reactor Controller Collins	**David Graham**
General Speyer	**Ray Barrett**
Professor Holden	**Peter Dyneley**
Reactor Control Assistant	**Shane Rimmer**
Press Officer	**Matt Zimmerman**
Plant Tour Guide	**David Graham**
1st Reporter	**Peter Dyneley**
2nd Reporter	**Matt Zimmerman**
Fire Chief	**Ray Barrett**
Guard	**Ray Barrett**

7. VAULT OF DEATH

Written by **Dennis Spooner**
Directed by **David Elliott**

'It's a very smooth ride. It feels as though we're hardly moving.'

Lady Penelope and Parker are invited to break into the vault of the Bank of England to illustrate that improved security is required. A new vault is fitted which can be opened only with an electronic key carried by the Bank's President, Lord Silton, in a briefcase which, he boasts, never leaves his side. But while Lord Silton dines with Lady Penelope at Creighton-Ward Mansion in Foxleyheath, the workaholic accountant Lambert is accidentally trapped inside the vault when it is closed for the next two years. The air is automatically pumped out to keep everything sterile, but with no manual shutdown Lambert will soon suffocate.

Parker reads in the newspaper that his old cell-mate, 'Light-Fingered' Fred, has just escaped from Parkmoor Scrubs. He remembers Fred telling him of his intention to break into the Bank of England as soon as he got out of prison, so when the bank manager Lovegrove uses the emergency call system to contact Lord Silton, Parker sabotages the phone lines into Creighton-Ward Mansion in the mistaken belief that the emergency at the bank is a break-in by Fred. Thwarted in their attempts to contact the bank, Lady Penelope and Lord Silton set off for London in FAB 1, but Penelope is puzzled and annoyed at Parker's unusual behaviour – at first driving extremely slowly, and then taking a wrong turn which sends them miles out of their way.

Unable to get in touch with Lord Silton, Lovegrove calls International Rescue. Scott arrives at the City of London Heliport in Thunderbird 1 and reports that it will be impossible to use the Mole in such a built-up area. Grandma suggests that they gain access to the vault from underneath the bank, via the old disused London subway which she remembers her grandmother talking about when she was a little girl. Virgil and Alan descend into the Underground tunnels, making their way to Bank station, and break into the bank with explosives.

Meanwhile, Lady Penelope has finally forced Parker to explain his misplaced loyalty to his former cell-mate and taken control of FAB 1 herself, although her driving leaves much to be desired. They finally arrive at the bank with just one minute to spare, but Lord Silton has left the key in his briefcase back at the mansion! Parker opens the vault within seconds using one of Lady Penelope's hairpins just as Virgil and Alan blast through the opposite wall. Lambert is amazed at the speed of his rescue – he had no sooner realized his predicament and attempted to call International Rescue than the brothers arrived!

Notes

This episode features the only appearance of a real human face (or, at least, part of one) in the series: when Penelope peeps through a spyhole in the door of the bank in the opening scene.

The City of London Heliport is partially constructed from the remains of STINGRAY's Marineville Tower.

Ray Barrett's voice for Lovegrove is a marvellously accurate impression of the distinguished actor Sir John Gielgud.

Vault of Death was adapted for audio on the Century 21 mini-album 'Lady Penelope and Parker' (MA 118), narrated by Sylvia Anderson as Lady Penelope.

When Lovegrove realizes that Lambert is still in the vault, he is talking with Carter, whose voice is initially that of Shane Rimmer but then changes to a completely different voice provided by David Graham.

Virgil and Alan arrive at Bank station via a tunnel from Piccadilly Circus, although the two stations are on different lines of the Underground: Piccadilly Circus is on the Piccadilly and Bakerloo lines, while Bank is on the Central, Northern, Waterloo & City, and Docklands Light Railway lines.

Original UK Broadcast:
> 7.00 p.m., Thursday 23 December 1965 (ATV Midlands)

Original Broadcast Episode Number: 13

First UK Network Broadcast:
> 6.00 p.m., Friday 1 November 1991 (BBC2)

Regular Cast:
> Jeff, Scott, Virgil, Alan, Gordon, John, Brains, Lady Penelope, Parker, Tin-Tin, Kyrano, Grandma

Major Equipment:
> TB1, TB2 (Pod 5), TB5, FAB 1, Hoverjets

Guest Voice Cast

Lord Silton	**Peter Dyneley**
Lovegrove	**Ray Barrett**
Lambert	**David Graham**
Lil	**Sylvia Anderson**
Light-Fingered Fred	**David Graham**
Taylor	**David Graham**
Carter	**Shane Rimmer**
Moore	**David Graham**
Longman	**Peter Dyneley**
Barrett	**David Graham**
Policeman	**David Graham**

8. OPERATION CRASH-DIVE

Written by **Martin Crump**
Directed by **Desmond Saunders**

'Sorry I'm late, folks. I had to milk the cows before I took off.'

Fireflash 3 crashes into the sea soon after taking off from London Airport *en route* to San Francisco and Air-Sea Rescue can find no trace of the wreckage. A test Fireflash is launched and this too experiences difficulties and crashes into the sea. However, on this occasion the flight has been monitored by Alan on Thunderbird 5 and he is able to report that the craft is actually some 180 miles north-west of the position given by the crew.

As Thunderbirds 1 and 2 are launched, the Fireflash sinks and the crew are trapped in the cabin when the emergency exit becomes jammed. Gordon searches the sea bed in Thunderbird 4 and finally locates the downed Fireflash. He uses Thunderbird 4's laser cutter to dislocate the airliner's heavy engines, enabling the Fireflash to float to the surface. There, the crew escape in Thunderbird 2's rescue capsule just as the cabin is engulfed in flames from the fused electrics.

The International Rescue team take a more active interest in the next Fireflash test, as Scott joins Captain Hanson on the flight deck to co-pilot the aircraft, while Virgil stands by in Thunderbird 2. Almost as soon as the Fireflash takes off, Alan reports that its position is 20 miles off course and soon, as with the previous planes, the elevator power unit fails and all power is lost. The Fireflash goes into a crash-dive, but Scott has brought along a back-up radio system to keep in contact with Thunderbirds 2 and 5.

> While Gordon searches for the Fireflash on the sea bed, the parting in his hair keeps changing sides. When he returns to Thunderbird 4 after making contact with the trapped crew, the configuration of the puppet-sized Thunderbird 4 doesn't match the model seen in long-shot.

Gordon enters the airliner's starboard wing via a line from Thunderbird 2. There, he finds that the EPU wiring has been cut by a saboteur, working for Benton Aircraft Espionage, who opens fire on him while attempting to escape. However, Gordon shoots him down and manually holds the EPU wiring in place, allowing the Fireflash to gain height and prevent another crash-landing into the sea.

Notes

The script shows that this episode was originally entitled *The Test Crew*. The events of *Trapped in the Sky* are mentioned by a TV reporter who was previously seen in *Sun Probe*.

After the second Fireflash crash, the saboteur is seen escaping in an EJ2 jet – later seen as the bogus Thunderbird 2 in *The Impostors*. Lt. Burroughs, Commander Norman's assistant at London Airport, was previously Solarnaut Asher in *Sun Probe*.

Original UK Broadcast:
    7.00 p.m., Thursday 16 December 1965 (ATV Midlands)

Original Broadcast Episode Number: 12

First UK Network Broadcast:
    6.00 p.m., Friday 8 November 1991 (BBC2)

Regular Cast: Jeff, Scott, Virgil, Alan, Gordon, John, Brains, Tin-Tin, Grandma

Major Equipment:
    TB1, TB2 (Pod 4), TB4, TB5, Fireflash, EJ2 jet

Guest Voice Cast

Commander Norman	**Peter Dyneley**
Captain Hanson	**David Graham**
Lt. Burroughs	**Ray Barrett**
International Air Minister	**Peter Dyneley**
Patterson	**David Graham**
Fireflash Pilot	**David Graham**
Fireflash Co-pilot Bob	**Ray Barrett**
Fireflash 3 Pilot	**David Graham**
TV Reporter	**Matt Zimmerman**
Seahawk Pilot	**Matt Zimmerman**
Farmer	**David Graham**
Radar Operator	**Shane Rimmer**
Saboteur	**Ray Barrett**
Newsreader	**David Holiday**

9. MOVE – AND YOU'RE DEAD

Written and Directed by **Alan Pattillo**

'It all started the day we went to Parola Sands. Everything was going the way we planned. It looked like nothing could go wrong...'

Alan and Grandma are trapped high on the girders of a recently completed suspension bridge over the San Miguel River. A sonic wave generator is positioned nearby. If either of them makes any move, the sonic wave device will register the movement and detonate a bomb attached to the underside of the bridge. Very slowly, Alan uses his Personal Intercall wrist communicator to call Tracy Island.

As Scott, Virgil and Brains set off in Thunderbirds 1 and 2, Jeff learns that even if Alan and Grandma manage to keep still in the hot noonday sun, the bomb is set to explode anyway at 13.00 hours. Grandma faints and in order to keep Alan from passing out too, Jeff makes him explain how they got into this fix.

In Thunderbird 2, Virgil and Tin-Tin ferry Alan to Parola Sands, where he is to take part in the Parola Sands Race to test a new engine designed by Brains and fitted into a BR2 Racing Car. After the race, Alan will collect Grandma Tracy from her house, as she is to join the rest of her family on Tracy Island. On arrival at Parola Sands, Alan meets his friend, engineer Kenny Malone, and an old racetrack rival, Victor Gomez. Gomez and his partner Johnnie Gillespie are desperate for the prize money and are prepared to go to any lengths to win the race.

The next day, the race is on and Alan leads the field down to the last lap. Gomez tries to force him off the road on a tight bend in a last-ditch attempt at victory, but in spite of Gomez's dirty tactics Alan wins the race. In the pits, Gillespie tells Gomez he has a plan to deal with Alan once and for all. While Alan calls Grandma from the parking lot, Gomez causes a car to fall from the automatic stacking system and crash on to Alan's telecall booth. However, Alan has already completed his call and left the booth.

In the BR2, Alan collects Grandma and heads for a rendezvous with Thunderbird 2, but their car is hijacked by Gomez and Gillespie, who force them at gunpoint to drive out on to the centre of the San Miguel Bridge. Alan and Grandma are made to climb up on to the girders of the bridge, then, with a sonic wave generator in place, Gomez and Gillespie steal the BR2, leaving the Tracys to their fate...

Alan's story has managed to keep him awake long enough for Thunderbird 2 to arrive. Using a Neutralizer Tractor, Brains neutralizes the sonic wave generator to enable Virgil to manoeuvre a Jet Air Transporter on to the bridge underneath Alan and Grandma. Alan falls from the girder, but is caught on a cushion of air emitted by a powerful jet engine on the back of the Transporter. Grandma jumps from the bridge and also safely lands on the cushion of air. They escape from the bridge just as the bomb explodes.

Meanwhile, Scott attempts to stop Gomez and Gillespie escaping in the BR2 by strafing the road with machine-gun fire. The two villains struggle for control of the steering wheel and crash the car over a cliff.

Notes

Grandma Tracy leaves her home to live on Tracy Island for the first time, so the events of this episode must precede those of other episodes (including *Sun Probe*, *The Uninvited*, *The Mighty Atom*, *Vault of Death* and *Operation Crash-Dive*) where she is already living on the Island.

Move – and You're Dead was adapted for audio on the Century 21 mini-album 'One Move and You're Dead' (MA 128), narrated by Christine Finn as Tin-Tin.

When Jeff is first contacted by Alan, he is sitting behind his desk, but when we cut back to him after a quick shot of Alan (a matter of only a few seconds), he is perched on the front of the desk reading a magazine.

Original UK Broadcast:
7.00 p.m., Thursday 10 February 1966 (ATV Midlands)

Original Broadcast Episode Number: 20

First UK Network Broadcast:
6.00 p.m., Friday 28 February 1992 (BBC2)

Regular Cast:
Jeff, Scott, Virgil, Alan, Gordon, Brains, Tin-Tin, Grandma

Major Equipment:
TB1, TB2 (Pods 1 and 5), Neutralizer Tractor, Jet Air Transporter, BR2, Racing Car

Guest Voice Cast

Victor Gomez	**David Graham**
Johnnie Gillespie	**Ray Barrett**
Kenny Malone	**Ray Barrett**
Billy Billoxi	**Matt Zimmerman**
Parola Sands Announcer	**Ray Barrett**
Timekeeper	**David Holliday**
Parola Sands Page	**Sylvia Anderson**

10. MARTIAN INVASION

Written by **Alan Fennell**
Directed by **David Elliott**

'Listen, pal. It's his money, he calls the tune. You start where he says or you don't start at all.'

Two policemen, responding to a flying saucer report, find themselves attacked by Martians and trapped in a cave. This is just part of a movie script to be directed by B-movie director Goldheimer under the supervision of the Hood in a devious plan to capture the secrets of International Rescue on film for sale to General X. Exerting his psychic control, the Hood forces Kyrano to switch off the automatic camera detector in Thunderbird 1, and then sets his plan in motion.

Filming begins in the Nevada Desert using automatic camera equipment. The first scenes involve the two policemen becoming trapped in the cave by the Martians, but the Hood has sabotaged a pyrotechnic effects sequence and the resulting explosion brings down the whole cliff face, trapping the two actors inside the cave. To make the situation worse, the cave begins to fill up with water from an underground river.

The film unit calls International Rescue and Thunderbirds 1 and 2 soon arrive. Virgil uses the Excavator, a drilling and crushing vehicle, to drill through the boulders at the cave entrance, creating an opening which lets the water drain out. The two actors are swept to safety as the cave roof collapses.

As the Thunderbird craft prepare to return home, Scott discovers that the automatic camera detector has been disabled. Using the film crew's video playback system, he learns that the entire rescue operation has been captured on film. The Hood

has already escaped in his Jeep to rendezvous with General X at his mansion. A desperate chase ensues, with the Hood eventually stealing an Angel Executive Aircraft from an aerodrome for the last leg of his journey. Unfortunately for the Hood, the plane is in need of an overhaul and it crashes into General X's mansion, destroying the film in the process.

Notes

Up to this point, the Hood has never been referred to by any name on screen – not even 'the Hood'. Here, he calls himself Agent 79 in his radio transmissions to General X. His price for the secrets of International Rescue is $200 million.

Martian Invasion was adapted as a comic strip by Keith Page and Alan Fennell for *Thunderbirds: The Comic* (issues 24–26, 1992).

Original UK Broadcast:
  7.00 p.m., Thursday 17 March 1966 (ATV Midlands)

Original Broadcast Episode Number: 24

First UK Network Broadcast:
  6.00 p.m., Friday 27 March 1992 (BBC2)

Regular Cast: Jeff, Scott, Virgil, Alan, John, Tin-Tin, Kyrano, the Hood

Major Equipment:
  TB1, TB2 (Pod 5), TB5, Excavator, Hoverjet, Hood's Jeep

Guest Voice Cast

Goldheimer	**Ray Barrett**
Bletcher	**David Graham**
General X	**Matt Zimmerman**
Maguire	**David Graham**
Slim	**Matt Zimmerman**
Martian Pete	**Peter Dyneley**
Martian Ray	**Ray Barrett**
Director of Photography	**Shane Rimmer**
Production Manager	**David Graham**
Make-up Girl	**Sylvia Anderson**
Brian	**Ray Barrett**

11. BRINK OF DISASTER

Written by **Alan Fennell**
Directed by **David Lane**

'What an extraordinary man. He didn't even touch his tea!'

While Lady Penelope eludes two villains in FAB 1, eventually blowing them off the road with the car's rear-mounted machine guns, Warren Grafton, a visitor to Creighton-Ward Mansion, disables the alarm systems as he waits for Lady Penelope's return. Meeting with Lady Penelope, Grafton explains that he is looking for investors in his Pacific–Atlantic Monorail company. Parker suspects a scam when he recognizes Grafton's chauffeur as a crook named Harry Malloy, so Lady Penelope puts Grafton in touch with Jeff Tracy, who investigates as an interested investor. Parker's suspicions are well founded: in a meeting in New York with his 'business partners', Grafton reveals his intention to make up his financial deficit on the project with Lady Penelope's jewel collection.

Grafton takes Jeff, Brains and Tin-Tin aboard the totally automated Pacific–Atlantic monotrain, assuring them of complete safety. However, a patrolling helijet is struck by lightning in a storm and crashes into a monorail bridge, bringing down part of the bridge and cutting off the automatic signals. The monotrain is out of control and heading for disaster!

In Foxleyheath, Grafton's men break into Creighton-Ward Mansion and plunder Lady Penelope's floor safe. However, the security devices on the safe itself are still intact and alert Lady Penelope and Parker, who use machine guns to disable the crooks' car. The villains steal FAB 1, but Lady Penelope locks the steering by remote control, leaving them going round in circles.

On the monotrain, Jeff calls International Rescue as Brains

attempts to re-activate the brakes. He fails twice, but eventually manages to stop the train – right in the middle of the collapsing bridge. Thunderbirds 1 and 2 arrive at the danger zone and Virgil lowers the magnetic grabs from Thunderbird 2 to remove the monotrain car to safety just as the bridge collapses. His scam revealed, Grafton and his cohorts are imprisoned.

Notes

Lady Penelope has clearly been taking lessons since her atrocious driving in *Vault of Death* – her driving in this episode is very proficient. The bogus telegram reveals the location of Creighton-Ward Mansion in Foxleyheath.

Brink of Disaster was adapted for audio on the Century 21 mini-album 'Brink of Disaster' (MA 124) narrated by David Graham as Parker. The episode was also adapted as a comic strip by Rod Vass and Alan Fennell in *Thunderbirds: The Comic* (issues 30–33, 1992).

Just as the villains' car goes out of control in the opening sequence, a huge lump of greenery falls out of the sky in the background. When Selsden and Malloy try to open Lady Penelope's safe, Malloy's torch begins to smoke – the torch bulb has become so hot, it has started to set the prop alight.

Original UK Broadcast:
    7.00 p.m., Thursday 24 February 1966 (ATV Midlands)
Original Broadcast Episode Number: 22
First UK Network Broadcast:
    6.00 p.m., Friday 13 March 1992 (BBC2)
Regular Cast:
    Jeff, Scott, Virgil, Alan, Brains, Lady Penelope, Parker, Tin-Tin
Major Equipment:
    TB1, TB2, TB5, FAB 1, Helijet, Monotrain
Guest Voice Cast

Warren Grafton	**David Graham**
Harry Malloy	**David Graham**
Doolan	**Matt Zimmerman**
Selsden	**Ray Barrett**
Hugo	**Peter Dyneley**
2nd Investor	**Ray Barrett**
Joe (Patrol 304)	**Ray Barrett**
Stan (Patrol 304)	**Matt Zimmerman**
Patrol Base	**Matt Zimmerman**
Crook with Machine Gun	**Ray Barrett**

12. THE PERILS OF PENELOPE

Written by **Alan Pattillo**
Directed by **Alan Pattillo and Desmond Saunders**

'I say! Open this door at once! We're British!'

A new rocket fuel produced from sea water, used to power the Sun Probe on its historic solar flight, has been developed by International Rescue's Sir Jeremy Hodge in partnership with Professor Borender. Sir Jeremy and Borender attend a conference in Paris two days after the Sun Probe launch, but then Borender disappears from a monotrain during a journey to Anderbad. Sir Jeremy calls in Lady Penelope to help find his friend.

They meet in a Parisian café, where Lady Penelope narrowly avoids drinking poisoned Pernod. As he flees, the culprit leaves behind a matchbook emblazoned with a heraldic crest. Tracking down the crest in the heraldic archive, Lady Penelope and Sir Jeremy are trapped in the basement as gas is pumped in, but they are rescued by Parker. Sir Jeremy explains that the process he and Borender have developed could contaminate the world's oceans and shift the balance of power if it falls into the wrong hands – and someone is clearly out to see that it does!

Lady Penelope and Sir Jeremy retrace Borender's steps by taking the express monotrain to Anderbad, but the evil Dr Godber is aboard. He arranges a power failure as the train enters the Anderbad Tunnel, and kidnaps Lady Penelope and Sir Jeremy, taking them to his tunnel hideout in a control sub-station where the pair are reunited with Professor Borender. To force Sir Jeremy and Borender to reveal the secret of their process, Godber ties Lady Penelope to a ladder and lowers her into the path of the Anderbad Express!

Virgil and Gordon arrive at Anderbad in Thunderbird 2,

meeting up with Parker in FAB 1. Realizing that Lady Penelope has gone missing, Virgil and Gordon set off into the tunnel on the Monobrake. As the Anderbad Express approaches, the brothers discover Godber's hideout. A gunfight ensues, but the control panel in the sub-station is destroyed and the train cannot be stopped! Virgil shoots the rope which holds Penelope in place and she falls out of the path of the train just as it comes hurtling through the tunnel.

Notes

The launch of the Sun Probe at the start of this episode is the same event that was seen in flashback at the start of *Sun Probe*. The events of that episode take place one week after the launch, so this episode takes place immediately before. Indeed, *The Perils of Penelope* and *Sun Probe* can be viewed as THUNDERBIRDS' only two-part story, although they have never been broadcast as consecutive episodes.

This is the only episode in which we see Scott piloting Thunderbird 1 without his International Rescue uniform – when he returns from leave.

The Anderbad Express monotrain is the same model as the one seen as the Pacific–Atlantic monotrain in *Brink of Disaster*.

The Perils of Penelope was adapted for audio on the Century 21 mini-album 'The Perils of Penelope' (MA 114), narrated by Sylvia Anderson as Lady Penelope.

As it bears down on Lady Penelope's perilous position, the leading car on the Anderbad Express monotrain keeps changing colour, from white and red to silver and blue.

Original UK Broadcast:
      7.00 p.m., Thursday 14 October 1965 (ATV Midlands)

Original Broadcast Episode Number: 3

First UK Network Broadcast:
      6.00 p.m., Friday 15 November 1991 (BBC2)

Regular Cast:
      Jeff, Scott, Virgil, Alan, Gordon, Lady Penelope, Parker, Tin-Tin

Major Equipment:
      TB1, TB2 (Pod 6), FAB 1, Monobrake, Monotrain, Sun Probe

Guest Voice Cast

Sir Jeremy Hodge	**Peter Dyneley**
Professor Borender	**David Graham**
Dr Godber	**Ray Barrett**
Albert	**Matt Zimmerman**
Roache	**David Graham**
Waiter	**David Graham**
Colonel Benson	**David Graham**

13. TERROR IN NEW YORK CITY

Written by **Alan Fennell**
Directed by **David Elliott and David Lane**

'Now we've gotta sit here and wait for our air to run out.'

National Television Broadcasting System reporter Ned Cook is determined to get pictures of the Thunderbird craft during a rescue operation at an oil well fire, but Thunderbird 1's automatic camera detector alerts Scott to Cook's transgression and he electromagnetically wipes the taped pictures after a brief chase. Returning from the rescue site, Thunderbird 2 strays into a Naval test area and is attacked by missiles launched from the USN Sentinel. The giant craft is badly hit and narrowly avoids crashing into the sea. Virgil pilots the stricken Thunderbird 2 to a crash-landing on Tracy Island. He is not badly hurt, but Thunderbird 2 will be out of action for weeks.

From his sickbed, Virgil watches Ned Cook reporting from New York on the ingenious operation to move the Empire State Building as part of the redevelopment of the surrounding area. The building is slowly moved along rail tracks, supported by a huge gantry tractor, but the ground gives way beneath it and, as the building comes crashing down, both Cook and his cameraman, Joe, fall into a deep cavern. The Empire State Building collapses over the hole and the men are trapped, with water seeping into their hollow from an uncharted underground river.

This is clearly a job for Thunderbird 4, which could navigate up the river from its outlet in the bay, but with Thunderbird 2 out of commission there is no way to get Thunderbird 4 to New York in time to save Ned and Joe, who will be under water within twenty-two hours. Jeff makes a priority call to Washington and arranges for Thunderbird 4 to be transported to New York by the USN Sentinel, but the journey will still take twenty-four hours. Scott races ahead in Thunderbird 1 and establishes radio contact with Ned and Joe. Breathing apparatus is passed down to the two men through a small hole in the cavern roof, but each has only two hours of air in the tanks so there is little margin for error.

Sentinel arrives in New York harbour and Gordon sets off in Thunderbird 4 to find the inlet to the underground river. Scott tells Ned and Joe, now completely submerged, to search for the river entrance from their end, but the nearby Fulmer Finance Building collapses, causing a tidal wave through the underground cavern. Ned and Joe manage to find the river entrance from the cavern, but their air has run out. From Thunderbird 4, Gordon spots the men and rescues them just as the tidal wave hits. Thunderbird 4 is swept back into the harbour by the powerful current.

Later, the Tracy family, with Brains and Tin-Tin, are in the audience at the next broadcast of THE NED COOK SHOW, as a wheelchair-bound Ned Cook pays tribute to the brave men and women of International Rescue.

Notes

Other guests in the audience at THE NED COOK SHOW include Dr Godber from *The Perils of Penelope* and film producer Bletcher from *Martian Invasion*.

While Sylvia Anderson is credited as a voice artist, she does not take part in this episode.

Terror in New York City was adapted for audio on the Century 21 mini-album 'Thunderbird 4' (MA 108), narrated by David Graham as Gordon Tracy. The episode was also adapted as a comic strip by Keith Page and Alan Fennell in *Thunderbirds: The Comic* (issues 9–11, 1992) and collected in the graphic album *Thunderbirds in Action* (Ravette Books, 1992).

Original UK Broadcast:
7.00 p.m., Thursday 21 October 1965 (ATV Midlands)

Original Broadcast Episode Number: 4

First UK Network Broadcast:
6.00 p.m., Friday 22 November 1991 (BBC2)

Regular Cast:
Jeff, Scott, Virgil, Alan, Gordon, Brains, Tin-Tin, Kyrano, Grandma

Major Equipment:
TB1, TB2 (Pod 6), TB4, Firefly, USN Sentinel

Guest Voice Cast:

Ned Cook	**Matt Zimmerman**
Joe	**David Graham**
Sentinel Commander	**Ray Barrett**
First Officer Clayton	**David Graham**
Scanners	**Shane Rimmer**
Policeman — Site Control	**Ray Barrett**
2nd Policeman — Site Control	**David Graham**
Police Patrol	**David Graham**
Newsreader	**Ray Barrett**
Washington	**Shane Rimmer**
Garner	**David Graham**
TV Compere	**Ray Barrett**

14. END OF THE ROAD

Written by **Dennis Spooner**
Directed by **David Lane**

'There's worse to come. I've still got a case of nutomic charges on board.'

The Gray & Houseman Construction Company is building a road through a mountain range in South-East Asia using its amazing road-building vehicle, but the contract must be completed before the monsoon season. Eddie Houseman has done his part by blasting a pathway through the mountains and now pays a call on his old friend Tin-Tin Kyrano on Tracy Island. Alan is less than pleased to see Tin-Tin's old flame sweeping her off her feet again.

Back at the road construction project, the mountain range is crumbling into the pathway cleared by Eddie and will never survive the monsoon. When Eddie hears the news, he immediately returns to the site. Realizing that the company is finished if the deadline is not met, Eddie recklessly sets off in an explosives tractor to plant charges on the unstable peak which will cause it to fall away from the road. With the peak about to collapse, Eddie fires the charges while still too close and the blast leaves his tractor teetering on the edge of the mountain trail. But there's worse to come: he still has a case of unstable nutomic charges on board and if he goes over the edge, he'll be blown sky high!

Bob Gray calls International Rescue, but the organization is faced with a dilemma: Eddie Houseman knows them, so by rescuing him security will be breached. Scott sets off in Thunderbird 1, followed by Virgil and Alan in Thunderbird 2. Falling rocks threaten to overbalance the tractor, but Scott fires long steel spears into the cliff face to protect Houseman from the boulders. As Virgil brings in Thunderbird 2 to pick up the tractor with the magnetic grabs, the craft's vertical jets start to tip the tractor over the edge and Virgil is forced to back off. Scott carefully manoeuvres Thunderbird 1 to prop up the tractor with the vehicle's nose cone, enabling Thunderbird 2 to descend and pick up the vehicle.

However, the tractor proves far too heavy for the grabs, which fail one by one as Thunderbird 2 moves away from the danger zone. Virgil manoeuvres the tractor near to the mountainside and Eddie leaps clear just before the tractor slips free of the grabs and the nutomic charges cause a massive explosion as the tractor crashes to the ground. With Eddie saved, Thunderbirds 1 and 2 immediately head for home. Eddie never saw the faces of the men piloting the vehicles, so International Rescue's security remains intact.

Notes

While Sylvia Anderson is credited as a voice artist, she does not take part in this episode.

End of the Road was adapted for audio on the Century 21 mini-album 'Thunderbird 2' (MA 109), narrated by David Graham as Brains.

Original UK Broadcast:
7.00 p.m., Thursday 25 November 1965 (ATV Midlands)

Original Broadcast Episode Number: 9

First UK Network Broadcast:
6.00 p.m., Friday 10 January 1992 (BBC2)

Regular Cast:
Jeff, Scott, Virgil, Alan, Gordon, John, Brains, Tin-Tin, Kyrano, Grandma

Major Equipment:
TB1, TB2, TB5, Road Construction Vehicle, Explosives Tractor, Helijet

Guest Voice Cast

Eddie Houseman	**Ray Barrett**
Bob Gray	**David Graham**
Cheng	**David Graham**
J. B. Lester	**Ray Barrett**
Chuck Taylor	**Matt Zimmerman**
Engineer	**David Graham**

15. DAY OF DISASTER

Written by **Dennis Spooner**
Directed by **David Elliott**

'He's still at it, poor fellow. Seems to be under some delusion that he's in charge of the rescue.'

A Martian Space Probe rocket is being transported to its launch site over the Allington Suspension Bridge. The load is well within the overall capacity of the bridge, but not as a concentrated mass, and as the MSP slowly travels over the bridge the suspension cables begin to snap and the bridge collapses, tipping the MSP from the transport vehicle into the Allington River. The rocket lands on the river bed in an upright launch position, but covered in debris from the bridge. The impact sets off the automatic launch countdown, which will blow the rocket to pieces, killing two engineers who are trapped in the command module.

Brains is visiting Lady Penelope in England and both witness the disaster taking place on television. They rush to the bridge in FAB 1, but the approach is blocked by sightseers. Brains makes his way to the bridge on foot, while Lady Penelope and Parker arrange a diversion by blowing up the disused Allington Research Centre nearby, drawing the crowd's attention away from the bridge so as not to hamper the rescue operation.

Brains arrives at the Allington Suspension Bridge control centre, where the Bridge Controller refuses to acknowledge the need for more sophisticated rescue equipment. Instead, he has brought in antiquated dock cranes to clear the debris from the MSP, but the attempt fails and the two cranes capsize. Brains contacts John in Thunderbird 5 on his Personal Intercall wrist communicator, directing the International Rescue operation himself.

Thunderbird 1 arrives at the bridge, closely followed by Thunderbird 2. Virgil releases Pod 4 and Gordon pilots Thunderbird 4 into the river to survey the wreckage. Gordon cuts through the debris with Thunderbird 4's lasers, while Virgil lifts the wreckage from the water with the magnetic grabs. With time running out, Brains suggests that Gordon should blow away the rest of the debris with missiles. The plan works and Gordon rams Thunderbird 4 into the MSP command module to knock it clear of the main craft. The module floats to the surface and is air-lifted away from the danger zone by Thunderbird 2 with only thirty seconds to spare. The MSP launches from the river bed and, after an erratic flight, explodes in mid-air.

The Bridge Controller turns Brains over to psychiatrist Dr

Korda, believing him to be insane after seeing him talking into his watch. Penelope 'rescues' Brains from the clutches of the psychiatrist, who then witnesses Penelope talking into her powder compact!

Notes

The music accompanying the journey of the MSP is entitled 'March of the Oysters'. Originally composed by Barry Gray for the STINGRAY episode *Secret of the Giant Oyster*, the piece is also heard in *30 Minutes After Noon*, *The Impostors* and *The Cham-Cham*.

Dr Korda appears to have the same taste in decor as the Hood – he has a statue in his office that is identical to one in the Hood's temple. Korda is named after the Hungarian film producer and director Sir Alexander Korda, who, as the head of London Films, is widely regarded as the saviour of the British film industry in the 1930s and 1940s.

Day of Disaster was adapted for audio on the Century 21 mini-album 'Thunderbirds' (MA 121), narrated by David Graham as Gordon Tracy.

Original UK Broadcast:
7.00 p.m., Thursday 4 November 1965 (ATV Midlands)

Original Broadcast Episode Number: 6

First UK Network Broadcast:
6.00 p.m., Friday 6 December 1991 (BBC2)

Regular Cast:
Jeff, Scott, Virgil, Alan, Gordon, John, Brains, Lady Penelope, Parker, Tin-Tin, Grandma

Major Equipment:
TB1, TB2 (Pod 4), TB4, TB5, FAB 1, MSP

Guest Voice Cast

Allington Bridge Controller	**Ray Barrett**
Dave Clayton	**David Graham**
Kirby	**Ray Barrett**
Chuck	**David Graham**
Bill Craddock	**Matt Zimmerman**
Frank	**David Graham**
Professor Wingrove	**Peter Dyneley**
NTBS Reporter	**Peter Dyneley**
2nd NTBS Reporter	**Matt Zimmerman**
Policeman	**David Graham**
Dr R. G. Korda	**Ray Barrett**
Crane Chief	**Peter Dyneley**

16. EDGE OF IMPACT

Written by **Donald Robertson**
Directed by **Desmond Saunders**

'They're crazy! It's probably a million to one chance we'd get hit!'

The Hood is hired by General Bron to sabotage the new Red Arrow fighter plane, ensuring that the plane crashes into the launch site on its test flight. World Space Control project supervisor Colonel Tim Casey is replaced for the test programme on Red Arrow 2, so he decides to pay an unexpected call on his old friend Jeff Tracy at Tracy Island. Brains suspects that the Red Arrow was sabotaged and provides Red Arrow 2 pilot Goddard with a diversion detector before he returns to base. The Hood has planted a homing device on an international television relay tower so that when Red Arrow 2 makes its test flight it is drawn off course. Goddard ejects, but the plane crashes into the tower, trapping two operatives, Jim and Stan, in the control cabin. The men call International Rescue as the tower disintegrates.

As a diversionary tactic to enable the launch of Thunderbirds 1 and 2 without compromising the security of International Rescue, Tin-Tin takes Colonel Casey scuba-diving under the pretext of searching for a rare water mamba. Arriving at the danger zone, Alan operates the Booster Mortar, a tracked vehicle with a mounted mortar cannon, which fires two low-altitude escape harnesses through the window of the relay tower's control cabin. Donning the escape harnesses, Jim and Stan climb on to the balcony, activate their jet packs and fly clear as the relay tower finally gives way, crashing to the ground.

Virgil finds the Hood's homing device in the wreckage and contacts the police. A patrol car spots the Hood's van and gives chase. The road ahead is closed because of a collapsed bridge, but the Hood mistakes the barrier for a police road block set to trap him, so he drives through and flies straight off the end of

the bridge into the river below.

Returning from his diving expedition none the wiser about the Tracys' secret activities, Casey is informed by Jeff that he has been reinstated at World Space Control and is to resume the Red Arrow tests.

Notes

This is the only occasion in which we see the Hood acting with motives that do not involve International Rescue. He gives his codename here as '671' when he contacts General Bron.

In a startling prediction of the future, the television relay tower is seen to be owned by British Telecommunications Ltd. The use of this company name in THUNDERBIRDS pre-dated the formation of the real-life British Telecommunications plc (a.k.a. BT) by nearly twenty years.

The TX 204 Target-carrying Aircraft originally seen in *Trapped in the Sky* appears briefly in an establishing shot of the airfield. Tim Casey previously appeared as a bank executive in the opening scenes of *Vault of Death*.

Tim Casey is a colonel, but Scott refers to him as 'General' in one scene.

Original UK Broadcast:
7.00 p.m., Thursday 28 October 1965 (ATV Midlands)

Original Broadcast Episode Number: 5

First UK Network Broadcast:
6.00 p.m., Friday 29 November 1991 (BBC2)

Regular Cast:
Jeff, Scott, Virgil, Alan, Gordon, Brains, Tin-Tin, the Hood

Major Equipment:
TB1, TB2 (Pod 3), Booster Mortar, Low-altitude Escape Harnesses, Remote Camera, Braman, Red Arrow 1, Red Arrow 2, TX204

Guest Voice Cast

Colonel Tim Casey	**David Graham**
Commander Norman	**Peter Dyneley**
General Bron	**David Graham**
Goddard	**Matt Zimmerman**
Jim	**David Graham**
Stan	**Ray Barrett**
Race	**David Graham**
Control Tower Lieutenant	**Ray Barrett**
Captain	**Matt Zimmerman**
1st Policeman	**David Graham**
2nd Policeman	**Ray Barrett**
Police Radio	**Christine Finn**

17. DESPERATE INTRUDER

Written by **Donald Robertson**
Directed by **David Lane**

'No man can stay in the burning sun for long without having his tongue loosened.'

Brains and Tin-Tin mount an expedition to find treasure in a temple on the bed of Lake Anasta in the Middle East, but the Hood learns of their plans through his psychic link with Kyrano. Ferried to the desert in Thunderbird 2, Brains and Tin-Tin make the final leg of their journey in a desert Jeep towing a pair of caravans, rendezvousing with archaeologist Professor Blakely before completing the journey. Unfortunately, the Hood gets to Lake Anasta ahead of them and unloads a 3E mini-submarine from his transporter truck into the water.

The expedition team arrive at Lake Anasta and Brains and Tin-Tin use scuba gear to dive in and take a first look at the lost temple. Brains removes a rock sample from the central column for later examination, but the Hood, observing from his submarine, believes that they have found the treasure already. Back in the laboratory caravan, Professor Blakely examines the sample and confirms that they are on the right track. That night, the Hood, disguised as a bedouin tribesman, steals into the expedition caravans and hypnotizes the three team members.

The next morning, Brains regains consciousness to find himself buried up to his neck in desert sand. He calls for help, but Tin-Tin and Blakely are still unconscious. The Hood appears, demanding to know where the treasure is, but Brains is unable to tell him. Back on Tracy Island, Jeff is worried that the team have not called in and dispatches Thunderbirds 1 and 2 to the scene. The Hood watches the arrival of the craft from his submarine, a new plan forming in his mind.

Scott, Virgil and Gordon rescue Brains and find Tin-Tin coming round in her caravan, although Blakely is still out cold. Scott reports that the camera detector in Thunderbird 1 has been activated, and Brains realizes that they have all walked into a trap. That night, Brains makes a second dive into the lake, discovering a treasure store hidden inside the column he had examined earlier. Unfortunately, he trips an alarm set by the Hood and, following a series of wires along the lake bed, soon runs into International Rescue's old enemy, who hypnotizes him once again. Tin-Tin raises the alarm as the Hood blows up the temple to reveal the treasure, trapping Brains beneath one of the columns in the process.

Thunderbird 4 is launched into the lake from Thunderbird 2, and Gordon finds the temple in ruins. He soon locates Brains, whose air is running out, but is fired upon by the Hood's submarine. Gordon pursues the Hood, scoring a direct

hit with his missiles and destroying the submarine, but the Hood manages to escape before the submarine explodes.

Brains is still trapped beneath the column, but Scott brings down a hydrostatic hoist, a huge air bag, with which he and Gordon are able to lift the column. Gordon pulls Brains clear just as the cords on the hoist snap and the column crashes back on to the lake bed.

Later, Brains and Tin-Tin visit Professor Blakely in hospital, where they find him planning his next expedition. He wants them to join him, but both would rather go on a nice, soothing rescue mission!

Notes

In a nod to continuity, Tin-Tin has an Air Terrainean flight bag (presumably acquired during that fateful trip on the Fireflash in *Trapped in the Sky*) with her on board Thunderbird 2 as they fly out to the Middle East.

Brains's desert Jeep was originally seen as the explorers' Jeep in *The Uninvited*. Tin-Tin wears the same diving outfit that she sported in *Edge of Impact*.

This episode has the smallest guest cast seen in THUNDERBIRDS, with only two characters other than the regulars. Matt Zimmerman and Sylvia Anderson do not take part, although both are credited on the closing titles.

Desperate Intruder was adapted for audio on the Century 21 mini-album 'Brains and Tin-Tin' (MA 119), narrated by Christine Finn as Tin-Tin.

When Brains falls under the Hood's influence, he collapses and between shots his glasses simply disappear. It subsequently becomes apparent that they have fallen off, but we don't see it happen – one moment they're on his face and the next they've vanished.

Original UK Broadcast:
7.00 p.m., Thursday 18 November 1965 (ATV Midlands)

Original Broadcast Episode Number: 8

First UK Network Broadcast:
6.00 p.m., Friday 3 January 1992 (BBC2)

Regular Cast:
Jeff, Scott, Virgil, Gordon, John, Brains, Tin-Tin, Kyrano, Grandma, the Hood

Major Equipment:
TB1, TB2 (Pods 4 and 5), TB4, Desert Jeep, Transporter Vehicle, 3E Submarine, Hydrostatic Hoist, Helijet

Guest Voice Cast

Professor Blakely	Peter Dyneley
Hassan Ali	David Graham

18. 30 MINUTES AFTER NOON

Written by **Alan Fennell**
Directed by **David Elliott**

'We're gonna get to the bottom of this – even if it means employing a little deception.'

Tom Prescott picks up a hitchhiker as he drives home after working late. As he drops the man off, a strange bracelet made of hydrochromatized steel is locked to his wrist and he is told that the key is in a filing cabinet in his office at the Hudson Building in Spoke City. Prescott races back to the building to unlock the bracelet before the explosive device set into it detonates. He arrives at the building just in time, but is still descending from his office in the elevator when the device explodes. The elevator plunges into the basement and Prescott is trapped at the bottom of the lift shaft.

With the sprinkler system sabotaged, the fire rages out of control and the Spoke City fire department is unable to contain the blaze, so Jeff dispatches Thunderbirds 1 and 2 to the scene. Virgil and Alan descend into the lift shaft in a specially cooled dicetylene cage fitted with grabs, recovering the elevator car and rescuing Prescott.

Prescott's amazing story appears to ring true in light of the discovery of the bracelet remains. The fire has also destroyed extensive files on several criminal organizations and Police Commissioner Garfield suspects the work of the Erdman gang. In order to draw the gang out, a story is released to the press that Prescott died in the Hudson Building inferno. The case is turned over to the British Security Service, and top agent Southern is assigned.

Southern infiltrates a meeting in Glen Carrick Castle in Scotland, posing as one of three men hired to break into a plutonium storage facility. By radio, the Leader of the gang explains how they must disable the store's guard robots and plant explosives in the main storeroom before escaping by helijet. The explosives are contained in the bracelets locked to their wrists, which are set to detonate at 12.30 p.m. They will find the keys to unlock the bracelets in the main storeroom.

The plan goes as scheduled, but on arrival in the storeroom Southern pulls a gun on the other two men, Dempsey and Kenyon. Unfortunately for Southern, he is attacked by a guard robot which has not been disabled and, held in its steel arms, he is helpless as Dempsey and Kenyon escape, trapping him in the storeroom with their bracelets. Southern uses his radio pen to contact his boss, Sir William Frazer, who calls International Rescue.

On the night of the Hudson Building fire, the Auto Date Fixer in Commissioner Garfield's office reads 12/7/65. The next day, it reads 13/7/65, illustrating attention to detail on the part of the set decorator. Unfortunately, the American convention is for the month numeral to appear first: either the first date should read 7/12/65 (12 July) with the next day as 7/13/65, or the second date should read 12/8/65 (8 December).

Scott and Virgil arrive at the plutonium store in Thunderbirds 1 and 2. Using the Laser Beam Equipment, they burn their way through the series of locked security doors, penetrating the main storage area. With just five minutes to go, Scott loads the three explosive bracelets on to Thunderbird 1 and dumps them in the sea as they detonate. Lady Penelope and Parker meet the Leader's helijet at the rendezvous point, bringing down the craft with FAB 1's cannon as it takes off.

Notes

30 Minutes After Noon pioneers the use of real hands in the same frame as puppet characters through a clever arrangement of perspective: in the scenes in Glen Carrick Castle, Southern's hand plays with a pen in the extreme foreground while the Dempsey and Kenyon puppets appear in the background.

30 Minutes After Noon was adapted for audio on the Century 21 mini-album 'Thirty Minutes After Noon' (MA 129), narrated by David Graham as Parker. The episode was also adapted as a comic strip by Malcolm Stokes and Alan Fennell for *Thunderbirds: The Comic* (issues 18–20, 1992) and collected in the graphic album *Thunderbirds in Action* (Ravette Books, 1992).

Original UK Broadcast:
  7.00 p.m., Thursday 11 November 1965 (ATV Midlands)
Original Broadcast Episode Number: 7
First UK Network Broadcast:
  6.00 p.m., Friday 13 December 1991 (BBC2)
Regular Cast:
  Jeff, Scott, Virgil, Alan, Gordon, John, Brains, Lady Penelope, Parker, Tin-Tin
Major Equipment:
  TB1, TB2 (Pod 5), TB5, FAB 1, Dicetylene Cage, Laser Equipment, Helijet
Guest Voice Cast

Southern (Tiger Four)	**Ray Barrett**
Sir William Frazer (Two-One)	**David Graham**
Tom Prescott	**Matt Zimmerman**
Commissioner Garfield	**David Graham**
The Leader	**David Graham**
Dempsey	**Peter Dyneley**
Kenyon	**David Graham**
Officer Flanagan	**Ray Barrett**
Officer Jones	**Peter Dyneley**
Stranger	**Ray Barrett**
Sam Saltzman	**David Graham**
Gladys Saltzman	**Sylvia Anderson**
Frank Forrester	**Matt Zimmerman**
BSS Assistant	**David Graham**
Erdman Gang Member	**Peter Dyneley**
Policeman (Police Barrier)	**Matt Zimmerman**

19. THE IMPOSTORS

Written by **Dennis Spooner**
Directed by **Desmond Saunders**

'Eat? I guess you ain't been round these parts long enough t've heard about Ma's beans, ma'am.'

A fake International Rescue team rescues a man from an underground well and makes off with the top-secret plans of the AL4, stolen from the nearby Aeronautical Center. When the robbery is discovered, General Lambert launches a worldwide search to track down International Rescue and bring them to justice. The Tracys are horrified, but have no choice but to shut down operations while the hunt is on.

However, International Rescue is not powerless in this crisis. Jeff contacts their many agents around the world to help them find the impostors. Lady Penelope and Parker fly to America to interview Eddie Kerr, the World Television reporter who covered the 'rescue' at the well, while in the southern states, hillbilly agent Jeremiah Tuttle finds aircraft tracks in the woods leading to an old mine. Jeremiah reports his findings to Jeff but, without any further evidence, Jeff decides to take no action.

Space Observatory 3, a scanning satellite covering the South Pacific region, is out of action with an antenna fault. Technician Elliott suits up and goes outside to effect repairs, but his jet pack goes haywire, thrusting him away from the satellite. Too small to register on radar, Elliott has just three hours of oxygen left. Only International Rescue can save him, but if they help, they will be spotted by Lambert's search team. Posing as a fellow reporter, Lady Penelope receives vital information from Eddie Kerr which enables Jeff to pinpoint the impostors in the area covered by Jeremiah Tuttle. Remembering Jeremiah's report of aircraft tracks, Jeff sends Lady Penelope to investigate, but FAB 1 is soon bogged down in mud, so she and Parker proceed on foot. Lady Penelope finds the going tough in her high heels.

Risking exposure, Jeff sends Scott and Alan in Thunderbird 3 to rescue Elliott. They soon get a bearing on the astronaut and

recover him from space. Meanwhile, Lady Penelope and Parker arrive at the abandoned mine, the impostors' hideout, but they are spotted by the villains, who open fire on them. Fortunately, Jeremiah and his mother have followed Lady Penelope and Parker into the woods and flush the two villains out of the cave with Ma Tuttle's explosive beans. International Rescue are exonerated.

Notes

The photographer who takes the picture of the impostor at the start of the episode previously appeared as Colonel Tim Casey in *Edge of Impact*. Also in the crowd at the bogus rescue is Blanche Carter from *City of Fire*. Eddie Kerr gets his office furnishings from the same place as Dr Korda and the Hood: he has the same statue from the Hood's temple that appeared in Dr Korda's office in *Day of Disaster*.

The Impostors was adapted for audio on the Century 21 mini-album 'International Rescue' (MA 120), narrated by Shane Rimmer as Scott Tracy.

Original UK Broadcast:
7.00 p.m., Thursday 13 January 1966 (ATV Midlands)

Original Broadcast Episode Number: 16

First UK Network Broadcast:
6.00 p.m., Friday 17 January 1992 (BBC2)

Regular Cast:
Jeff, Scott, Virgil, Alan, Gordon, John, Lady Penelope, Parker, Tin-Tin

Major Equipment:
TB3, TB5, FAB 1, Fireflash, EJ2 Jet, Helijet

Guest Voice Cast

General Lambert	**Ray Barrett**
Elliott	**David Graham**
Eddie Kerr	**Matt Zimmerman**
Jeremiah Tuttle	**Peter Dyneley**
Ma Tuttle	**Sylvia Anderson**
Jenkins	**Ray Barrett**
Carela	**David Graham**
Hale	**Ray Barrett**
Captain Hanson	**David Graham**
Fireflash Co-pilot	**Ray Barrett**
Fireflash Stewardess	**Sylvia Anderson**
Colonel	**Ray Barrett**
Wakefield	**Matt Zimmerman**
Air Force Officer	**Peter Dyneley**
Air Force Lieutenant	**Peter Dyneley**
Speed Merchant	**Matt Zimmerman**
Helijet Pilot	**David Graham**
Search Control	**David Graham**
Jack	**David Graham**

When they board Thunderbird 3, Alan does another quick change into different clothes before climbing into the elevator (see The Uninvited). This time, Scott does a quick change too: initially he is wearing a yellow suit and orange shirt, but just before blast-off we see him in his blue roll-neck sweater and checked jacket.

After he is rescued, Elliott tells Scott and Alan that it is great that they have been cleared. Scott replies, 'You can say that again,' without moving his lips.

20. THE MAN FROM MI.5

Written by **Alan Fennell**
Directed by **David Lane**

'My! This is a deserted area! One just wouldn't know where one was, would one?'

A frogman steals aboard a ship anchored in harbour on the French Riviera, shooting Captain Blacker before thoroughly searching his desk and eventually locating secret papers. He then places a limpet mine on the ship's hull and makes his escape. The ship explodes just as MI5 agent Bondson arrives on the scene. Bondson contacts International Rescue, warning of the destruction of the world, so Lady Penelope agrees to meet with Bondson in the Forest of Digne, where he tells her that the plans of a nuclear device have been stolen.

Lady Penelope sets herself up as a target for the thieves, posing as model Gayle Williams, newly arrived on the French Riviera to expose those who blew up Blacker's boat. She gives Parker the night off, so she is alone on her luxury yacht, FAB 2, when Carl, the leader of the crooks, kidnaps her. She is tied up in a lonely boathouse, where Carl plants a radio-controlled bomb, explaining that the explosion will create a diversion for the harbour patrol, enabling Carl and his cronies to escape in their mini-submarine. Lady Penelope manages to get a message to Jeff on her powder compact radio, and Scott, Virgil and Gordon are soon on their way.

Lady Penelope tells Jeff of the villains' plan, while Scott tracks down the mini-sub with Thunderbird 1's sonar sounding equipment. Thunderbird 4 is launched into the harbour and Gordon soon pinpoints the sub. He launches the paralyser, a magnetic clamp fitted with a drill which cuts through the submarine's hull and pipes tranquillizer gas inside, knocking out the crooks. Gordon retrieves the plans of the nuclear device, while Scott rescues Penelope from the boathouse. Penelope returns the plans to Bondson, and then learns that Parker has gambled away FAB 2 at a casino in Monte Carlo!

Notes
This episode features the first full Thunderbird 4 launch sequence shown from inside Pod 4. Prior to this, we have only seen Thunderbird 4 emerging down the ramp from outside the pod door. This is also the only occasion in which Thunderbird 2 gently rests the pod on the surface of the water and then rises clear of the pod with lifting jets. Normally, the pod is simply dropped on to the water.

There is another use of a real hand in the same frame as a puppet character (see *30 Minutes After Noon*) as Captain Blacker is shot down in the opening sequence. Lady Penelope wears the orange hat with the huge brim that she sports in her picture caption in the opening titles of every episode. Brains's test submarine is a small model of the Hood's 3E submarine seen in *Desperate Intruder*.

The Man from MI.5 was adapted as a comic strip by Jon Haward and Alan Fennell for *Thunderbirds: The Comic* (issues 24–26, 1992).

Original UK Broadcast:
7.00 p.m., Thursday 20 January 1966 (ATV Midlands)

Original Broadcast Episode Number: 17

First UK Network Broadcast:
6.00 p.m., Friday 24 January 1992 (BBC2))

Regular Cast:
Jeff, Scott, Virgil, Alan, Gordon, John, Brains, Lady Penelope, Parker, Tin-Tin, Grandma

Major Equipment:
TB1, TB2 (Pod 4), TB4, TB5, FAB 1, FAB 2, Fireflash

Guest Voice Cast

Bondson	**Ray Barrett**
Carl	**David Graham**
Ritter	**Ray Barrett**
Third Man	**Matt Zimmerman**
MI5 Agent Tidman	**David Graham**
Fireflash Stewardess	**Sylvia Anderson**

21. CRY WOLF

Written by **Dennis Spooner**
Directed by **David Elliott**

'So you never did need rescuing? I think someone had better do some explaining.'

Two boys, Tony and Bob Williams, unwittingly call out International Rescue on their walkie-talkies while playing in the Australian desert near their home at Charity Springs in the Northern Territory. To explain how their games are dangerous to International Rescue, Scott takes the boys back to Tracy Island for a guided tour, but the story makes headlines in the local newspapers which worries the boys' father. Under the guise of a weather station, he runs a satellite tracking station and is engaged in top-security research for the military. The story is picked up on by the Hood, who realizes the true nature of the apparently innocent weather station. In disguise, he encourages Tony and Bob to play in the old Charity Springs tin mine at Dunsley Hill and, once the boys are inside, fires a grenade into the entrance, causing a cave-in that traps the boys. Tony and Bob call International Rescue on their walkie-talkies but their rescue plea is assumed to be another game and no action is taken.

The Hood attempts to break into Williams's control room, but Williams gets a message to Colonel Jameson, who orders him to destroy the top-secret photos from the spy satellite, as it will take three hours to get help out to the remote station. Williams suggests that Jameson call International Rescue, who can get there within thirty-five minutes. The call goes out and Jeff realizes that the boys' call for help was genuine. Scott, Virgil and Alan race to Charity Springs, but the Hood has already burned his way through Williams's security door with a welding torch. The Hood hypnotizes Williams before he can destroy the photos and then escapes with them in his Jeep.

Thunderbird 2 arrives at the old tin mine and Alan and Virgil lower themselves on ropes into the mine shaft. They rescue Tony and Bob as the mine crumbles around them. Meanwhile, Scott chases the Hood on his hoverjet. The Hood carelessly drives into a ravine and Scott believes that he cannot have survived the crash. But he has, after becoming entangled in branches half-way down the ravine, although the secret photos are destroyed.

All of the characters refer to Williams's station as Dunsley Tracker, but a caption on an alert signal reads 'Densley Tracker'.

Back at the Williams's house, Tony and Bob show Scott their home-made International Rescue base with table-top launching facilities, but Scott proves too heavy for the boys' set-up and crashes their soapbox Thunderbird 2 into the chicken coop.

Notes

Tony and Bob's tour of Tracy Island takes in the hangar bay for the Thunderbird 2 pod vehicles, and we see the Mole, the Firefly, the Transmitter Truck (*Sun Probe*), the Excavator (*Martian Invasion*) and the Monobrake (*The Perils of Penelope*), as well as a civilian fire truck and a yellow fire vehicle first seen in *City of Fire*.

Colonel Jameson was originally seen as General Lambert in *The Impostors*. Satellite HQ and the tracker satellite itself were also previously seen in *The Impostors*. One of the technicians at Satellite HQ previously appeared as BSS agent Southern in *30 Minutes After Noon*.

Original UK Broadcast:
7.00 p.m., Thursday 27 January 1966 (ATV Midlands)

Original Broadcast Episode Number: 18

First UK Network Broadcast:
6.00 p.m., Friday 31 January 1992 (BBC2)

Regular Cast:
Jeff, Scott, Virgil, Alan, Gordon, John, Brains, Tin-Tin, Grandma, the Hood

Major Equipment:
TB1, TB2, TB3, TB5, Hoverjets, Hood's Jeep, Mole, Firefly, Transmitter Truck, Excavator, Monobrake

Guest Voice Cast:

Williams	**Ray Barrett**
Bob Williams	**Sylvia Anderson**
Tony Williams	**Christine Finn**
Colonel Jameson	**David Graham**
Lt. Lansfield	**Matt Zimmerman**
Sergeant	**David Graham**

26. SECURITY HAZARD

Written by **Alan Pattillo**
Directed by **Desmond Saunders**

'Look, fellers, if that kid is roaming around the base on his own, Dad's gonna go berserk.'

While Scott, Virgil and Alan are fighting a fire in an English mine, a young boy, Chip Morrison, stows away in Thunderbird 2's Pod 1. As Thunderbird 2 arrives back at Tracy Island, the intruder alert signals and the Tracys find themselves with a security hazard on their hands. While Jeff tries to think of a solution to their problem, Chip is looked after by each of the brothers in turn and he exhibits a rare talent for encouraging them to expose International Rescue secrets, as they recall rescues which highlight the importance of their individual rescue vehicles.

First up is Virgil, who shows Chip Thunderbird 2 and tells how the craft was instrumental in the rescue of Eddie Houseman, trapped in his explosives truck and balanced precariously on a mountain ledge. Next, in the Thunderbird 3 hangar, Alan recounts the story of the Sun Probe rescue mission, explaining how Thunderbird 3's radio safety beam was used to activate the Probe's failed retro rockets. Then Scott shows Chip round Thunderbird 1, remembering International Rescue's very first mission: saving the passengers and crew of the Fireflash at London Airport. Finally, Chip is left with Gordon, who gives the boy a guided tour of Thunderbird 4 and relates the story of the recovery of the Martian Space Probe nose cone from the Allington River. Realizing too late what they have done, the brothers anxiously wonder what their father will say when he finds out. They are understandably surprised to discover Jeff giving Chip a full run-down of the importance of his own position in International Rescue!

Chip's father previously appeared as Dave Clayton in *Day of Disaster*, as we clearly see during the excerpts from that episode.

When Thunderbird 2 returns to its hangar, smoke can be seen flowing back down into units inside the hangar, revealing that this is simply reversed footage of the regular Thunderbird 2 launch sequence. This sequence appears again in *Ricochet*.

Once inside the hangar, Thunderbird 2 unloads Pod 1, but the numeral on the puppet-sized pod door in the close-up shots doesn't match that on the model-sized long shot.

To prevent Chip from innocently leaking the secrets of International Rescue, they wait until he falls asleep and then take him home aboard Thunderbird 2. Chip wakes up in his own bed, believing that his trip to Tracy Island was all a dream.

Notes

A sort of 'Greatest Rescues', this episode features extensive flashback footage from *End of the Road*, *Sun Probe*, *Trapped in the Sky* and *Day of Disaster* – so extensive, in fact, that it contains only seventeen minutes of new material.

The International Rescue fire truck seen during the mine fire rescue in the opening sequence previously appeared as the Gray & Houseman explosives tractor in *End of the Road*. Chip Morrison was last seen as Bob Williams in *Cry Wolf*.

Original UK Broadcast:
7.00 p.m., Thursday 31 March 1966 (ATV Midlands)

Original Broadcast Episode Number: 26

First UK Network Broadcast:
6.00 p.m., Friday 10 April 1992 (BBC2)

Regular Cast:
Jeff, Scott, Virgil, Alan, Gordon, Brains, Lady Penelope

Major Equipment:
TB1, TB2 (Pods 1 and 2), TB3, TB4, FAB 1, Fireflash, Fire Truck, Elevator Cars, Magnetic Grabs, Sun Probe, Road Construction Vehicle, Explosives Tractor, MSP

Guest Voice Cast

Chip Morrison	**Sylvia Anderson**
Morrison	**David Graham**
Eddie Houseman	**Ray Barrett**
Bob Gray	**David Graham**
J. B. Lester	**Ray Barrett**
Colonel Harris	**Ray Barrett**
Solarnaut Asher	**David Graham**
Solarnaut Camp	**John Tate**
TV Reporter	**Matt Zimmerman**
Controller Norman	**Peter Dyneley**
Captain Hanson	**David Graham**
Fireflash Co-pilot	**Ray Barrett**
Control Tower Lieutenant	**Ray Barrett**
Bill Craddock	**Matt Zimmerman**
Frank	**David Graham**
Allington Bridge Controller	**Ray Barrett**
Dave Clayton	**David Graham**

Second Season (1966)

1. ATLANTIC INFERNO

Written by **Alan Fennell**
Directed by **Desmond Saunders**

'No one has been hurt and Scott will keep a check on the situation. He'll realize that this is not a job for International Rescue.'

Lady Penelope invites Jeff to join her for a holiday at her farm in Bonga Bonga. Jeff is reluctant, but his sons convince him to take a break and Scott is placed in temporary command.

The World Navy is testing gyropedoes in the Atlantic Ocean. The captain of the World Navy flagship Atlantic warns the men on the drilling rig Seascape – Hooper, O'Shea and Cravitz – that there will be underwater nuclear explosions but insists that this poses no danger to them. Two gyropedoes are launched at a target sub, but the second missile is a maverick and explodes on the sea bed. It ignites a gas field beneath the sea bed, throwing up a flame 200 feet high. Scott is in two minds about whether to involve International Rescue, but eventually decides to launch Thunderbirds 1 and 2.

Gordon takes Thunderbird 4 to the sea bed and caps the escaping gas with a sealing device, putting out the flame. Jeff is furious when he finds out that International Rescue has been involved and tells Lady Penelope that he is abandoning his holiday. She manages to persuade him otherwise, but Jeff is clearly uncomfortable with the idea of leaving Scott in control.

In the Atlantic, however, the gas field remains ignited beneath the sea bed. The gas eventually breaks through again, shooting another column of flame above sea level and high into the air. Feeling themselves in danger, Hooper and O'Shea call for International Rescue but, once bitten, Scott decides not to get involved and recommends that the Navy evacuate Seascape. Unfortunately, it will take the Navy two hours to get there. Another jet of gas bursts through the sea bed and the resulting wave fractures one of the rig's legs. Hooper and O'Shea go down in a diving bell to check the damage, but a third column of flame then explodes, causing the rig to slip further and the diving bell crashes to the sea bed. Hooper and

O'Shea are trapped!

Scott launches Thunderbirds 1 and 2, and Alan, Virgil and Gordon fly to the danger zone. Time is running out, as the next place that the fire will spread to is Seascape's bore hole. Alan lands Thunderbird 1 on Seascape, while Gordon goes down to the diving bell in Thunderbird 4. Seascape collapses even further and Alan has to lift Thunderbird 1 from the rig to prevent it from sliding into the ocean. Gordon cuts through the diving bell's cables with Thunderbird 4's laser beam equipment before clearing the debris, attaching magnetic grabs to hoist the bell to the surface and getting clear just as Seascape explodes in flames.

Jeff returns to Tracy Island to supervise the rescue operation, but Scott refuses to grant him landing permission as Thunderbirds 1 and 2 are due back shortly. Back behind his desk at last, Jeff is glad to return to work – it is the only way he can relax!

Notes

Now painted yellow, the road construction vehicle seen in the opening sequence previously appeared as the Gray & Houseman road construction vehicle in *End of the Road*.

The World Navy Commander was last seen as the Commander of Matthews Field in *The Cham-Cham*. Cravitz was formerly Bob Gray in *End of the Road*.

Atlantic Inferno was adapted for audio on the Century 21 mini-album 'Atlantic Inferno' (MA 125), narrated by David Graham as Gordon Tracy. The episode was also adapted as a comic strip by Keith Page and Alan Fennell in *Thunderbirds: The Comic* (issues 27–29, 1992).

Original UK Broadcast:
> 5.05 p.m., Sunday 2 October 1966 (ATV London)

Original Broadcast Episode Number: 27

First UK Network Broadcast:
> 6.00 p.m., Friday 17 April 1992 (BBC2)

Regular Cast:
> Jeff, Scott, Virgil, Alan, Gordon, John, Brains, Lady Penelope, Parker, Tin-Tin

Major Equipment:
> TB1, TB2 (Pod 4), TB4, TB5, FAB 1, Magnetic Grabs, Sealing Device, Seascape, Road Construction Vehicle, Desert Jeep, Jeff's Jet

Guest Voice Cast

Frank Hooper	**John Tate**
Dick O'Shea	**Jeremy Wilkin**
World Navy Commander	**Peter Dyneley**
Atlantic Captain	**David Graham**
Sir Harry	**John Tate**
Atom Sub Reefer Captain	**Ray Barrett**
Atom Sub Reefer Lieutenant	**Matt Zimmerman**
Cravitz	**Jeremy Wilkin**
TV Reporter	**Ray Barrett**

> Lady Penelope's sheep-counting meter is useless to her as it counts to only five digits. She would need six for her 200,007 sheep.

2. PATH OF DESTRUCTION

Written by **Donald Robertson**
Directed by **David Elliott**

'...and believe me, fellers, Sanchos cooks his beef in a very special way.'

Crablogger 1, a huge tree-felling machine, arrives at base camp in South America in preparation for its first mission. The base commander, Jansen, takes the crew for a meal at a local restaurant in nearby San Martino and all but Jansen have the 'special'. The next morning, when the Crablogger sets off from the camp, both of the two-man crew collapse, the victims of food poisoning, and the Crablogger veers off course, heading straight for San Martino. To make matters worse, the vehicle has to be constantly relieved of the supplies of wood pulp that it produces while in motion, for if the machinery jams the resulting explosion of the Superon-fuelled atomic reactor would lay waste to everything within a 50-mile radius. The one way to stop the huge machine is to activate the secret reactor shut-down procedure from inside the control cabin, which can be accessed only through the roof of the vehicle. Jansen calls International Rescue and Scott sets off in Thunderbird 1, while Jeff apprises Lady Penelope of the situation.

San Martino is evacuated just as the Crablogger ploughs through the village, destroying everything in its path. Scott arrives at the base camp and learns that they have just forty-two minutes to break into the control cabin and shut down the reactor. Thunderbird 2 reaches the danger zone, and Virgil and Brains set off in pursuit of the Crablogger in a Mobile Crane driven by Scott. At Robotics International in England, Lady Penelope is unable to persuade the security guard to let her have the address of Jim Lucas, inventor of the Crablogger, so Parker uses a hypnotic ray on the guard while Lady Penelope plunders the personnel files. They race to Lucas's house but are delayed *en route* by a road accident. Stealing into Lucas's bedroom, Lady Penelope wakes Lucas and puts a gun to his head. She tells him that it is vital that he reveal the Crablogger shut-down procedure, but time prevents her from explaining further.

Lady Penelope transmits Lucas's information to Brains,

who, with Virgil, has gained access to the Crablogger control cabin by cutting through the roof. The vehicle is heading straight for the San Martino Dam along a narrow mountain track as Brains activates the reactor shut-down. However, there is a three-minute time-lag before the machine will actually come to a halt and they must drain the tanks of the explosive Superon fuel. Scott brings up a fuel truck and Virgil and Brains attach siphons to the fuel outlets. The Crablogger finally stops, but the ledge is crumbling away beneath its immense weight. At the last minute, the tanks are finally drained and Virgil and Brains leap clear with their hover packs as the Crablogger tumbles from the cliff road. The dam is saved.

Notes

Base-camp operative Simms previously appeared as Dave Clayton in *Day of Disaster*, but was last seen as Chip Morrison's father in *Security Hazard*. Dam site manager Manuel was previously seen as General Bron in *Edge of Impact*.

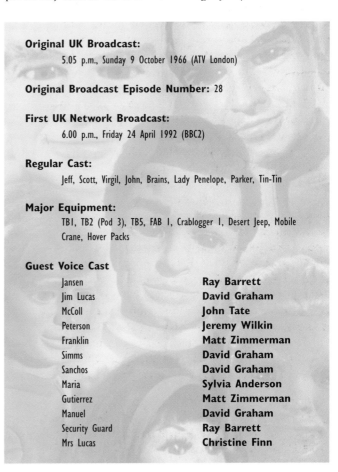

Original UK Broadcast:
5.05 p.m., Sunday 9 October 1966 (ATV London)

Original Broadcast Episode Number: 28

First UK Network Broadcast:
6.00 p.m., Friday 24 April 1992 (BBC2)

Regular Cast:
Jeff, Scott, Virgil, John, Brains, Lady Penelope, Parker, Tin-Tin

Major Equipment:
TB1, TB2 (Pod 3), TB5, FAB 1, Crablogger 1, Desert Jeep, Mobile Crane, Hover Packs

Guest Voice Cast

Jansen	**Ray Barrett**
Jim Lucas	**David Graham**
McColl	**John Tate**
Peterson	**Jeremy Wilkin**
Franklin	**Matt Zimmerman**
Simms	**David Graham**
Sanchos	**David Graham**
Maria	**Sylvia Anderson**
Gutierrez	**Matt Zimmerman**
Manuel	**David Graham**
Security Guard	**Ray Barrett**
Mrs Lucas	**Christine Finn**

3. ALIAS MR. HACKENBACKER

Written by **Alan Pattillo**
Directed by **Desmond Saunders**

'Bugs in the flowers, peeping Thomases at the windows, pens that send messages...I need reviving!'

Using the alias Hiram K. Hackenbacker, Brains has designed a revolutionary new airliner, the Skythrust, for Atlantic Airlines. Skythrust incorporates a top-secret design feature which has made it the safest craft in the skies. Lady Penelope believes that the vehicle, due to fly on its maiden flight from Paris to London, will make the ideal location for the unveiling of the new fashion collection designed by her friend François Lemaire, which she has agreed to model. Lemaire has developed an incredible new fibre, Penelon (named after Lady Penelope), which can fold up so compactly that a complete outfit will fit into a matchbox without creasing. What's more, the fibre can perfectly duplicate numerous other fabrics, from cotton and nylon to wool and even leather! Lemaire's secret is highly sought after by his competitors, as his studio is littered with bugging devices and he is under constant observation by industrial spies. Brains agrees to Lady Penelope's plan.

Skythrust takes off, London-bound, and the fashion show begins. Penelon is a huge success with the invited guests, but Lemaire's assistant, Madeline, hijacks the airliner, giving Captain Ashton instructions to fly to the Sahara Desert, where the rest of her gang awaits. Her co-conspirator Mason, the steward, gets Lemaire to pack the costumes, for they are going to steal the entire collection!

Penelope sends an alarm signal to Tracy Island and Thunderbirds 1 and 2 are soon on their way. Scott and Virgil pinpoint Skythrust's position and Scott radioes Ashton, insisting that he returns to London. Madeline is not impressed. Brains suggests that Virgil and Alan fire a missile at Skythrust's undercarriage, locking the wheels in the raised position. They do so and Ashton tells Mason that there is no alternative but to head for London Airport, where they at least have the facilities to handle a crash-landing. Reluctantly, the hijackers agree.

The aircraft crash-lands at London Airport, but the secret 'Hackenbacker Device' comes into play: a rear-mounted ejectable fuel pod flies free and is detonated before the plane lands, leaving Skythrust free of major fire hazard as it skids to a standstill on the runway. In the Sahara, Alan dispatches the rest of Madeline's gang with a well-aimed missile launched from Thunderbird 2.

Notes

This features the largest cast of characters (in speaking roles) seen in any single THUNDERBIRDS episode or either of the feature films. Hiram Hackenbacker is clearly used as an assumed name, not as Brains's real one.

Alias Mr. Hackenbacker was adapted for audio on the Century 21 mini-album 'Brains' (MA 123), narrated by David Graham as Brains.

Original UK Broadcast:
5.05 p.m., Sunday 16 October 1966 (ATV London)

Original Broadcast Episode Number: 29

First UK Network Broadcast:
6.00 p.m., Friday 1 May 1992 (BBC2)

Regular Cast:
Jeff, Scott, Virgil, Alan, Gordon, Brains, Lady Penelope, Parker, Tin-Tin

Major Equipment:
TB1, TB2 (Pod 3), FAB 1, Skythrust, D103

Guest Voice Cast

Captain Ashton	**Paul Maxwell**
François Lemaire	**Ray Barrett**
Controller Norman	**Peter Dyneley**
Madeline	**Sylvia Anderson**
Mason	**Jeremy Wilkin**
Deirdre	**Christine Finn**
Captain Saville	**Ray Barrett**
Skythrust Co-pilot	**David Graham**
Control Tower Lieutenant	**Ray Barrett**
D103 Pilot	**Jeremy Wilkin**
Reporter 1	**Jeremy Wilkin**
Reporter 2	**Paul Maxwell**
Officer, London Airport	**David Graham**
Saville's Secretary	**Christine Finn**
Telephone Operator	**Sylvia Anderson**
Waiter	**David Graham**
Fashion Buyer 1	**David Graham**
Fashion Buyer 2	**David Graham**
Ross	**David Graham**
Co-conspirator	**Ray Barrett**

Penelope says that 1993 is the best year for champagne, but she must be just being polite – 1993 wasn't a particularly good year for champagne at all!

4. LORD PARKER'S 'OLIDAY

Written by **Tony Barwick**
Directed by **Brian Burgess**

'It will be a great disaster!'

Professor Lungren has developed a solar generator which will, as its first test, power the sleepy Mediterranean town of Monte Bianco from a vantage point on a mountain overlooking the town. Lady Penelope and Parker are among the invited guests at the hotel to witness this historic event, which all goes according to plan until a violent storm hits the surrounding area. The solar reflector dish is repeatedly struck by lightning and eventually buckles, crashing down the mountainside and lodging half-way, with the reflector pointing directly at the village. The village is plunged into darkness as the solar power cuts off but then, as the storm clears, Monte Bianco is bathed in moonlight reflected by the huge dish. Everyone enjoys the spectacle, but Penelope suddenly realizes the potential disaster: as the sun rises in the morning, the sunlight will be magnified and reflected on to the town, which will burn under the intense heat!

The mountains surrounding Monte Bianco block all radio signals, so Penelope takes FAB 1 out to sea to call International Rescue. Meanwhile, Parker and the hotel waiter, Bruno, make plans to keep the hotel guests occupied so that panic doesn't set in. Thunderbirds 1 and 2 set off for Monte Bianco, with Alan and Brains joining Virgil in Thunderbird 2, while Penelope drives up to the solar station on the mountainside, where Lungren's assistant, Mitchell, tells her that the sun will be high enough for the reflector to start burning the village at 6.30, in just one hour's time! As the sun begins to rise, Parker and Bruno wake the hotel guests and drag them to the ballroom to play 'Lord Parker's Bingo'.

Brains plans to tilt the reflector dish upwards, away from the town. Wearing a heat suit, he is lowered from Thunderbird 2 to take a closer look at the mechanism, attaching the Magno-Grip, a large electromagnet on a cable winch, to the dish. But even the power of Thunderbird 2 cannot shift the dish and Brains realizes that he must fix the rotation mechanism to enable it to be tilted. Time is running out and the hotel roof starts to

smoulder. In a flash of inspiration, Brains gets Scott to generate smoke from Thunderbird 1's exhaust and pass in front of the reflector, blocking out the sun and giving him time to work.

The gear is fixed and Virgil is able to move the reflector, but the huge dish begins to slip and overbalance. As the dish tips over, Alan thinks he sees Brains fall down the mountainside and land at the bottom, where he is crushed by falling rocks and the reflector dish when it lands on top of him. However, to everyone's relief, it was only Brains's empty heat suit that Alan saw falling – having found it too cumbersome, Brains had taken it off. With Monte Bianco returning to normal, 'Lord' Parker has to explain his sudden elevation to the peerage.

Notes

It appears that Señor Faccini has hired Cass Carnaby to perform at his hotel on this prestigious occasion, as the pianist from *The Cham-Cham* is seen in a brief clip from that episode. Professor Lungren's assistant, Mitchell, previously appeared as Captain Ashton in *Alias Mr. Hackenbacker*. The STINGRAY tune 'Blues Pacifica' is heard playing on the radio in FAB 1.

While credited, Ray Barrett does not take part in this episode.

Original UK Broadcast:
    5.05 p.m., Sunday 23 October 1966 (ATV London)
Original Broadcast Episode Number: 30
First UK Network Broadcast:
    6.00 p.m., Friday 8 May 1992 (BBC2)
Regular Cast:
    Jeff, Scott, Virgil, Alan, Brains, Lady Penelope, Parker, Grandma
Major Equipment:
    TB1, TB2 (Pod 3), FAB 1, Magno-Grip
Guest Voice Cast

Professor Lungren	**Peter Dyneley**
Mitchell	**Charles Tingwell**
Señor Faccini	**Jeremy Wilkin**
Bruno	**Charles Tingwell**
Party Goer	**David Graham**

5. RICOCHET

Written by **Tony Barwick**
Directed by **Brian Burgess**

'As long as we're in one piece, the show goes on.'

Telsat 4 is launched from Sentinel Base, but the second stage fails to separate, even under manual control. International Space Control are contacted to allocate safe co-ordinates for the destruction of the rocket, but, unknown to ISC, the co-ordinates they provide are dangerously close to those of an unlicensed pirate television satellite, KLA. On board are DJ Rick O'Shea and his engineer, Loman. The explosion of the rocket damages the satellite, but O'Shea continues his illegal broadcasts as normal. Meanwhile, Gordon and John are fitting a new component to Thunderbird 5, and this means that the International Rescue satellite will be non-operational for three hours.

Loman realizes that their satellite is headed for re-entry and their breaking parachutes will not operate. In a spacesuit, Loman goes outside to assess the damage but becomes trapped in the airlock when the inner door will not open on his return. O'Shea uses their transmitter to call for help, but the call goes unheard on Thunderbird 5. Fortunately, Tin-Tin is watching KLA and alerts Jeff, who dispatches Virgil and Brains in Thunderbird 2 and Alan with Scott in Thunderbird 3. As KLA begins re-entry, Alan space-walks across to the satellite using rocket thrusters, rescues the unconscious Loman from the airlock and returns him to Thunderbird 3. He then makes the journey back to KLA, cutting through the inner door with laser beam equipment to rescue O'Shea. O'Shea suits up, but suffers badly from vertigo and is terrified of the space-walk across to Thunderbird 3. He refuses to leave.

ISC targets KLA as crash-landing on the oil refinery at A'Ben Duh, so Virgil heads for the refinery, planning to shoot down the satellite. But then Brains picks up O'Shea's broadcast, indicating that he must still be aboard the satellite. With Thunderbird 5 still out of action, Virgil cannot check with Jeff if this is so, and Brains feels that he cannot simply shoot down the satellite if O'Shea is still on board. Virgil angles Thunderbird 2 to catch the satellite on its wing, carrying it away

from the refinery, but KLA eventually falls clear of Thunderbird 2 and crashes into the desert.

Returning dejectedly to Tracy Island believing that O'Shea has died in the crash, Virgil and Brains are delighted to learn from Alan that he did manage to rescue O'Shea after all. In his panic, the DJ switched on a pre-recorded programme by accident and it was this broadcast that Brains and Virgil heard. Alan admits that he had to blacken the DJ's eye as it was the only way he could get O'Shea to step outside!

Notes

The Rick O'Shea puppet was created by sculptor Terry Curtis, who loosely based the character's features on those of Sean Connery (see *Thunderbirds Are Go*).

The song 'Flying High' that O'Shea plays as a request from Tin-Tin was originally written and recorded as the end-titles song for the series. Performed by Gary Miller, it was abandoned in favour of the familiar instrumental march. Also heard on Rick's show are the main theme from *The Man from MI.5* and an instrumental version of 'I've Got Something to Shout About' from the STINGRAY episode *Titan Goes Pop*.

The ISC building previously appeared as the Satellite HQ tracking station seen in both *The Impostors* and *Cry Wolf*.

This is the only second-season episode in which Lady Penelope does not appear, and the only episode in the whole series in which we see Virgil piloting Thunderbird 3.

Ricochet was adapted for audio on the Century 21 mini-album 'Ricochet' (MA 126), narrated by David Graham as Brains.

Original UK Broadcast:
5.05 p.m., Sunday 6 November 1966 (ATV London)

Original Broadcast Episode Number: 31

First UK Network Broadcast:
6.00 p.m., Friday 15 May 1992 (BBC2)

Regular Cast:
Jeff, Scott, Virgil, Alan, Brains, Tin-Tin, Grandma

Major Equipment:
TB2 (Pod 3), TB3, TB5, KLA Satellite, Telsat 4

Guest Voice Cast:

Rick O'Shea	**Ray Barrett**
Loman	**David Graham**
Professor Marshall	**Sylvia Anderson**
Power	**Jeremy Wilkin**
International Space Control	**Charles Tingwell**
DJ Tom	**Jeremy Wilkin**
Sentinel Base Computer	**David Graham**

6. GIVE OR TAKE A MILLION

Written by **Alan Pattillo**
Directed by **Desmond Saunders**

'I don't like it, Scobie. That gold's too heavy.'

December 2067: it is Christmas on Tracy Island and, as the sun beats down, 'Santa' Jeff Tracy allows young Nicky to watch the launch of Thunderbird 3. Nicky is visiting as a very special Christmas present and Jeff recalls how it all started...

In conjunction with Harman's department store, the directors of the Coralville Children's Hospital arrange to drop a container full of presents, launched by rocket from the roof of Harman's in a publicity stunt which benefits everybody. A trial run for the rocket is a success and International Rescue agrees to provide a special Christmas gift for one of the Coralville children: a visit to Tracy Island to spend Christmas with International Rescue! The invitation is to be placed inside one of the gift boxes.

On Tracy Island, Scott and Tin-Tin fly to the mainland to do the Christmas shopping, while Grandma and Kyrano make the preparations for Christmas dinner and the boys hang decorations and wrap presents. Only Brains does not take part, as he is up to something in his laboratory.

Christmas Eve comes and as the rocket is being packed with presents two crooks, Scobie and Straker, break into the Second National Bank from the toy department of Harman's, which is just next door. They drill a hole in the vault wall large enough to climb through and fire a cable across to the opposite wall, being careful not to allow anything to fall on the touch-sensitive vault floor, which is connected to the security system. Scobie is then pulled across on a harness to steal the gold reserves stacked on the shelves of the vault.

Virgil is preparing to leave for Coralville in Thunderbird 2 and Tin-Tin is heading for bed when both hear a noise coming from the roof. Is it Santa? No, it's just Brains, but what is he up to? Back in the vault, Scobie is getting greedy and has overloaded himself with gold. He slips nearer and nearer the floor, but eventually manages to get clear. Unfortunately, he has dislodged a pencil from a table and this falls to the floor, setting off the alarm. The two crooks hide in the container of toys, just as it is loaded on to the rocket.

Virgil overflies Coralville Hospital as the rocket drops its payload by parachute. The container is opened and the crooks are discovered inside, unconscious. The reward money for the capture of the crooks will go to the hospital, so it's a very merry Christmas for everyone – except Scobie and Straker.

Nicky is the lucky youngster who finds the invitation to

Tracy Island in his Christmas present and the boy is ferried to International Rescue's secret base in Thunderbird 2. After Christmas dinner, the brothers sing carols around the piano and then Brains unveils his party piece: a snow-making device. It is the first ever White Christmas on Tracy Island.

Notes

The models of the Thunderbird vehicles seen on the table in front of Jeff and Nicky in the opening scene were commercially available at the time of this episode's initial broadcast. They are the THUNDERBIRDS model toys produced by J. Rosenthal (Toys) Ltd. Unfortunately, Rosenthal's Thunderbird 5 didn't look very much like the genuine article, so it does not appear in this scene.

The 'new' Thunderbird 3 launch footage seen here was shot for *Thunderbirds Are Go*. Jeff tells Nicky that Thunderbird 3 is 287 feet high.

Lucky coincidence or attention to detail? We see calendars which indicate that Christmas Day is a Sunday, which it actually will be in 2067, when this episode is set.

Original UK Broadcast:
    5.05 p.m., Sunday 25 December 1966 (ATV London)
Original Broadcast Episode Number: 32
First UK Network Broadcast:
    6.00 p.m., Friday 20 December 1991 (BBC2)
Regular Cast:
    Jeff, Scott, Virgil, Alan, Gordon, John, Brains, Lady Penelope, Tin-Tin, Grandma, Kyrano
Major Equipment:
    TB2 (Pod 3), TB3, TB5, Ladybird Jet
Guest Voice Cast:

Nicky	**Sylvia Anderson**
Scobie	**Ray Barrett**
Straker	**David Graham**
Dr Pringle	**Jeremy Wilkin**
Dr Lang	**Charles Tingwell**
Nurse Nimmo	**Sylvia Anderson**
Harman	**Ray Barrett**
Saunders	**Jeremy Wilkin**
TV Reporter	**Jeremy Wilkin**
Santa 1	**Jeremy Wilkin**
Santa 2 (Leo)	**David Graham**
Tanner	**Charles Tingwell**
Preston	**Peter Dyneley**
Security Chief Joe	**Ray Barrett**

Tin-Tin tears a page off a calendar which shows the date as 2026. As mentioned opposite, we see other calendars which indicate that Christmas Day falls on a Sunday, but 25 December 2026 will be a Friday.

It is supposed to be the middle of the night when Virgil sets off in Thunderbird 2 for Coralville Hospital, but the Thunderbird 2 launch takes place in full daylight.

The Feature Films

THUNDERBIRDS ARE GO

Screenplay by **Gerry and Sylvia Anderson**
Directed by **David Lane**

'I've always been fascinated by that phrase, "Life as we know it." I have a feeling that we may encounter life as we don't know it.'

2065: the massive Zero X space vehicle, commanded by Captain Paul Travers, takes off from Glenn Field on the first manned expedition to Mars. However, the Hood is secretly on board, photographing the wing mechanisms, and his foot becomes trapped in the wing's control mechanics, jamming the systems. He manages to free himself and bail out, but Zero X goes out of control and the mighty craft plunges into the sea. The crew eject to safety in an escape pod.

Two years later, the Martian Exploration Center's report concludes that the crash was caused by sabotage. A second mission is approved, but only on the understanding that International Rescue will organize security for the launch. Jeff agrees and Scott is sent in Thunderbird 1 to oversee the operation. Virgil will follow Zero X through the atmosphere in Thunderbird 2 and Alan will then escort the craft into outer space in Thunderbird 3. Lady Penelope goes undercover as a reporter for *Universal Mirror* magazine to look out for saboteurs at Glenn Field.

At the pre-launch press conference, Penelope presents Paul Travers and each of the four members of his Zero X crew with St Christophers to wear during the flight. These are in fact homing devices that will enable her to keep track of them. The next day, the devices reveal that the Dr Grant who has joined the crew on board Zero X is an impostor: the Hood in disguise! Scott unmasks him but he escapes, so Lady Penelope and Parker give chase in FAB 1. When the Hood takes to the sea in a motor boat, Parker lowers the car's hydrofoils and FAB 1 launches into the sea in hot pursuit. The Hood is picked up by a helicopter which fires on FAB 1, but Parker shoots the craft down and it crashes into the sea. The real Dr Grant is located and takes his place on board Zero X as it lifts off safely and heads for Mars.

The emergency over, Lady Penelope invites Scott and Virgil to join her at the Swinging Star, a nightclub near her hotel. Alan is annoyed that he has been left out, and even more annoyed that Jeff refuses to allow him to go to the mainland with Tin-Tin as this would leave the base unmanned. That night, he dreams that he visits the Swinging Star after all, but this is a nightclub in outer space! He is escorted there by Lady Penelope in a flying FAB 1, and they watch Cliff Richard Jr and the Shadows performing 'Shooting Star'. The dream comes to an end when Alan falls out of bed!

22 July 2067: after a six-week flight, the Zero X Martian Exploration Vehicle lands on Mars. The crew explore and discover a series of strange coiled rock formations. Intending to take a sample back to Earth, they destroy one of the formations with the MEV cannon, but soon realize that they have unwittingly killed a living creature: the coils of rock are Martian rock snakes, creatures which shoot balls of fire from their mouths. The other rock snakes open fire on the MEV and only after a furious fight with the creatures do the crew escape from the planet in the MEV and link up with the main body for the return to Earth.

2 September 2067: Zero X begins Earth re-entry and is joined by the vehicle's lifting bodies for the controlled descent. Suddenly, the rear lifting body goes out of control, damaging the main vehicle's locking gear before exploding. The missing lifting body cannot be replaced and the crew's escape pod eject mechanism fails as the space vehicle heads for a crash-landing on the American town of Craigsville, population 4,800!

Jeff sends Scott and Brains to the scene in Thunderbird 1, while Virgil, Alan and Gordon rendezvous with Zero X in Thunderbird 2. Using air-to-air rescue gear, Alan ascends into Zero X through the undercarriage doors and Brains relays instructions on how to repair the escape pod wiring, which is preventing the pod's use. Sending the rest of the crew into the escape pod, Travers pilots Zero X until the last possible moment in an attempt to control its descent. He over-runs the engines to give Alan more time, but the movement causes Alan to drop his screwdriver, so he has to make the last connection by hand. Alan jumps from the ship and the escape pod ejects just before Zero X crashes into Craigsville.

Gordon cannot pull Alan back into Thunderbird 2 as the rope is snagged, but Lady Penelope is waiting below in FAB 1 to pick him up. She takes Alan (wearing a false moustache) to the real Swinging Star nightclub to celebrate his successful rescue of the Zero X crew. Once there, he is surprised to find the rest of the family there also, all wearing false moustaches!

Notes

Jeff calculates that as it is 11 a.m. on Tracy Island, it is 4 a.m. in England and, indeed, Lady Penelope is just sitting down to tea. Unless the world's time zones have changed by 2067, this puts Tracy Island somewhere just off the coast of Chile or Peru.

Having already created a puppet with some resemblance to

The Assembly Controller's map gives the name of the Zero X launch site as 'Glenn Field', but a sign on the gate of the press enclosure when Lady Penelope arrives in FAB 1 has it written as 'Glenfield'.

Alan is justifiably aggrieved by Jeff's refusal to allow him to go to the mainland with Tin-Tin. After all, only Kyrano was left to mind the store when the entire family went to see THE NED COOK SHOW at the end of Terror in New York City.

Sean Connery in Rick O'Shea (*Ricochet*), sculptor Terry Curtis here created a perfect Sean Connery puppet in the character of Zero X pilot Paul Travers. He later sculpted another Connery lookalike puppet in Captain Grey for CAPTAIN SCARLET AND THE MYSTERONS.

London Airport's Commander Norman appears to have been promoted to the board of the Space Exploration Center: he is seated to the right of the SEC President during the meeting. The Public Relations Officer at the press conference previously appeared as the Commander of Matthews Field in *The Cham-Cham* and Dr Pringle in *Give or Take a Million*. The Zero X MEV later appeared in the pilot episode of CAPTAIN SCARLET AND THE MYSTERONS. Lady Penelope's St Christopher homing device was introduced in *The Duchess Assignment*.

The script of the film was novelized as *Thunderbirds Are Go* by Angus P. Allan and published by Armada Paperbacks in 1966. United Artists released a soundtrack album of Barry Gray's film score (ULP 1159), which also included four tracks of incidental music from the television series. The album was re-released by Silva Screen on vinyl in 1987 and then on CD in 1990. It was re-released again by EMI in 1992.

Premiere:
8.30 p.m., Monday 12 December 1966
(London Pavilion, Piccadilly, London)

Regular Cast:
Jeff, Scott, Virgil, Alan, Gordon, John, Brains, Lady Penelope, Parker, Tin-Tin, the Hood

Major Equipment:
TB1, TB2 (Pod 5), TB3, TB5, FAB 1, Zero X (with MEV)

Voice Cast:

Jeff Tracy	**Peter Dyneley**
Scott Tracy	**Shane Rimmer**
Lady Penelope Creighton-Ward	**Sylvia Anderson**
Virgil Tracy	**Jeremy Wilkin**
Alan Tracy	**Matt Zimmerman**
Brains	**David Graham**
Aloysius Parker	**David Graham**
Tin-Tin Kyrano	**Christine Finn**
Gordon Tracy	**David Graham**
John Tracy	**Ray Barrett**
Kyrano	**David Graham**
The Hood	**Ray Barrett**
Captain Paul Travers	**Paul Maxwell**
Space Captain Greg Martin	**Alexander Davion**
Space Navigator Brad Newman	**Bob Monkhouse**
Dr Ray Pierce	**Neil McCallum**
Dr Tony Grant	**Charles Tingwell**
Controller — Glenn Field	**Ray Barrett**
Space Exploration Center President	**Jeremy Wilkin**
Public Relations Officer	**Charles Tingwell**
Messenger	**Matt Zimmerman**
Angry Young Man	**Charles Tingwell**
Swinging Star Compere	**Bob Monkhouse**

C R E D I T S

Executive Producer	**Gerry Anderson**
Producer	**Sylvia Anderson**
Supervising Visual Effects Director	**Derek Meddings**
Music Composed, Arranged and Directed by	**Barry Gray**
Supervising Art Director	**Bob Bell**
Assistant to the Executive Producer	**Norman Foster**
Associate Producer	**John Read**
Editor	**Len Walter**
Assistant Editor	**George Randall**
Lighting Cameraman	**Paddy Seale**
Camera Operator	**Alan Perry**
Puppet Operators	
Christine Glanville	**Mary Turner**
Wanda Webb	**Judith Shutt**
Wardrobe	**Elizabeth Coleman**
Wardrobe Assistant	**Zena Relph**
Visual Effects Director	**Shaun Whittacker-Cooke**
Visual Effects Lighting Cameraman	**Harry Oakes**
Visual Effects Camera Operators	**Ted Cutlack**
	Richard Conway
Visual Effects 2nd Unit Director	**Peter Wragg**
Visual Effects 2nd Unit Lighting Cameraman	**Ted Fowler**
Visual Effects 2nd Unit Camera Operators	**Ron Gallifant**
	Ron Ashton
Model Building Supervisor	**Ray Brown**
Properties Made by	**Tony Dunsterville**
	Plugg Shutt
	Arthur Cripps
Property Master	**Brian Burgess**
Production Co-ordinator	**Ken Turner**
Assistant Directors	**Harry Ledger**
	Ian Spurrier
Lip Sync Operator	**Grenville Nott**
Art Director	**Keith Wilson**
Designers	**John Lageu**
	John F. Brown
Sculpting Supervision	**Terry Curtis**
Sculptors	**Tim Cooksey**
	John Peverill
Sound Editors	**Brian T. Hickin**
	Maurice Askew
Sound Mixer	**Ken Scrivener**
Dialogue Recorder	
End Title Played by	**The Band of HM Royal Marines**
Conducted by	**Lt.-Col. F. Vivian Dunn**
'Shooting Star' Sung by	**Cliff Richard**
Written and Accompanied by	**The Shadows**
'Lady Penelope' Written and Played by	**The Shadows**

THUNDERBIRD 6

Written by **Gerry and Sylvia Anderson**
Directed by **David Lane**

'I thought it would be a good idea, in this day and age of speed and things like that, to build an airship.'

Using the pseudonym Mr X, Brains has designed a revolutionary new aircraft for the New World Aircraft Corporation, an airship called Skyship One. Penelope, Alan and Tin-Tin will be aboard the airship on its maiden voyage, but Brains will be tied up designing a new Thunderbird craft for International Rescue, Thunderbird 6. Unfortunately for Brains, although Jeff knows that he needs a new vehicle of some description, he cannot give Brains any specifications to work to and rejects each of his designs.

Alan and Tin-Tin travel by Tiger Moth biplane to rendezvous with Lady Penelope in England. Suitably attired in Edwardian outfits, they set out for the airfield with the Tiger Moth and FAB 1, escorted by Scott and Virgil in Thunderbirds 1 and 2. Meanwhile, aboard Skyship One, an intruder guns down the entire crew, who are replaced by impostors. The ship is completely automated, so the only way that they will be discovered is if anything breaks down. Lady Penelope, Alan, Tin-Tin and Parker board the airship, the gravity compensators are turned on and Skyship One takes off on the first leg of a round-the-world cruise. As the airship crosses the Atlantic *en route* for New York, the bodies of the real Skyship crew are dumped overboard.

The International Rescue team meet their charming host, the fake Captain Foster. Down in the gravity compensator room, his men are in contact with the Hood, who is using the codename Black Phantom. They have bugged every part of the ship that will be used by Lady Penelope in order to record her voice and rearrange her words to create a false message which will lure Thunderbirds 1 and 2 to a disused airfield 10 miles south of Casablanca. During the course of the voyage, Foster will steer conversation in the right direction so that Lady Penelope will say the words that they need to make up their bogus message.

Skyship One stops in various exotic locations around the world, flying over the Empire State Building, the Grand Canyon and the pyramids. Parker tells Lady Penelope that he feels the crew don't seem to know as much about the ship as they should. Lady Penelope and Alan also have doubts about their hosts, and as they speak a lamp falls over, revealing a bug. Lady Penelope sends a coded message to Jeff via Thunderbird 5, revealing her suspicions, but the Hood's bogus message is finally completed when Lady Penelope reads aloud from a false newspaper story planted by Foster.

Skyship One makes its final stop, in Switzerland. While the rest of the International Rescue team are entertained by Foster at the Whistle Stop Inn, Parker locates the villains' base in the gravity compensation room and determines that they have been editing recordings of Lady Penelope's voice. With everyone back on board, Lady Penelope and Alan soon realize that all the bugs have been removed and Alan hands out guns to everyone,

putting them on emergency stand-by. The next day, the bogus message is relayed to Thunderbird 5. Jeff launches Thunderbirds 1 and 2, *en route* for Casablanca, but before they arrive, Lady Penelope makes a direct call to Jeff to tell him that the message was false and the rendezvous is a trap. Forewarned is forearmed, and Thunderbirds 1 and 2 obliterate the opposition on arrival at the disused airfield.

The team prepare to round up the villains in the gravity compensation room, but a gun battle ensues and the gravity compensators are damaged. The villains capture Tin-Tin and hold her hostage to enforce the surrender of the others. However, Skyship One is in a slow descent as it crosses the English coastline, now low enough to hit radio masts at an early warning station near Dover. The airship crashes into the masts and comes to rest precariously balanced on one of the radio towers. When the compensators fail altogether, the weight of the ship will send it crashing on to the missile base below!

The villains gather on the deck, with their hostages held at gunpoint. Scott pulls up alongside in Thunderbird 1 and secures a line to the airship to steady it, but conventional rescue with International Rescue equipment is out of the question as a lightweight vehicle is required, one that will not tip the airship off balance. On Gordon's suggestion, Brains pilots Alan's Tiger Moth and effects a landing on the Skyship deck, while Virgil secures a second line from Thunderbird 2, assisting Thunderbird 1 to steady the ship. Foster takes control of the biplane, climbing aboard with Lady Penelope and ousting Brains. Alan shoots him as he tries to take off, but Foster's hand knocks the accelerator and the biplane launches across the deck. Alan, Brains, Tin-Tin and Foster's henchmen leap on to the wings as the craft takes off, but Penelope is in the cockpit and doesn't know how to fly the biplane. Alan shouts instructions while exchanging gunfire with Foster's men. The villains are shot and fall off, but the fuel tank has been holed by a stray bullet. Lady Penelope tries to land the Tiger Moth on the new M104 motorway, but the throttle is stuck.

Skyship's gravity compensators finally give out, but the evacuation of the missile base is complete. Scott and Virgil release their safety lines and Skyship One crashes on to the base with a mighty explosion. Back on the Tiger Moth, Lady Penelope performs an aerial roll to dump Foster's body so that

Tin-Tin claims never to have seen the pyramids before, but she must surely mean that she has never visited them before, as she previously saw them when Thunderbird 2 flew over them in Desperate Intruder.

Penelope is so concerned with the fate of the Air Terrainean DX 102 airliner, she doesn't notice that the second paragraph in the bogus newspaper report of the crash is exactly the same as the first.

Virgil tells Scott that he has 'a tiger in his tank', a humorous reference to a contemporary advertising campaign for Esso petrol ('Put a Tiger in your Tank'). Unfortunately, the joke presupposed that the cinema audience was familiar enough with vintage aircraft to recognize Alan's biplane as a Tiger Moth – it isn't mentioned anywhere in the film's dialogue.

Alan can climb into the rear cockpit. The biplane stalls and Alan brings it to a crash-landing in a field. No one is hurt, but there is no sign of Parker and everyone believes that he was left on board Skyship One. Fortunately, he is safe: he was hanging on to the Tiger Moth's undercarriage until just prior to the crash-landing, when he fell off into a tree. Back on Tracy Island, Brains finally unveils Thunderbird 6, the ideal lightweight supplementary rescue vehicle, already tested on a rescue operation: the Tiger Moth!

Notes

The newspaper that Penelope reads on the morning of Skyship One's arrival in Egypt clearly shows the date as 11 June 2068. It can be inferred that FAB 1 is completely destroyed in the climax of the film, since the car is still in the hold of Skyship One when it crashes into the missile base.

Several of the puppets created for *Thunderbirds Are Go* are seen again here: Foster's henchman Carter previously appeared as Zero X pilot Paul Travers, the President of New World Aircraft was previously seen as the Assembly Controller at Glenn Field and Cliff Richard Jr also makes a cameo appearance – disguised in thick glasses and a moustache, he is sitting behind Lady Penelope at the Whistle Stop Inn.

During the evacuation of the missile base, one of the cars that drives through shot is Sam Loover's car from JOE 90. Footage of the destruction of the missile base reappears in *The Most Special Agent*, the opening episode of JOE 90.

Pemiere:
2.30 p.m., Monday 29 July 1968
(Odeon Cinema, Leicester Square, London)

Regular Cast:
Jeff, Scott, Virgil, Alan, Gordon, John, Brains, Lady Penelope, Parker, Tin-Tin, Grandma, the Hood

Major Equipment:
TB1, TB2 (Pod 5), TB3, TB4, TB5, TB6, FAB 1, Hover Pack, Skyship One

Voice Cast:

Jeff Tracy	**Peter Dyneley**
Scott Tracy	**Shane Rimmer**
Lady Penelope Creighton-Ward	**Sylvia Anderson**
Virgil Tracy	**Jeremy Wilkin**
Alan Tracy	**Matt Zimmerman**
Brains	**David Graham**
Aloysius Parker	**David Graham**
Tin-Tin Kyrano	**Christine Finn**
Gordon Tracy	**David Graham**
John Tracy	**Keith Alexander**
Kyrano	**David Graham**
The Hood/Black Phantom	**Gary Files**
Captain Foster/White Ghost	**John Carson**
New World Aircraft President James Glenn	**Geoffrey Keen**
Captain Foster	**Gary Files**
Hogarth	**Jeremy Wilkin**
Lane	**Gary Files**
Carter	**Matt Zimmerman**
Indian Fortune-teller	**Christine Finn**
Narrator	**Keith Alexander**

Executive Producer	**Gerry Anderson**
Producer	**Sylvia Anderson**
Supervising Visual Effects Director	**Derek Meddings**
Music Composed, Arranged and Directed by	**Barry Gray**
Art Director	**Bob Bell**
Production Manager	**Norman Foster**
Assistant Director	**Peter Anderson**
Lip Sync Operator	**Ian Spurrier**
Director of Photography	**Harry Oakes**
Camera Operator	**Peter Nash**
Focus Operator	**Ian Vinson**
Editor	**Len Walter**
Assistant Editor	**Len Cleal**
Puppet Co-ordinator	**Mary Turner**
Puppet Operators	
Wanda Webb	**Linda Rutter**
Sheena McGregor	**Charmaine Wood**
Wardrobe	**Kim Martin**
Puppet Workshop	**Terry Curtis**
	Tim Cooksey
	Plugg Shutt
Model Makers	**Ray Brown**
	Peter Ashton
	Eric Backman
Visual Effects Assistant	**Ian Wingrove**
Model Workshop	**Brian Smithies**
Sets Designed by	**Keith Wilson**
	John Lageu
	Tony Dunsterville
Properties Made by	**Peter Holmes**
Property Master	**Ted Fowler**
Location Unit Cameraman	**Derek Black**
Location Unit Camera Operators	**Tommy Fletcher**
Tiger Moth Flown by	**Joan Hughes, MBF**
Remote Control Flying	**Eric Faulkner**
Supervising Sound Editor	**John Peverill**
Sound Editors	**Peter Pennell**
	Brian Hickin

SPIN-OFF ADVENTURES 4

During the original broadcast run of THUNDERBIRDS, International Rescue's adventures were not confined solely to television and film. THUNDERBIRDS stories were expanded into other media by the writers and producers at Century 21, providing opportunities to exploit the concept through the various merchandising arms of the Century 21 Organization, primarily Century 21 Publishing (books and comics) and Century 21 Records (mini-albums and LPs). Keen to ensure levels of quality and consistency with the format of the television series, the Century 21 company directors were closely involved with the development of many of these merchandising projects.

Continuity was carefully maintained between the various storytelling formats to a remarkable degree. As might be expected, the books, records and comics all referred back to characters, vehicles and incidents that had appeared in the television episodes. More surprising, however, is the discovery that the spin-off formats also all cross-referenced each other: supporting characters and vehicles introduced in the comics reappeared in the novels and the records, those introduced on the records turned up in both the comics and the novels, stories told in the novels were recalled in the comics, and so on. This all helped to reinforce the idea of THUNDERBIRDS having a fictional 'life' that crossed the boundaries of the television screen into other media, and that these alternative storytelling methods were parts of the THUNDERBIRDS canon that were just as relevant as the stories that had been committed to film.

THE MINI-ALBUMS

As a subsidiary company of the Century 21 Organization, Century 21 Records was launched in September 1965 to meet the increasing demand in the children's record field (as opposed to the teenage and adult market which had, until that time, dominated record sales). Promoted as 'the toys you hear!', the first Century 21 release was a FIREBALL XL5-based LP *Journey to the Moon*, which featured an original FIREBALL XL5 story performed by the programme's voice cast. With the intention of educating the listener about space travel, British Interplanetary Society member Patrick Moore was hired as scientific adviser, but the album also featured songs and music by Barry Gray, including the TV theme song 'Fireball'. An edited version of the album was also released on a 7-inch EP, and this was the first of the company's thirty-six mini-albums.

Covering a variety of subjects, the mini-albums were primarily spin-offs from the popular Gerry Anderson television series: in addition to the FIREBALL XL5 record, there were three STINGRAY, nineteen THUNDERBIRDS and five CAPTAIN SCARLET EPs, as well as four EPs of themes and incidental music tracks from the various series. Several EPs also appeared that presented recordings of other properties licensed by Century 21: The Daleks from the BBC's DOCTOR WHO, Mario Perego's puppet mouse Topo Gigio (then appearing in ITV's Saturday afternoon show TOPO GIGIO COMES TO TOWN) and Jean Morton's cuddly koalas Tingha and Tucker, who had been popular fixtures of ITV children's television since 1959. But it was the Anderson-based mini-albums that were the best-sellers, so much so that a number of them were re-released in pairs as LPs.

Of the nineteen THUNDERBIRDS story EPs, sixteen featured edited recordings from the soundtracks of the television episodes with additional narration, in character, by a number of the series' voice artists. The three remaining EPs presented entirely new THUNDERBIRDS stories, with the television voice artists re-creating their puppet roles for complete authenticity. All three were written by people with close links to the television series: scriptwriter Alan Fennell, director Desmond Saunders and voice artist David Graham.

'INTRODUCING THUNDERBIRDS'
Written by **Alan Fennell**

On the invitation of Jeff Tracy, Lady Penelope and Parker visit Tracy Island for the first time, crossing to the island from Lady Penelope's cruiser in FAB 1. Jeff shows her around the Tracy Villa, explaining that everything to do with the running of International Rescue must remain concealed to prevent their secrets from falling into the wrong hands. While Parker struggles with Lady Penelope's luggage, Jeff explains the function of International Rescue and reveals that Lady Penelope will control the British end of the set-up.

Brains reports that Jeff's sons are all in position aboard their respective vehicles, so Jeff takes Lady Penelope on a tour of the island. She insists that Parker should carry Jeff's heavy portable remote control console. The trio drive around the island in FAB 1, stopping at various vantage points to observe the launching of Thunderbirds 1, 2, 3 and 4 before returning to the house for dinner.

Jeff takes Lady Penelope to the library to present her with the International Rescue codes and call signs, but he is surprised to find that his supposedly impregnable safe, hidden behind a bookshelf, is empty. Lady Penelope quickly realises what has happened: calling Parker, she tells him to put everything back. Jeff is amused and remarks that with characters like the two of them around, International Rescue can't go wrong. Thunderbirds are definitely go!

Notes

This story clearly takes place prior to the events of *Trapped in the Sky*. Released in advance of the launch of the series on British television, the record was intended to introduce the concepts and characters of the series and stimulate the interest of potential viewers.

Although Lady Penelope's boat is unnamed here, the inference is that it is Seabird, an ocean-going cruiser used by Penelope in her *TV Century 21* comic adventures, rather than her yacht FAB 2.

The title on the record label ('Introducing the Thunderbirds') differs slightly from that on the sleeve. Originally released as Century 21 mini-album MA 107, 'Introducing Thunderbirds' also appeared on side one of the Century 21 LP *Lady Penelope Presents* (LA 2), and was re-released on the Marble Arch LP *Gerry Anderson Presents TV Favourites – Volume 1* (MAL 770).

VOICE CAST	
Jeff Tracy	**Peter Dyneley**
Lady Penelope Creighton-Ward	**Sylvia Anderson**
Aloysius Parker	**David Graham**
Brains	**David Graham**
Kyrano	**David Graham**

'FAB'
Written by **Desmond Saunders and David Graham**

John reports that alarm calls from the Everest area about attacks by the so-called Abominable Snowman are still coming through and three more people have disappeared in the last two weeks. On Scott's suggestion, Jeff contacts Lady Penelope, who is holidaying in Delhi, and she readily agrees to look into the matter. She and Parker contact Gallup Din, the International Rescue agent for the Nepal area, in the village of Borapur. Din reveals that the only evidence at the scene of each incident are footprints of an enormous circumference, which Lady Penelope asks to see for herself. None of the local people is prepared to act as a guide into the

mountains, but Din has contacted a well-known Asiatic explorer who has worked in the area for a number of years and has agreed to act as their guide. Unknown to Lady Penelope and Parker, however, this man is the Hood in disguise.

The Hood takes Lady Penelope and Parker by ski-copter into the mountains. Arriving at their destination, Lady Penelope twists her ankle as she alights, so the Hood suggests that she remain behind while he takes Parker to view the footprints. Instead, Parker is taken to an ice cave, where the Hood pulls a gun on him and reveals that he is the Abominable Snowman. Like all of the other men he has captured, he has lured Parker to the cave to become a slave in his uranium mine.

The Hood locks Parker in the cave and returns to the ski-copter to deal with Lady Penelope. Parker immediately contacts her to warn her and she in turn contacts Jeff for International Rescue's assistance. Scott sets off in Thunderbird 1, but there is no sign of Lady Penelope when he gets there. The Hood takes her to the cave and straps her to a metal girder, threatening to cut her head off with his laser beam device unless she reveals the codes used by International Rescue to send secret messages.

Brains's new metal detector enables Scott to locate the Hood's ski-copter. He bursts into the cave, shoots the Hood with his tranquillizer gun and destroys the laser beam controls, shutting down the device in the nick of time. Scott reveals that the Hood will be out cold until the arrival of the airborne police, who will also help to return the captured slave workers to their homes. Penelope calls Jeff to report the successful conclusion of their mission. The legend of the Abominable Snowman can be buried for ever.

Notes
This story is preceded by a song, 'The Abominable Snowman', composed by Barry Gray and performed by Sylvia Anderson and David Graham as Lady Penelope and Parker. Originally released as Century 21 mini-album MA 107, the story also appeared on side one of the Century 21 LP *Lady Penelope Investigates* (LA 4). Under the title 'The Abominable Snowman', a synopsis of the story appears alongside those of five television episodes in the third of Century 21's THUNDERBIRDS annuals (1968).

VOICE CAST	
Jeff Tracy	**Peter Dyneley**
Lady Penelope Creighton-Ward	**Sylvia Anderson**
Scott Tracy	**Shane Rimmer**
Aloysius Parker	**David Graham**
John Tracy	**Ray Barrett**
The Hood	**Ray Barrett**
Gallup Din	**David Graham**
Threatened Explorer	**David Graham**

'THE STATELY HOMES ROBBERIES'
Written by Alan Fennell
From a story by **Jim Watson**

A series of robberies at English stately homes has culminated in a theft at the home of Lord and Lady Donnington-Brown, neighbours of Lady Penelope – the twelfth such robbery in a month. The thief steals only priceless family heirlooms, leaving cash and contemporary works of art untouched. The police are baffled, as there are no clues or signs of forced entry at the crime scenes. Penelope is concerned that Creighton-Ward Mansion could be the next target, for even the strongest locks and the most sophisticated vaults seem to be no match for the thief.

Parker contacts his former underworld associates to try to determine the identity of the villain, but even 'Fingers' Fred is unable to shed any light on the matter. Jeff offers to send Brains over with some gadgets to improve security at the Mansion, but Penelope feels that it won't deter the thief. She is determined to go about her normal business and plans a trip to Wickfen's to buy a new outfit, staying on in town afterwards to dine out and see a show. Parker contacts

Elaine Wickfen to arrange an appointment, unaware that his call is being monitored by Mr Charles and his manservant, Dawkins.

At Wickfen's, Elaine Wickfen and her model, Cynthia, prepare for Lady Penelope's arrival. Lady Penelope arrives in FAB 1 and tells Parker to return for her at 6.00 p.m. Back at the Mansion, Mr Charles and Dawkins approach the house in a stealth helijet and drop gas capsules down the chimneys to knock out the servants. On her way home, Lady Penelope asks Parker to call ahead so that Lil can prepare a nightcap, but there is no response from the Mansion and she suspects trouble. Spotting a helijet taking off from the front lawn, she uses Parker's pneumatic machine pistol to fire a suction microphone at the craft. Listening in to the on-board conversation between Mr Charles and Dawkins, they learn that the next target will be the Crown Jewels in the Tower of London.

Realizing that the authorities will not believe her story, Lady Penelope decides to take matters into her own hands. She and Parker are lying in wait at the Tower when Mr Charles and Dawkins arrive by helijet the following evening. With breathing masks in place, the thieves use gas capsules to incapacitate the Beefeaters and gain access to the Tower. Following them inside, Lady Penelope and Parker confront Mr Charles and Dawkins just as they are putting the Crown Jewels into a sack. Parker puts the jewels back, while Lady Penelope finds out more about Mr Charles's motives. He reveals that his ancestors, the Granvilles, were once noble peers and the owners of all of the heirlooms that he has stolen. They were stripped of their title and property by Richard the Lionheart after being convicted of cowardice during the Crusades. Their property was then distributed among the King's loyal friends, including the Creightons and the Wards, Penelope's ancestors.

Mr Charles asserts that Lady Penelope will not be able to prove anything to the authorities, but she reveals that she has made a tape recording of his confession and this will be enough to make the police search his home. The microphone that she has used was designed by Brains to record only male voices, so Lady Penelope's cover will not be compromised. She and Parker leave Mr Charles and Dawkins handcuffed in the Tower to await the arrival of the police.

The next morning's paper reveals that the police have recovered the stolen heirlooms, but have disregarded Mr Charles's accusations of Lady Penelope's involvement in his arrest, believing that it is impossible to associate her with criminals in any way.

Notes
Prior to the release of this record in June 1966, fashion designer Elaine Wickfen and her exclusive boutique had already appeared in the first 'Lady Penelope' strip in *Lady Penelope* comic. Originally released as Century 21 mini-album MA 110, the story was also issued on side two of the Century 21 LP *Lady Penelope Investigates* (LA 4).

Creighton-Ward Mansion, stately home of Lady Penelope Creighton-Ward.

VOICE CAST	
Lady Penelope Creighton-Ward	**Sylvia Anderson**
Aloysius Parker	**David Graham**
Jeff Tracy	**Peter Dyneley**
Mr Charles	**Peter Dyneley**
Dawkins	**Ray Barrett**
Elaine Wickfen	**Sylvia Anderson**
Cynthia	**Sylvia Anderson**
Beefeater	**David Graham**
Newspaper Vendor	**David Graham**

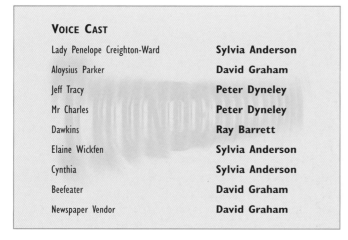

TV Century 21,
issue 73 (11 June 1966).

THE COMICS

Century 21 Merchandising (then known as AP Films Merchandising) launched *TV Century 21*, a quality weekly comic, in January 1965. The brainchild of the company's managing director Keith Shackleton and scriptwriter Alan Fennell, *TV Century 21* was a joint venture with City Magazines, part of the News of the World group, which handled publishing and distribution, while Century 21 produced the contents. Fennell, who became the comic's editor and head writer, brought in assistant editor Tod Sullivan, script editor Angus Allan and art editor Dennis Hooper as his production team. Featuring strip stories based on the Gerry Anderson television series, *TV Century 21* presented the work of some of British comics' most admired artists, Mike Noble, Ron Embleton, Don Lawrence and Ron Turner among them, with high-quality production values which readers appreciated. Within weeks of its launch, *TV Century 21* was Britain's top-selling comic.

At the time of the comic's first publication, THUNDERBIRDS was still in production and SUPERCAR, FIREBALL XL5 and STINGRAY were the only Gerry Anderson properties regularly seen on British television. But for the first year of the comic's publication, strips based on those three series were joined by one charting the adventures of Lady Penelope and Parker (in advance of their television debut for the first nine months). Set at a time prior to Lady Penelope's involvement with International Rescue, the first strip (written by Fennell and illustrated by Eric Eden) told of her original meeting with Parker and went on to pit them against the villainous Mr Steelman, who became Lady Penelope's arch-enemy in both the comic strip and the Lady Penelope novels.

Other elements from THUNDERBIRDS appeared in the STINGRAY strip ahead of the series' television premiere (both the Fireflash and the Sidewinder from *Pit of Peril* appeared in the second STINGRAY strip story), but it was not until January 1966 that a THUNDERBIRDS strip appeared in the comic. By this time, the series was well established on television and the arrival of the strip in *TV Century 21* was heralded by various feature articles in the weeks leading up to the strip's first appearance in issue 51. The 'Lady Penelope' strip transferred to *Lady Penelope*, a new comic for girls, but in the final instalment of her *TV Century 21* strip, Lady Penelope was contacted by Jeff Tracy, who invited her to join International Rescue.

THUNDERBIRDS made a triumphant debut in *TV Century 21*, dominating three pages of the comic (including the full-colour centre spread) with artwork by British comics legend Frank Bellamy. A former artist for *Mickey Mouse Weekly* and *Swift* comics, Bellamy made his name as the successor to Frank Hampson on the 'Dan Dare' strip in *Eagle* comic. Between 1959 and 1965, he contributed a succession of outstanding strips to *Eagle*, culminating in the epic 'Heros of Spartan' immediately ·
before starting work on THUNDERBIRDS for *TV Century 21*.

Bellamy's THUNDERBIRDS strip used unusually stylistic framing techniques which made every instalment dynamic and action-packed. Purists argue about his stylized depictions of the International Rescue vehicles (particularly Thunderbirds 2 and 4), but few other artists have been able to transfer the essence of the series and its characters to the printed page so successfully. Apart from a six-week period in mid-1966 (during which time he was replaced by Don Harley), Bellamy had an uninterrupted run on the strip from January 1966 to October 1969, producing an amazing 360 pages of artwork over thirty stories in 186 issues of the comic.

In 1971, Bellamy replaced John Allard on the *Daily Mirror*'s long-running 'Garth' strip, which he concentrated on solely until his untimely death in 1976. His

The Sidewinder from Pit of Peril *appears on the cover of* TV Century 21, *issue 9 (20 March 1966).*

THUNDERBIRDS strips were all reprinted in Fleetway's *Thunderbirds: The Comic* from October 1991 to March 1994, and thirteen of the stories were collected in a series of six graphic albums published by Ravette Books in 1992.

The first six THUNDERBIRDS strips in *TV Century 21* were written by Alan Fennell and are, therefore, the ones with the most legitimate claim to the THUNDERBIRDS canon.

1. BLAZING DANGER

Written by **Alan Fennell**

Art by **Frank Bellamy**

Published in *TV Century 21*, issues 52–58 (15 January–26 February 1966)

In a Canadian Forest, Sam Lincoln plans to kill his business partner Jack Farrel and take control of Canada Engineering Inc. He sets off incendiary charges which start a forest fire, but both men are trapped by a fast-flowing river as the fire rages out of control. Gordon rescues the men in Thunderbird 4, but when he and Virgil take Thunderbird 2 to help combat the fire Lincoln steals International Rescue's Master Fire Fighter vehicle and attempts to escape through the flames. Lincoln is trapped by falling trees, so Virgil takes an auxiliary vehicle to pull him clear before the master vehicle explodes, but Lincoln overpowers Virgil and steals the auxiliary vehicle, leaving Virgil unconscious in the middle of the inferno. Gordon rescues Virgil in a second auxiliary vehicle, while Scott heads off Lincoln in Thunderbird 1.

> ### REPRINT HISTORY
> TV ACTION + COUNTDOWN, issues 71–77
> (Polystyle Publications, 17 June–29 July 1972)
> ACTION 21, issues 1–7 (Engale Marketing, July 1988–July 1989)
> THUNDERBIRDS: THE COMIC, issues 32–38
> (Fleetway Editions, 26 December 1992–20 March 1993)
> THUNDERBIRDS ARE GO, issues 1–7 (Leaf Publishing, 1995)

TV Century 21,
issue 53 (22 January 1966).

2. MISSION TO AFRICA

Written by **Alan Fennell**

Art by **Frank Bellamy**

Published in *TV Century 21*, issues 59–65 (5 March–16 April 1966)

Heart specialist Dr Adams is being rushed to Madagascar to save the life of African General N'Mobo when his plane crashes in a Kenyan game reserve. Canisters of medical compound Rexsta Seven, designed to stimulate life, break open and get into the local water supply, stirring the animals into a frenzy. Meanwhile, Adams and his pilot, Peters, are captured by Masai warriors, who want Adams to cure their dying sacred albino rhinoceros. Scott flies to the reserve in Thunderbird 1 and manages to save the life of Peters, who has escaped from the Masai but has been attacked by a lion. Brains suggests a plan to replace the dying rhinoceros with a healthy duplicate and sets to work on an antidote for the compound, while Scott locates a second albino rhino. Using hastily modified equipment, Scott and Virgil capture the rhino, and Virgil causes a diversion in Thunderbird 2 which enables Scott to replace the dead rhino with the duplicate and rescue Dr Adams.

> ### REPRINT HISTORY
> COUNTDOWN, issues 24–30
> (Polystyle Publications, 31 July–11 September 1972)
> ACTION 21, issues 8–10
> (Engale Marketing, August–October 1989; parts 1 to 3 only)
> THUNDERBIRDS: THE COMIC, issues 39–45
> (Fleetway Editions, 3 April–26 June 1993)

TV Century 21,
issue 64 (9 April 1966).

TV Century 21,
issue 67 (30 April 1966).

3. THE TALONS OF THE EAGLE (A.K.A. NEAR MISS)

Written by **Alan Fennell**
Art by **Frank Bellamy**
Published in *TV Century 21*, issues 66–72 (23 April–4 June 1966)

As Thunderbirds 1 and 2 return to Tracy Island from Africa, Thunderbird 2 is attacked by the Eagle, a USAF jet equipped with sophisticated jamming equipment. To escape, Virgil climbs above the atmosphere but is trapped in orbit when his fuel runs out. Scott and Alan take Thunderbird 3 to refuel Thunderbird 2 and both vehicles return to the island. Determined to protect the security of the organization, Jeff sets in motion a desperate plan to locate and shoot down the Eagle so that they can learns its secrets. Scott disables the jet with Thunderbird 1's missiles and it crash-lands into the sea. Gordon uses gas capsules to knock out the crew and Virgil uses Thunderbird 2 to airlift the Eagle to Mateo Island, where Brains can examine the jamming equipment while the brothers effect repairs to the jet's tail section. When the pilots recover consciousness they are alone on the island and fly the Eagle back to base none the wiser about International Rescue's involvement.

> **REPRINT HISTORY**
> THUNDERBIRDS HOLIDAY SPECIAL (Polystyle Publications, Summer 1984)
> THUNDERBIRDS: THE COMIC, issues 10–13
> (Fleetway Editions, 22 February–4 April 1992)
> THUNDERBIRDS: LIFT OFF! (Ravette Books, 1992)

4. THE ATLANTIC TUNNEL (A.K.A. SHAFT K279)

Written by **Alan Fennell**
Art by **Frank Bellamy**
Published in *TV Century 21*, issues 73–82 (11 June–13 August 1966)

TV Century 21,
issue 75 (25 June 1966).

Jeff acquires a permit to survey his privately leased offshoot excavation of the Atlantic Tunnel, man's greatest engineering project, for the rare mineral mozatinum, the base compound in a tough metal alloy that Brains has invented. At the Boston entrance of the tunnel, Alan and Brains meet up with Brains's old university colleague Vincent Baker, who is surveying the same section of the tunnel for a man named Shendon. But Shendon is actually the Hood, who has learned of the project from Kyrano and covets the mozatinum. When traces of the rare mineral are found in rock samples drawn from his own leased shaft, the Hood defies tunnel regulations and begins his own excavations. His blast charges cause a series of cave-ins in the Tunnel which trap Alan and Brains in Shaft K279, but they are rescued by Virgil using the Excadigger. A second rockfall traps a group of tunnel workers and the atomic reactor on a rock cutter is damaged, exposing the men to deadly radiation. Virgil rescues the men in the nick of time, using the Mole, but not before the Hood has taken photographs of Thunderbird 1 and made his escape in a private jet. Scott chases after the jet and shoots it down. The Hood ejects to safety, but his pictures are destroyed.

> **REPRINT HISTORY**
> THUNDERBIRDS HOLIDAY SPECIAL (Polystyle Publications, Summer 1984)
> THUNDERBIRDS: THE COMIC, issues 1–4
> (Fleetway Editions, 19 October–30 November 1991)
> THUNDERBIRDS: THE COLLECTION (Fleetway Editions, March 1992)
> THUNDERBIRDS IN SPACE (Ravette Books, 1992)

5. SOLAR DANGER

Written by **Alan Fennell**
Art by **Frank Bellamy and Don Harley**
Published in *TV Century 21*, issues 83–98
(20 August–3 December1966)

A series of freak disasters on Earth is being caused by unprecedented solar activity. Alan and Brains journey to the Sun in Thunderbird 3 and discover that the ejection of a massive build-up of solar waste matter could upset the natural balance of the solar system and destroy the Earth. The World President authorizes International Rescue to use a planetomic missile to destroy the solar debris, but the explosion creates a shock wave which throws Thunderbird 3 out of control. The spacecraft crash-lands in a sulphur lake on Venus, where Alan and Brains are menaced by strange Venusian monsters as they attempt to make repairs. Booster rockets are fitted to Thunderbirds 1 and 2 so that they can make the journey to Venus. On arrival, Gordon dives into the lake in Thunderbird 4 to secure winch cables to Thunderbird 3, enabling Virgil to lift the rocket clear of the lake in Thunderbird 2.

Reprint History

THUNDERBIRDS HOLIDAY SPECIAL (Polystyle Publications, June 1971; parts 11 to 16 only)
THUNDERBIRDS HOLIDAY SPECIAL (Fleetway Editions, April 1992)
THUNDERBIRDS ARE GO, issue 8 (Leaf Publishing, 1995; part 1 only)

6. THE BIG FREEZE
(A.K.A. ARCTIC MENACE)

Written by **Alan Fennell**
Art by **Frank Bellamy**
Published in *TV Century 21*, issues 99–104
(10 December 1966–14 January 1967)

Right: TV Century 21, *issue 86 (10 September 1966).*
Below: TV Century 21, *issue 100 (17 December 1966).*

During extreme weather defence tests at the World Army's Camp 21st Century base 50 feet beneath the Arctic icecap, a wayward missile destroys the nuclear power plant. The ice-breaker Shackleton, bringing a replacement reactor, can't get through the ice, the radiation shielding on the base's blazing atomic reactor begins to crack, and sparks from the fire ignite the emergency diesel generator fuel stores, leaving 1,000 trapped men to face death by freezing or radiation contamination. Thunderbirds 1 and 2 race to the Arctic and while Gordon uses Thunderbird 4's laser to melt the ice hindering the Shackleton, Alan uses the Firefly to blow out the power plant fire with nitro-glycerine shells. The brothers then ferry the replacement reactor from the Shackleton to the base on special transporters and help the army personnel to fit it.

Reprint History

THUNDERBIRDS HOLIDAY SPECIAL (Polystyle Publications, June 1971)
THUNDERBIRDS HOLIDAY SPECIAL (Polystyle Publications, Summer 1984)
CENTURY 21, issue 5 (Engale Marketing, Summer 1991)
THUNDERBIRDS: THE COMIC, issues 1–3 (Fleetway Editions, 19 October–16 November 1991)
THUNDERBIRDS: THE COLLECTION (Fleetway Editions, March 1992)
THUNDERBIRDS TO THE RESCUE (Ravette Books, 1992)

THUNDERBIRDS Annual,
1966; Lady Penelope
Annual, 1966; and Lady
Penelope, issue 2
(29 January 1966).

Lady Penelope, meanwhile, continued her solo adventures in her own comic and was only rarely seen alongside her International Rescue colleagues in the *TV Century 21* strips. The artwork on the 'Lady Penelope' strip in *Lady Penelope* comic became the almost exclusive domain of Frank Langford, whose stylish interpretation of the THUNDERBIRDS world and its characters was radically different from that of Frank Bellamy, but no less breathtaking. International Rescue made occasional appearances, as did other characters from the television episodes, such as Jimmy Bondson from *The Man from MI.5*, and in one story Penelope was invited to star in a film being made at the Century 21 Film Studios – the film's producer was a Mr Andershill. Many of these and the earlier *TV Century 21* strips were also reprinted in Fleetway's *Thunderbirds: The Comic* in the early 1990s.

Each year from 1965 to 1969, Century 21 and City Magazines also published a collection of hardback annuals tied into the comics. Unlike today's disappointing lightweight equivalents, these ninety-two-page annuals were heavy, robust A4-size coffee-table style books, packed with strips, text stories, relevant feature articles, vehicle cutaways, character biographies and photos. THUNDERBIRDS was absent only from the first of the *TV Century 21* (later simply *TV21*) annuals, and also featured in a separate THUNDERBIRDS annual from 1966 to 1968, the first of which sported a cover painted by Frank Bellamy. In 1969, the series shared the spotlight with CAPTAIN SCARLET in a combination *Captain Scarlet and Thunderbirds* annual. *Lady Penelope* (later simply *Penelope*) annuals were also published from 1966 to 1969 but, like the comic, were generally much less focused on THUNDERBIRDS: the first featured articles on hairdressing, astrology, fashion boutiques, actress Adrienne Posta, pop trio the Walker Brothers and recipes for swinging parties!

A frame from the opening
instalment of 'The Atlantic
Tunnel' in TV Century 21,
issue 73 (11 June 1966).
Art by Frank Bellamy.

THE NOVELS

Between 1966 and 1967, AP Films/Century 21 Films authorized the publication of eight original novels based on the exploits of International Rescue and its London agent, Lady Penelope. All but two of these were written by the highly prolific British writer John William Jennison, who, prior to his Supermarionation-based novels, was the author of more than a hundred novels for different UK paperback publishers. Working in a variety of genres (primarily Westerns and thrillers), under at least forty pseudonyms, he made his debut as a science-fiction author in 1951 with *Conquerors of Venus*, using the pen name Edgar Rees Kennedy. Other works were credited to Neil Charles, Gill Hunt, King Lang and Matthew C. Bradford, although Jennison was perhaps best known as John Theydon, a name he had used since 1946.

Jennison began writing fiction based on the various Gerry Anderson series in 1965 with World Distributors' hardback illustrated storybook *Supercar on the Black Diamond Trail*, and followed this with a pair of Stingray storybooks, *Danger in the Deep* and *The Deadly Alliance*. As John Theydon, he then penned two Stingray paperbacks, *Stingray* and *Stingray and the Monster*, for Armada Books (a division of May Fair Books), which led to him being commissioned to write the Thunderbirds novels. Later, he authored three Captain Scarlet novels for Armada and ended his literary career with two novels based on The Secret Service. He is believed to have died shortly after.

Jennison's Thunderbirds novels fully utilized the different medium to tell more wide-ranging stories than was possible within the fifty-minute television episodes. His science-fiction background also encouraged him to introduce more fantastic elements (such as lost civilizations and alien invaders) into the stories, but even these aspects were presented in a manner that was 'true' to the Thunderbirds format. After all, the precedent had already been set with the Zombites in *Martian Invasion* and the Martian rock snakes in *Thunderbirds Are Go*.

Jennison was also keen to establish a continuity between his novels, so while each could be read as a stand-alone work there was also a clear chronological progression. This was most apparent in the ongoing thread of International Rescue's encounters with the Hood in which the Tracys' increasing awareness of his identity, motives, powers and influence over Kyrano eventually leads them into open conflict with the villain.

THUNDERBIRDS

Written by **John Theydon (John W. Jennison)**
Published 1966 by Armada Books (paperback, 126 pages),
illustrated by **Peter Archer**
Reprinted October 1989 as *Thunderbirds 1:
Thunderbirds* by Titan Books

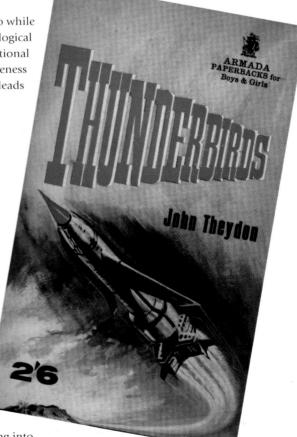

A strange meteor passes close to Thunderbird 5 and John is rendered unconscious. Shortly after, the same fate befalls Alan and Scott when they arrive in Thunderbird 3, but none of the brothers suffers any after-effects. The meteor is tracked to a 'landing' in the Gobi Desert and Thunderbird 5 intercepts a peculiar radio message from the area. Believing the meteor to have been an alien spaceship and the message a call for help from its occupants, Jeff dispatches Scott to the area in Thunderbird 1, unaware that the Hood has learned of Scott's mission from Kyrano.

Arriving in the deserted town of Obo, Scott is menaced first by a giant mountain goat, mutated by radioactive fall-out, and then by the Hood masquerading as a prospector. He eventually pinpoints the source of the alien message to a well in an ancient fort and, descending into the well, he makes contact with a microscopic alien colony contained within a glowing sphere. The alien intelligence takes control of Scott's mind, forcing him to take the sphere in Thunderbird 1 to London, where it intends to use an underground reservoir as a means to take over the Earth by possessing the bodies of everyone on the planet.

Lady Penelope and Parker trail Scott to Dartmoor, where they manage to free him from the aliens' influence, but the Hood, who has followed Scott to England, steals the sphere and soon falls under alien control. The International Rescue team race to London for a subterranean showdown with the Hood and the alien intelligence. Gordon, in Thunderbird 4, manages to retrieve the sphere from the reservoir before the colony can escape into the water.

Notes

This being the first novel in the range, character background is understandably sparse, although everyone is certainly 'in character', with dialogue that accurately reflects that of their screen counterparts. The author is clearly familiar with the television episodes and works in some nice continuity, with references to the events of *Trapped in the Sky* and *Desperate Intruder*.

CALLING THUNDERBIRDS

Written by **John Theydon (John W. Jennison)**
Published 1966 by Armada Books (paperback, 125 pages), illustrated by **Peter Archer**
Reprinted March 1990 as *Thunderbirds 2: Calling Thunderbirds* by Titan Books

Lady Penelope travels to Peru to help her cousin Gus search for hidden treasure, the lost emerald mines of the Incas. She is trailed by the Hood, who has learned of her plans after breaking into Creighton-Ward Mansion in a failed attempt to determine the secret location of International Rescue. Shortly after her arrival in Lima, Penelope is kidnapped by an unscrupulous adventurer named Morales, who is also after the Inca treasure.

Parker seeks the assistance of Scott and Virgil, already in Lima helping to rescue the survivors of a devastating earthquake. The trio learn that Gus has also been kidnapped, but after a daring rescue in the cellar beneath the ruins of Gus's hotel, they find a *quipu*, an ancient Inca cord of coloured threads that Gus had left in the hotel safe. Scott and Parker take FAB 1 to San Pedro to consult Professor Carlos de Sabata, an expert on *quipus*. The Hood attempts to obtain the *quipu* by impersonating the Professor, but his plan is foiled by Parker.

The real Professor translates the *quipu*, which points to a further clue hidden in an Inca temple in Cuzco, but Morales and his gang have already beaten them to it and found a map which reveals the location of the emerald mine beneath the temple of Illa Ticca, deep in the Peruvian jungle. Scott, Parker and the Professor follow Morales's truck to Illa Ticca, rescuing Penelope from a savage tribe of jungle Indians *en route*. At Illa Ticca, the quartet encounter both Morales and the Hood, but manage to rescue Gus and escape from the bowels of the temple as it is destroyed by an earth tremor which seals the emerald mine for ever.

Notes

Once again there are some nice continuity references, not only to the events of *Desperate Intruder* but also to the previous novel, *Thunderbirds*, as the International Rescue team finally learn the name by which the Hood prefers to be known. Lady Penelope travels to South America in her ultra-modern ocean-going cruiser Seabird IV and the previous three Seabirds are described as having been sunk in the line of duty. Unfortunately, the author doesn't appear to have seen *Move – and You're Dead*, as Thunderbird 1 is described as carrying no weapons or missiles.

THUNDERBIRDS: OPERATION ASTEROIDS

Written by **John W. Jennison**
Published 1966 by World Distributors Ltd (hardback, 202 pages)

Scott, Alan and Tin-Tin head for the Moon in Thunderbird 3 to rescue a technical supervisor and robot miners who have become trapped in a duranium mine shaft. The rescue operation requires the Mole, so Jeff arranges for Virgil and Brains to accompany the vehicle as it is ferried to the Moon on board a space freighter from the Lunar Mining Corporation base at Woolamoroo in Australia. The Hood learns of International Rescue's plans from Kyrano, but

Jeff recognizes the symptoms of the villain's power over his old friend and contacts Lady Penelope, holidaying in Australia, to watch out for the Hood at Woolamoroo. Unfortunately, the Hood captures Lady Penelope and takes her on to the freighter.

After the freighter is launched with Virgil, Brains and the Mole on board, the Hood hijacks the ship, paralysing the International Rescue trio. His plans go awry when he tries to pilot the craft back to Earth and the freighter goes out of control on a course that will take it out of the solar system. Scott, Alan and Tin-Tin set off in pursuit and track the freighter to the asteroid Ceres, where it has crash-landed. Once again, the Hood gains the upper hand, marooning Scott, Virgil and Alan on the asteroid when he makes his escape with Lady Penelope, Brains and Tin-Tin in Thunderbird 3. However, the brothers manage to repair the freighter and use it to make their way back to Earth.

Responding to an emergency call to rescue a pair of geologists trapped in their diving machine in the flooded crater of an extinct volcano, Jeff pilots Thunderbird 2 with Gordon and Parker aboard. After completing the rescue operation, they are perfectly placed to follow the errant Thunderbird 3 through the atmosphere and track it to a landing in Tibet. Leaving Parker behind to locate the Hood's hideout, Jeff returns to Tracy Island to refuel.

In the Hood's secret base hidden beneath a monastery, Lady Penelope and Brains learn of the villain's plans. He has kidnapped four of the world's top scientists and set them to work on a satellite capable of targeting nuclear devices on any city in the world. Threatening Lady Penelope and Tin-Tin, he forces Brains to complete the work, but Lady Penelope escapes and links up with Parker. In disguise, Scott and Alan penetrate the monastery and, fighting off the Hood's android guards, rescue Brains, Tin-Tin and the scientists. They make their escape in Thunderbird 3 as a nuclear device explodes in the Hood's laboratory.

Notes

Jeff refers to the events of *Calling Thunderbirds* as he realizes that the Hood is responsible for the mental attacks on Kyrano. Reluctantly, Jeff leaves Grandma and Kyrano in charge of the base as he is the only pilot available to fly Thunderbird 2 on the mission to rescue the geologists trapped in the volcano. The cover illustration by R. W. Smethurst suggests that Thunderbirds 1 and 2 accompany Thunderbird 3 to the mining base on the Moon, but this is not so.

THUNDERBIRDS: LOST WORLD

Written by **John W. Jennison**
Published 1966 by World Distributors Ltd (hardback, 205 pages)

Fireflash IV vanishes during a flight over New Guinea, in exactly the same spot that Meteor Seven disappeared the previous month. Jeff decides to send Scott to investigate in Thunderbird 1 and he flies the same route as Fireflash. Approaching an area of intense turbulence, Scott's instruments suddenly go dead and the craft is drawn down. Scott manages to ease the vehicle out of the dive and crash-lands on a sandbank in a deep valley. Exploring the jungle to find a safe landing site for Thunderbird 2, he is caught in a torrential rainstorm and Thunderbird 1 is swept away downriver. Scott finally locates his vehicle and it is safely air-lifted out of the valley by Thunderbird 2.

Jeff is contacted by his old friend Professor Peterkin, who, with his daughter, Moira, plans an expedition into the jungles of New Guinea in search of an advanced race of people hidden from the outside world for thousands of years. Penelope discovers that the Hood has taken a keen interest in Peterkin's expedition, so Jeff provides the Professor with a small distress beacon which he can activate should an emergency arise.

A week later, John picks up a signal from Peterkin's beacon and Scott immediately flies to New Guinea in Thunderbird 1. With the help of a tribe of natives, he learns that Peterkin's helicopter has been carried by an unknown force into a river tunnel at the base of a white cliff that is sacred to the natives. Inside the tunnel, Scott finds Moira Peterkin's diary, proving that he is on the right trail. Virgil, Gordon and Tin-Tin arrive in Thunderbird 2, bringing with them a hovercraft on which they plan to make their journey through the tunnel, but the Hood lies in wait. He overpowers the International Rescue team and steals the hovercraft to make his own way into the tunnel. Following him using Brains's new hoverbelt devices, Scott, Gordon, Brains and Tin-Tin discover a hidden valley on the other side of the mountain. There, they are captured by the Yassamalek, the descendants of an ancient civilization possessed of incredibly advanced anti-gravity technology.

Taken to the Yassamalek city, which is hidden inside an extinct volcano, the quartet discover that the Hood has befriended their fanatical hosts and persuaded them to use their technology to conquer the outside world. Unfortunately, the Hood's plans are ruined when volcanic activity destroys the Yassamalek's generators, enabling the International Rescue team, Peterkin's party and the passengers and crew of the two missing airliners to escape from the city as it is destroyed by lava.

Notes

Discussing the Hood, Jeff refers directly to the events of *Trapped in the Sky* and *The Mighty Atom*. The events of *Operation Asteroids* are also referred to a number of times as the Hood blames Scott for the destruction of his laboratory in Tibet.

The cover illustration is terribly misleading, suggesting not only that Thunderbird 1 flies into the hidden valley (which it doesn't), but also that the valley is populated by dinosaurs (which it isn't). The artist, R. W. Smethurst, must have assumed that the book was related in some way to Sir Arthur Conan Doyle's 1912 novel *The Lost World*, in which an expedition discovers dinosaurs on a plateau in South America.

LADY PENELOPE: COOL FOR DANGER

Written by **Kevin McGarry**
Published 1966 by World Distributors Ltd (hardback, 172 pages)

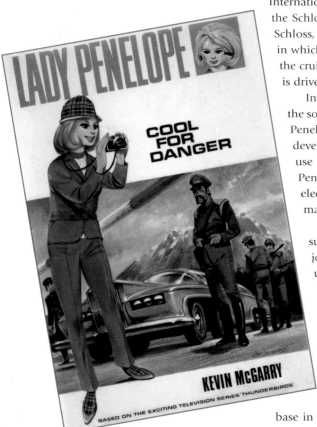

With the aid of a petty thief, Flaginne, Lady Penelope and Parker set out to rescue International Rescue agent Roger Lyon, imprisoned on a trumped-up charge in the Schloss Stillban in the Alpine country of Revonia. A former inmate of the Schloss, Flaginne is familiar with the location of the solitary confinement cell in which Lyon is being held. The trio sail to the Mediterranean in Seabird, but the cruiser is caught up in a hurricane which appears to pursue them. Seabird is driven on to the Needles, so the group make their way ashore in FAB 1.

Investigating the unusual weather conditions in the area, they pinpoint the source as an old shooting lodge in the Maritime Alps. There, they discover Penelope's arch-enemy Mr Steelman and his robot servants. Steelman has developed a device which can create storms on command, enabling him to use weather as a weapon and dominate the world. He captures Lady Penelope and Parker and imprisons them in the lodge, setting the electronic furnace which powers the weather machine to run wild. The pair manage to escape before the lodge explodes.

While Lady Penelope, Parker and Flaginne enter Revonia and successfully engineer Lyon's escape from the Schloss Stillban, Steelman joins up with the Revonian revolutionary General Lazlo, who plans to use Steelman's storm machine to 'liberate' the country. Resting up in the Hotel St Goar, Lyon remembers that, prior to his imprisonment, he had discovered Steelman's hideout in the Emodisk valley, but Steelman captured him and used one of his robots to erase Lyon's memory. During their stay in the hotel, two unsuccessful attempts are made on Lyon's life by Lazlo's agents, but Lazlo's daughter, Tania, poses as a chambermaid and steals a bottle of Lady Penelope's exclusive perfume.

Lyon leads Lady Penelope, Parker and Flaginne to Steelman's base in the mountains, where they discover Lazlo's rebel troops preparing to make their assault on the Revonian capital, Sangreb. Steelman programmes his robots to home in on Lady Penelope's perfume and the group are pursued down the mountain, but Lady Penelope lays a false trail for the robots with the help of a mountain goat. She makes contact with an Army patrol and reveals the rebels' location. The Army rounds up Lazlo and his troops, but Steelman escapes to Sangreb, where he breaks into the vaults of Monte Paradiso and steals the greatest treasures of Revonia. Lady Penelope and Parker finally trail Steelman to Wadi Zem Zem, an air base in the desert known to Parker from his time as a radio operator in the Air Force. There, they recover the stolen treasures, but Steelman once again evades capture.

Notes

Mr Steelman, Roger Lyon and Seabird all made their debuts in Lady Penelope's first comic strip in *TV Century 21*. Seabird 1 was destroyed by Steelman in that story, so the vessel used by Penelope here should really have a different numeral. There are also references to the events of Mr Steelman's second comic strip appearance in later issues of *TV Century 21*.

LADY PENELOPE: A GALLERY OF THIEVES

Written by **Kevin McGarry**

Published 1966 by World Distributors Ltd (hardback, 161 pages)

No sooner has Lady Penelope discovered that one of her paintings has been stolen and replaced with a clever fake than she has been kidnapped by Parker, who has fallen under the influence of Mr Steelman's hypnotic robot. Steelman fakes Lady Penelope's death in a hoverjet crash and imprisons her in the Castello Malatesta, the family home of the Contessa Malatesta in Pontiora, Italy. There, the Contessa's silk-making industry covers Steelman's plans to ransom priceless works of art that he has stolen from galleries around the world and replaced with perfect forgeries. Lady Penelope learns that the forgeries are being created by a team of highly skilled artists whom Steelman has also kidnapped, working to specifications provided by a special computer of his own design. To ensure the co-operation of the Contessa's loyal servants, Steelman has imprisoned the Contessa and assumed her identity.

Breaking Steelman's hold over Parker, Lady Penelope escapes from her cell with Pierce, one of the artists, and the trio rescue the Contessa. Evading Steelman and his robot guards, they escape from the Castello and contact the authorities, but by the time the police return to the Contessa's home, Steelman and the paintings have gone.

Back home in England, Lady Penelope recruits the assistance of art expert Fritz Creoni, who allows himself to become a target for Steelman in his bid to steal a priceless Cézanne from the National Gallery in London. But Steelman is one step ahead of Lady Penelope and uses Creoni to decoy her while he steals the painting. However, Lady Penelope has secreted a homing device on the back of the picture and she, Creoni and Roger Lyon track it to a big old house outside Camusfecken in the Highlands of Scotland, which Steelman has made his new headquarters. Unfortunately, they fall into Steelman's hands once again, but are rescued by Parker, who uses the house's reputation for being haunted to frighten the villain and his guards.

Steelman escapes and the police recover the stolen paintings, but Steelman's former associate Estelle de Sale makes off with the Cézanne and attempts to ransom the picture at the Monaco Arts Ball. Her plan is foiled when she is tracked down and killed by Steelman, but she reveals the hidden location of the painting to Roger Lyon before her death.

Notes

The Kevin McGarry novels are the weakest of the range and this, unfortunately, is the poorer of the two. The author's only reference seems to have been the 'Lady Penelope' strip in *TV Century 21*, as this book displays no real understanding of the International Rescue set-up: Lady Penelope goes swanning around telling everyone she meets that she is the London agent for International Rescue, abandoning all pretence of secrecy.

THUNDERBIRDS: RING OF FIRE

Written by **John Theydon** (John W. Jennison)
Published 1966 by Armada Books (paperback, 125 pages),
illustrator unknown

The Yelcho atomic power station, the only one in South America fitted with a Cobaltium 5 reactor, is threatened by the eruption of Mount Yelcho. The station is evacuated, but Professor Jorge Silva is trapped in an elevator as he attempts to shut down the reactor before the lava engulfs it. Scott flies out to the station in Thunderbird 1 and rescues Silva, but then becomes trapped himself as he attempts to access the reactor vault. Virgil rescues Scott in the Mole, but they have run out of time to shut down the reactor. The lava hits and detonates the reactor, causing a massive Cobaltium explosion. The resulting radiation cloud is carried by a stratospherical gale across Patagonia and disperses harmlessly over the Antarctic Circle, but the explosion splits the Earth's crust along the line of a rift in the Yelcho valley. The crust continues splitting past the continental shelf into the South Pacific.

While Scott and Virgil fly to Palena to assist with the evacuation, Jeff learns that the World Navy intends to commandeer Tracy Island for tests of their new Cobaltium 5 surface-to-surface missiles. His protests to Admiral Obergaus fall on deaf ears. Jeff is given twenty-four hours to evacuate the island and starts making preparations to transfer all of the International Rescue equipment to the organization's auxiliary repair shops and storerooms on Mateo Island.

Then trouble hits Thunderbird 1. A boulder ejected from a volcano damages the tail section and Scott is unable to land without a RONTGEN unit, which can be acquired only from a component factory in Cairo. Penelope and Parker oblige by breaking into the factory, and Kyrano flies Brains out to Tunisia in Jeff's private jet to rendezvous with FAB 1. As the jet crosses the Sahara, the Hood contacts Kyrano to learn of International Rescue's plans. Kyrano passes out, leaving Brains to fight with the controls and the plane crash-lands in the desert. Racing against time, Lady Penelope and Parker rush to locate the downed jet, hindered by the Hood, who attempts to steal the RONTGEN unit. His plans are foiled and Parker shoots down his plane as he makes his escape.

In a tricky operation, Brains is winched aboard Thunderbird 1 from Thunderbird 2 and replaces the RONTGEN unit. Returning to Tracy Island, Brains realizes that the rift eruption is getting worse and the undersea disturbance is set to cause massive tidal waves all over the world. To make matters even worse, he calculates that the potential line of fracture passes directly beneath Tracy Island, and if the island is destroyed by the World Navy's Cobaltium 5 missiles the rift will accelerate on across the Pacific to New Zealand and Australia, causing disaster on a colossal scale.

Admiral Obergaus refuses to recognize the danger and only the World President, Nikita Bandranaik, can countermand Obergaus's orders, but Jeff obtains his top-secret location from the sympathetic Commander Craddock, leader of the Navy task force. Bandranaik is an old friend of Lady Penelope, so she makes contact with him and explains the position. He returns immediately to the world capital, Unity City, cancels the naval operation and authorizes International Rescue to use the Cobaltium 5 missiles in Brains's desperate plan to divert the rift eruption. The plan is a complete success: the rift eruption hits a vast submarine cavern and the lava flows into it, ultimately dissipating beneath the Antarctic icecap.

Notes

Without question the best of the eight novels, *Ring of Fire* fully utilizes every main character in a clever and tightly written plot filled with incident and packed with tense action sequences. Any film producers looking for inspiration for their live-action THUNDERBIRDS movie need look no further.

Lady Penelope and Parker drive past the fabulous new Egyptian city of Oasis, which they previously visited in her first comic strip in *Lady Penelope*. She travels to a meeting with the World President in FAB 2 (from *The Man from MI.5*), while the rescue operation in Palena uses the Mole and the Firefly, as well as the Domo (from *The Duchess Assignment*) and the Excadigger (previously seen in the *TV Century 21* THUNDERBIRDS strip 'The Atlantic Tunnel').

LADY PENELOPE: THE ALBANIAN AFFAIR

Written by **John Theydon (John W. Jennison)**
Published 1967 by Armada Books and Century 21 Publishing Ltd (paperback, 128 pages), illustrated by **Chris Higham**

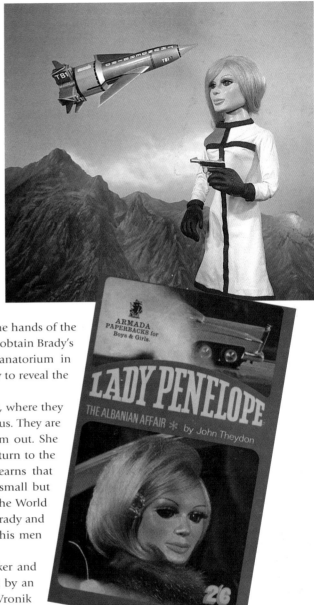

During a rescue operation at the Turkey end of the Black Sea–Iran monorail tunnel, Thunderbirds 1, 2 and 4 are photographed by Ace Brady, an unscrupulous freelance reporter. Despite Scott's attempts to stop him, Brady escapes with the photos, but his helijet later crashes in the Balkans. He hides the photos, still in his camera, in the mountains before falling into the hands of the Gryphus, a secret international crime organization determined to obtain Brady's photos. Gryphus leader Zurov takes Brady to the St Denis Sanatorium in Geneva, where Zurov's colleague Dr Vronik intends to force Brady to reveal the location of the pictures, but Brady falls into a coma.

Lady Penelope and Parker break into Brady's office in Geneva, where they discover a secret file that the reporter has compiled on the Gryphus. They are disturbed by Zurov's henchmen, but Lady Penelope knocks them out. She and Parker then follow them in FAB 1 when they recover and return to the sanatorium. Lady Penelope breaks into the sanatorium and learns that Zurov intends to sell the Thunderbirds pictures to Bereznik, a small but powerful Balkan state that refuses to recognize the authority of the World Government, which it is determined to undermine. She rescues Brady and escapes from the sanatorium in an ambulance, with Zurov and his men hard on her heels.

After a long chase around Lake Geneva, Lady Penelope, Parker and the unconscious Brady find refuge at a villa in Montreux owned by an old friend of Penelope. The Gryphus learns of their location and Vronik masquerades as a local doctor to gain access to Brady. He is discovered and knocked out by Lady Penelope, but Brady recovers, takes Vronik's clothes and money, and makes his escape. Fortunately, Lady Penelope has secreted a strip of sensitized metal inside the bandage on his head. This enables her and Parker to track Brady as he makes his way back to Albania, after an interlude in Venice where they elude more Gryphus agents. Trailing Brady to the site of his crashed helijet, Lady Penelope recovers the photos, which are then destroyed in a final showdown with Zurov and Vronik.

Notes

A marked improvement on Kevin McGarry's Lady Penelope novels. While Lady Penelope and Parker are clearly the focus of the story, their close involvement with International Rescue is never forgotten: Jeff, Scott, Virgil, Gordon, Alan, Grandma and Tin-Tin all make appearances, and the Mole and Firefly are both used in the Aziban rescue mission. The whole story revolves around the need to protect the organization's secrecy and Lady Penelope is very careful not to reveal that she is acting for International Rescue (compare *A Gallery of Thieves*).

Although the cruiser in which Penelope travels to Nice is not named, it is clearly intended to be Seabird (the boat is berthed at Smugglers' Cove and has a bomb-proof garage and an auto-pilot named George). Roger Lyon also makes a couple of brief appearances. Bereznik is another recurring 'villain' from the *Lady Penelope* comic strips: the state's agents made their first appearance in Penelope's second strip story in *TV Century 21* (issue 12).

BEYOND THUNDERBIRDS 5

REWRITING THE FUTURE

While the original television series has continued to delight new generations of viewers, over the last thirty years a number of attempts have been made to re-create the winning THUNDERBIRDS formula, with varying degrees of success.

The first of these was a puppet stage show developed and performed by former Century 21 puppeteers Christine Glanville and Rowena White, who, with their business partner David Ross, had formed a company called Stage Three. With the permission of Century 21 Merchandising, the trio pooled their talents to create a *Thunderbirds* show as an alternative to the successful *Rupert Bear and His Puppet Pals* show that they had been performing at the Pier Theatre in Bournemouth. Christine Glanville created the stage puppets, Rowena White made the costumes and wrote the scripts for three fifteen-minute episodes, while David Ross supervised the stage design, the construction of sixteen different sets and the voice recording. Sylvia Anderson's actress daughter Dee provided the voice for Lady Penelope, Kerry Jewel, son of comedian Jimmy Jewel, voiced Parker and Brains, and actors Malcolm Storry and David Schofield portrayed Jeff Tracy, Virgil, Alan and the Hood.

After eight months of planning, building and rehearsal, the *Thunderbirds* show opened at the Chancellor Hall, Chelmsford, on 15 April 1974, before moving to the Woodville Halls in Gravesend, where it was a great success. On 17 June 1974, the show opened in Bournemouth for a summer season at the Pier Theatre, but, inexplicably, audience figures were poor and the Bournemouth engagement was cancelled after only a four-week run. Performances at other venues in Bedworth, Nantwich and Gloucester

Stage versions of the THUNDERBIRDS characters for the Stage Three show.

were much more popular and enthusiastically received, but the word spread in theatrical circles that the show had flopped in Bournemouth and there were no further bookings. The curtain closed on Stage Three's *Thunderbirds* show at the Gloucester Leisure Centre in April 1975.

In 1976, during production of the second season of SPACE: 1999, Gerry Anderson attempted to revive the THUNDERBIRDS concept as a live-action series. In collaboration with SPACE: 1999 producer Fred Freiberger, he conceived RESCUE 4 (also known as INTER-GALACTIC RESCUE 4), which followed the exploits of the crew of a multi-purpose space rescue vehicle, patrolling the northwest quadrant of space. Equipped for many different operations, the rescue vehicle was extremely versatile. Launched from a vertical position, it had the ability to fly horizontally in a planet's atmosphere or in the vacuum of deep space, while watertight bulkheads enabled the craft to sail, submerge or hover-skim across water.

Reg Hill developed story ideas and storyboards for RESCUE 4 with visual effects designer Brian Johnson, while model-maker Martin Bower designed the Rescue 4 vehicle itself and built a 6-inch model which formed part of the development package for potential financiers. The concept was presented to America's NBC network as a series of thirteen half-hour episodes for their 1976–7 season, but the option was not picked up.

In 1980, the legacy of THUNDERBIRDS made a very significant impact on the world with the formation of a real-life International Rescue organization. In November that year, southern Italy was hit by an earthquake that measured 7.2 on the Richter scale and killed 4,500 people. Some 500 British firemen approached the Italian authorities with an offer to fly out and help in rescue operations, but their offer was refused on the grounds that they were unable to finance their own rescue equipment, food, shelter and transport.

Brian Catton, a fire officer from Buckinghamshire, realized that the volunteer firemen had to organize themselves into a self-sufficient operation that could be funded as a recognized charity, backed by the Red Cross. Inspired by THUNDERBIRDS, Catton's group was named International Rescue Corps. They soon became involved in rescue operations at earthquake disaster sites in North Yemen, Mexico City and Colombia, and are still in operation today, providing invaluable assistance to locate survivors trapped in the rubble of towns and cities that have been levelled by earthquakes.

The first (and least offensive) of three attempts to repackage THUNDERBIRDS for American viewers came in 1981. Working closely with *Starlog* magazine correspondent (and keen Anderson fan) David Hirsch, Robert Mandell, the Vice-President of Creative Services at ITC's New York office, supervised the production of a series of feature-length Gerry Anderson presentations, created by splicing together similarly themed TV episodes. Packaged under the banner 'Super Space Theatre', these TV movies were then sold to pay-cable and syndicated stations as ideal family programming.

Three THUNDERBIRDS features were made: THUNDERBIRDS TO THE RESCUE (which paired *Trapped in the Sky* with *Operation Crash-Dive*), THUNDERBIRDS IN OUTER SPACE (*Sun Probe* and *Ricochet*) and COUNTDOWN TO DISASTER (*Terror in New York City* and *Atlantic Inferno*). All three abandoned the existing opening title sequence in favour of a new video-animated title sequence and cut some two minutes from each of the episodes to bring the total combined running time to ninety-five minutes (the maximum length for a two-hour commercial slot on American television), but were otherwise faithful to the original programmes.

Although they are generally reviled by the series' fans, these three films nonetheless had a beneficial effect in two respects. First, they gave American viewers the opportunity to see at least some episodes of a television series that had not been shown there since the late 1960s. Second, their UK home video release by Channel 5 Video was so successful in the mid-1980s that the company was encouraged to issue the remaining twenty-six episodes in their original uncut format.

In 1983, a Japanese animated series originally broadcast as KAGAKU KYUUJO-TAI TECHNOVOYAGER (SCIENCE RESCUE TEAM TECHNOVOYAGER) was revoiced for English-language countries as THUNDERBIRDS 2086. Produced by Robert Mandell with dialogue supervision by Peter Fernandez, this re-working of

THUNDERBIRDS
2086
INTERNATIONAL
RESCUE VEHICLES

TB-1	ADVANCED SPACE SHUTTLE
TB-2	HYPERSONIC TRANSPORT
TB-3	RECONNAISSANCE GROUND VEHICLE
TB-4	SUBMARINE
TB-5	SPECIAL GROUND OPERATIONS VEHICLE
TB-6	SPACE STATION
TB-7	MINI-AIRCRAFT
TB-8	COMPUTER-CONTROLLED AIR TRANSPORT
TB-9	ONE-MAN SPACE WALKER
TB-10	ULTRA-HIGH-SPEED MINI-ROCKETSHIP
TB-11	HIGH-SPEED GROUND VEHICLE
TB-12	MULTI-FUNCTION FLATBED
TB-13	FLYING MINI-SUB
TB-14	DEEP SEA BATHYSCAPHE
TB-15	MOBILE COMPUTER
TB-16	THE MOLE
TB-17	LONG-RANGE SPACE PROBE

The Arcology, Pacific island base of International Rescue in THUNDERBIRDS 2086.

Thunderbird 1 (top), an advanced space shuttle, and Thunderbird 4 (above), the submarine, both used by International Rescue in THUNDERBIRDS 2086.

the THUNDERBIRDS format (made without the knowledge or involvement of Gerry Anderson or any members of the Century 21 team) took the basic idea of the International Rescue organization and its rescue vehicles, but repopulated it with unrelated characters and an entirely different set of Thunderbird machines.

Operating from the Arcology, a vast city complex housed on 4 square miles of buildings and grounds located on a remote island in the Pacific, this new International Rescue was authorized by the World Federation Supreme Council and commanded by Dr Warren Simpson, a fifty-five-year-old former NASA astronaut. Simpson was the chief engineer and designer of the organisation's Thunderbirds vehicles who had hand-picked the other members of the International Rescue team.

Captain Dylan Beyda, the twenty-eight-year-old son of space explorer Harrison Beyda, was the pilot of Thunderbird 1, an advanced space shuttle and flight command centre for International Rescue.

Captain Jesse Rigel, a twenty-nine-year-old lunar-born space cowboy trained at NASA, piloted Thunderbird 2, a hypersonic transport vehicle capable of ferrying pods containing disaster equipment and additional machinery both on Earth and into deep space.

Rigel's Thunderbird 2 co-pilot was thirty-year-old Johnathan Jordan Jr, also known as Little John or JJ, a graduate of NYU and former Olympic gymnast.

Captain Greg Hanson, a forty-five-year-old former miner for the Rama Space Seed project, piloted Thunderbird 3, a reconnaissance ground vehicle and mobile multi-functional laboratory.

Captain Kallan James, the only female member of the team, was an oceanographer and former Olympic gold-medal swimmer who piloted Thunderbird 4, a submarine capable of descending to depths that could be reached by no other vehicle.

The final member of the team was seven-year-old Paul 'Skipper' Simpson, Commander Simpson's nephew, who hoped to become a space explorer after completing his studies at the Arcology's Elementary Grade School.

The International Rescue of THUNDERBIRDS 2086 operated a fleet of seventeen Thunderbirds craft. The other main vehicles were Thunderbird 5, a special ground operations vehicle used for fire-fighting and disposal of highly toxic or explosive substances, and Thunderbird 6, a space station Emergency Alert Communications Centre in Earth orbit that monitored signals from anywhere on Earth or in space. The other craft were various specialist units – the equivalent of the original series' pod vehicles.

The music of THUNDERBIRDS 2086 was credited to Kentaro Haneda and Koji Makaino, although a number of incidental tracks composed by Barry Gray for the original Supermarionation series also cropped up during the proceedings. Character voices were provided by John Bellucci, Maia Danziger, Earl Hammond, Keith Mandell, Alexander Marshall and Lucy Martin. Distributed internationally by ITC Entertainment, twenty-four half-hour episodes premiered on the Prism cable network in the United States in 1983. They were eventually broadcast in the UK in 1986.

In 1984, mime artists Andrew Dawson and Gavin Robertson, the founders of the Mime Theatre Project, devised a stage show entitled *Thunderbirds: F.A.B.* Neither was a particular fan of THUNDERBIRDS, but both had fond memories of the series from their childhood and saw its continuing popularity as an ideal way to introduce new audiences to mime. Originally planning to incorporate elements from THUNDERBIRDS into a larger show, they soon realized that there was such a wealth of material to draw on that they decided to base the whole performance around this and some of the other Gerry Anderson series. Funded by the Arts Council with the full support of Anderson himself, Dawson and Robertson created an affectionate and hilarious parody of THUNDERBIRDS and CAPTAIN SCARLET in which the two performers played all of the roles themselves (including the Thunderbirds vehicles) with numerous costume changes. The show successfully toured the UK in 1985 and then went on to tour Hong Kong, Singapore, the USA and Australia. The crowing glory came in 1989 when *Thunderbirds: F.A.B.* opened in the West End and set a new box-office record for the Apollo Theatre in Shaftesbury Avenue.

A new, more elaborate version of the show, *Thunderbirds: F.A.B. – The Next Generation*, opened in 1991, with Paul Kent and Wayne Forester replacing Dawson and Robertson.

This incarnation added characters from STINGRAY to the plot, as well as additional, previously unseen characters from THUNDERBIRDS and CAPTAIN SCARLET, and went on to even greater success both in the West End and on international tour. Tristan Sharps joined Paul Kent on stage for a further revival of the show in 1995, which then went on a tenth anniversary UK tour with Richard James in place of Sharps.

As anyone who saw *Thunderbirds: F.A.B.* will attest, the show was fully deserving of its critical and commercial acclaim, but it did have a rather unfortunate side-effect. What began as an affectionate parody ended up causing ridicule to its source, as media attention focused increasingly on a stylized 'puppet' walk developed by Dawson and Robertson. As the actors themselves admitted, this walk more closely resembled the movements of the simple string puppets seen in BILL AND BEN, THE WOODENTOPS and ANDY PANDY than those in the Supermarionation productions, where the puppets' legs were only rarely seen moving at all. The media, however, were unwilling or unable to recognize the difference. Suddenly, at the mere mention of THUNDERBIRDS, television presenters were encouraging members of the public and film industry professionals to embarrass themselves on national television by 'doing the Thunderbirds walk', as if an interest in the series (whether professional or personal) instantly bestowed upon them body skills that had taken the Mime Theatre performers years to perfect. This and other aspects of the *Thunderbirds: F.A.B.* show helped to create a bizarre urban myth that the puppetry of THUNDERBIRDS was extremely crude, with visible

Above: Wayne Forester as Thunderbird 2.
Below: Paul Kent (left) and Wayne Forester (right)
in **Thunderbirds F.A.B. – The Next Generation.**

Paul Kent (left) and Wayne Forester (right) in **Thunderbirds F.A.B. – The Next Generation.**

strings, mouth movements that didn't match the voices and silly, unnatural ambulation.

At the time of the initial performances of *Thunderbirds: F.A.B.*, Gerry Anderson was involved in his own revival of THUNDERBIRDS as a new television series. Having just completed production on the Supermacromation series TERRAHAWKS, he began planning T-FORCE, an updated version of his best-known creation, working with TERRAHAWKS' visual effects supervisor Steven Begg to create a variety of new Thunderbird vehicles.

Although he now recognizes that a new version of THUNDERBIRDS would be acceptable to viewers only if it retained the format and design of the original series, in the mid-1980s Anderson was keen to make adjustments in areas that he felt audiences would find unbelievable. To this end, International Rescue's base of operations was to become a huge submarine which would be shielded from detection, Thunderbird 2 would be a much larger rescue vehicle, housing a hangar bay of interchangeable component parts from which Brains would be able to create vehicles that were custom-designed for each emergency situation, and Lady Penelope would have abandoned the Rolls-Royce for a pink Porsche. Among some of the wackier ideas suggested were that Lady Penelope would have gold-plated hair that could pick up radio waves and would take pills that turned her eyes purple so that she could see in the dark. Suitable finance was not forthcoming and the project collapsed.

In November 1987, voice artists Shane Rimmer, Matt Zimmerman and David Graham re-created their THUNDERBIRDS roles to help promote the BBC's Children in Need appeal. The characters appeared in a humorous serial story broadcast in short segments on Radio 2 in the four days leading up to that year's BBC Television and Radio appeal programme on 27 November. Produced by Dirk Maggs, the programmes followed Scott and Alan as they raced to rescue Parker, trapped in the vault of the BBC Record Library while attempting to make a secret donation to Children in Need on Lady Penelope's behalf.

Although T-FORCE had failed to materialize, a genuine all-new THUNDERBIRDS episode was produced by Gerry Anderson in 1990. *Parker's Day Off* was a commercial for Swinton Insurance featuring Lady Penelope and Parker. Designed to look as though it had been shot in the 1960s, the short film followed Penelope as she caused havoc on the roads in FAB 1 until the car was plucked to safety by Parker piloting Thunderbird 2. Directed by Gerry Anderson, with Christine Glanville operating the puppets, visual effects by Steven Begg and production design by Bob Bell, the commercial featured Anderson's own original studio puppet of Parker and stunningly accurate replica models of FAB 1 and Thunderbird 2, built by (respectively) David Sisson and Richard Gregory.

The following year, Anderson was invited by director Steve Barron to contribute a

THUNDERBIRDS section for Dire Straits' 'Calling Elvis' video. For this, Bob Bell reconstructed the Tracy lounge set and Christine Glanville created new puppets of Jeff Tracy and Brains, as well as Supermarionation-style puppets of the five Dire Straits band members. Directed by Gerry Anderson and produced by his wife, Mary, the new puppet footage was then edited with clips from the television series and live-action footage of the band performing the song. The video was broadcast on a number of music programmes throughout the summer of 1991 and later commercially released as part of a *Best of Dire Straits* compilation videotape.

In 1993, Gerry Anderson took another look at some of the concepts of T-FORCE and redeveloped them as a cel-animated THUNDERBIRDS-style television series. Originally titled G-FORCE, GFI was planned as a series of thirteen episodes that would combine conventional animation (for the characters) created in Moscow with computer-assisted animation (for the vehicles) completed in London.

GFI (Gee Force Intergalactic) followed the adventures of a rapid-response task force created by the Ruling Council of the United Planets to combat major crime and deal with large-scale disasters within their solar system. Based at Star City, a secret HQ hidden within an asteroid orbiting the Myson planetary system, G-Force was commanded by Professor James Gee, a highly respected scientist from Earth. Gee recruited two of his brightest students, a white male and a black female, who became known as Wungee and Tugee respectively, and the team was completed by a pair of aliens, electronics specialist Argent and engineering expert D'Or. The Professor's small dog, Megabyte, was also along for the ride.

The main vehicle used by G-Force was a 250,000-ton spacecraft known as Galaxy which housed a completely automated factory manned by robots and capable of building any form of vehicle or equipment needed to help in a mission. The craft also contained a gene laboratory and the Gene Machine, which was able to create or modify life forms by advanced genetic engineering. The team were supported by a group of robots named after American presidents and other Western leaders (Franklin, Abraham, Dickie, Maggie and so on), each capable of exhibiting human characteristics. These robots were all controlled by a massive central computer, George Washington, based within Galaxy in a room known as Washington Square.

When embarking upon a mission, the team would launch Star Probe, a small unmanned vehicle with faster-than-light capability, to the danger zone. Star Probe would create virtual-reality images from the information it gathered and this was then used by the G-Force team to rehearse the more dangerous parts of a mission before arriving at the scene. The team also used Star Streak, a high-speed single-seater reconnaissance space vehicle piloted by Wungee.

G-Force dealt with both natural disasters and those created by outside agencies, such as the evil Diados, an insect-like Mafia with their own spaceship, the Decimator. Angered by the formation of G-Force, the Diados drafted their hitman Head Case, an android with the ability to assume any identity, to destroy James Gee and his team.

The stories for all thirteen episodes were drafted and over half of them were worked up into full scripts by Tony Barwick, but only one complete episode, *Warming Warning*, was produced before the series was cancelled. The problem was that the Russian animation turned out to be remarkably poor and looked even worse in comparison with the high-tech computer animation produced in London. The cost of re-doing the Russian footage elsewhere made the completion of the series financially prohibitive, so the project was abandoned.

In 1994, ITC Entertainment's Los Angeles head office announced that a live-action THUNDERBIRDS movie, budgeted at $40 million, was in development and would be completed for a Christmas 1995 release. *Die Hard 2* and *Cliffhanger* director Renny Harlin was linked to the project, with Bob Hoskins being suggested to play Parker. Tom Cruise was reportedly interested in playing Scott Tracy and various actresses were under consideration to play Lady Penelope, including Emma Thompson, Patsy Kensit and Joanna Lumley.

So as to acquaint 1990s American children with the franchise in advance of the film's release, ITC Entertainment reformatted thirteen of the television episodes, cutting each down to a running time of twenty-three minutes (a standard US television half-hour) for broadcast on the Fox Broadcasting System's Fox Kids' Network as THUNDERBIRDS USA. The dialogue was rewritten and the entire original soundtrack was dropped in favour of new music (by Randall Chrissman), new sound effects and new voices (performed by Dena Mauer, G. King, Scott Brotherton and Mike Gibbons) in an ill-advised attempt to make the new version of the series more comparable to the then-popular children's series MIGHTY MORPHIN POWER RANGERS. The result was a sorry bastardization of a classic television show.

Tripp (Travis Webster) and Roxette (Johna Stewart) aboard Thunderbird 5 on 'Yo alert' in TURBOCHARGED THUNDERBIRDS.

ITC's feature film project ultimately collapsed and, in 1995, ITC was sold to the Dutch media conglomerate PolyGram for $156 million. Keen to exploit the potential of their new acquisition, PolyGram followed ITC's lead and also set about reformatting THUNDERBIRDS for 1990s American children. The result was the abominable TURBOCHARGED THUNDERBIRDS, a co-production with Bohbot for US syndication which combined new live-action footage with material from the original series, re-edited and, again, re-voiced with new dialogue, music, graphics and sound effects.

The concept of the re-designed show was that the action took place in the year 2096 on a planet called Thunderworld, populated by simulated life forms (the THUNDERBIRDS puppets). In the series, the planet was discovered by a pair of teenagers, Tripp and Roxette, who slipped into an alternative universe on their way home from school one day. They made contact with Thunderworld's International Rescue, who invited the teenagers to use their sophisticated interplanetary surveillance system to become the eyes and ears for the organization. The pair forged a mutual pact with the Tracy family to take on an unseen enemy, the evil Atrocimator, who revelled in wreaking intergalactic havoc and frequently threatened International Rescue directly using his 'hench-honcho' the Hood.

Roxette was played by Johna Stewart, a professional singer/writer who had previously guest-starred in episodes of BOY MEETS WORLD, THE NANNY, GROWING PAINS, CAGNEY AND LACEY, DALLAS and KATE AND ALLIE. Tripp was played by the largely unknown Travis Wester, whose career to that point had been mainly in television commercials. *The Rocky Horror Show*'s Tim Curry provided the voice of the Atrocimator.

The creative forces behind TURBOCHARGED THUNDERBIRDS were Robert A. Tercek and Sally DeSipio, described in the series' promotional brochure as 'two highly prominent production executives whose cutting edge work as a creative team has generated much acclaim' and 'recognized throughout the industry as visionaries in setting new production standards', none of which was readily apparent from their work here. Recognizing that a cool catchphrase such as 'Cowabunga, Dude!' or 'Don't have a cow, man!' was a vital ingredient for a truly successful children's series, Tercek and DeSipio filled TURBOCHARGED THUNDERBIRDS with hip dialogue that was guaranteed to catch on in playgrounds all over the United States, including 'Dock it, lock it and rock it', 'You're kickin' asteroids', 'Jock with her jive jargon', 'Booyah!' and 'Yo alert!' The latter even had its own arm actions to join in with.

Thirteen episodes were given the TURBOCHARGED treatment and the original episode titles were replaced with limp new ones: for example, *The Uninvited* became *The Lost Pyramid* and *Atlantic Inferno* became *Home Alone*. Gerry Anderson quite rightly insisted on the removal of his name from the title sequence.

Turbocharged Thunderbirds debuted on American syndicated television on 18 December 1994. It was not renewed for a second season and has never been broadcast in the UK.

The announcement of PolyGram's acquisition of the ITC catalogue came with further promises of a Thunderbirds feature film developed by Working Title Films, a subsidiary of PolyGram Filmed Entertainment. A variety of different approaches by which to accomplish this (including stop-motion animation and computer-generated digital animation) were proposed amidst media speculation that the project would be filmed live action, with the actor brothers Alec, William, Daniel and Stephen Baldwin as the Tracy brothers, Sean Connery as Jeff Tracy and Joanna Lumley as Lady Penelope.

At the Cannes Film Festival in 1997, Working Title announced that Peter Hewitt, director of *Bill and Ted's Bogus Journey* and *The Borrowers*, was assigned to the project, which had been awarded a budget of $60 million. *The English Patient* star Kristin Scott-Thomas (previously seen as a cool secret agent in Tom Cruise's *Mission: Impossible* feature film) was announced to play Lady Penelope and Pete Postlethwaite (seen in *Brassed Off, Amistad* and *The Lost World: Jurassic Park*) revealed that he had been offered the role of Parker. A script by Karey Kilpatrick (*James and the Giant Peach*) was circulated around various London-based digital and visual effects houses, who were invited to tender for work on the film, and those who read it reported that it was very true to the spirit and format of the original series and should make the exciting, action-packed spectacular that everyone expected.

This all sounded very promising, but then rumours began to surface in the press of interference by American film executives, who felt that certain elements of the original series' premise would be unacceptable to a contemporary audience. One executive reportedly asked if a couple of the Tracy brothers could be black, while others apparently suggested cutting down on the number of brothers as, they argued, audiences would otherwise perceive Tracy Island as a gay commune.

Whether or not there was any truth to these stories, it was more than apparent that the project had run into difficulties in execution. Over the summer of 1998, the massive success of Michael Bay's *Armageddon* (which had the essence of a potential Thunderbirds feature film written all over it in its story of a mission into space to save the Earth from collision with a huge meteor) was overshadowed by the devastating failure of two other big-budget feature film adaptations of 1960s television series, *Lost in Space* and *The Avengers*. Thunderbirds' planned principal photography start date of August 1998 came and went, and pre-production work was suspended while the script was rewritten in an attempt to rein in the budget. Despite these drawbacks, as the twentieth century drew to a close, PolyGram and Working Title remained determined that a live-action Thunderbirds feature film would eventually be made, bringing to fruition more than five years of development work in a faithful adaptation of a much-loved and immensely popular television property.

Whatever the outcome of any future revival of Thunderbirds as either a feature film or a television series, British audiences are likely to have a much harder time accepting any variations from the well-established Thunderbirds format than, say, American audiences. This is because Thunderbirds has become ingrained in the consciousness of the British people. Whereas the majority of the American public may never have seen the show, or perhaps barely remember something of it from long ago, for the British public Thunderbirds has never really been away.

Roxette (Johna Stewart) and Tripp (Travis Webster) prepare to 'Dock it, lock it and rock it' in Turbocharged Thunderbirds.

LIGHTNING IN A BOTTLE

Long after the first screening of the last new episode on Christmas Day 1966, THUNDERBIRDS continued to attract viewers in the UK with repeat runs of all thirty-two episodes well into the early 1970s. These repeats were, however, sporadic and unevenly distributed across the different regions on the ITV network.

The best-served area for all of the Gerry Anderson series was the one covered by ATV Midlands, weekday franchise holder for the Birmingham transmitter, which also took over the weekend franchise from ABC in 1968. ATV Midlands transmitted THUNDERBIRDS almost continually from September 1966 to March 1973 – a total of six complete runs of the series. The other ITC Anderson series were treated just as favourably with even the earliest, SUPERCAR and FIREBALL XL5, receiving repeat screenings as late as 1973.

Viewers in the Yorkshire Television area were not so lucky. Up to 1968, the area was served by Granada, who faithfully repeated the first series in the latter half of 1966 before screening the second series for the first time in January 1967. But when the newly formed Yorkshire Television was awarded the franchise for the Yorkshire area in 1968, they refused to buy any of the Gerry Anderson series until the advent of UFO in 1971, denying Yorkshire viewers not only new Supermarionation series such as JOE 90 and THE SECRET SERVICE but also repeats of old favourites such as STINGRAY, THUNDERBIRDS and CAPTAIN SCARLET that could be seen by viewers in many of the other regions. The first Yorkshire Television broadcast of THUNDERBIRDS did not, in fact, take place until April 1976, when it was billed in the Yorkshire editions of *TV Times* as a 'new series'. The programme was, by then, more than ten years old.

THUNDERBIRDS was screened by the ITV regions for the last time in 1981 and was then absent from British television for a decade, but the series returned in triumph in 1991 when it received its first UK network (all parts of the country receiving the same episode simultaneously) broadcast on BBC2. Relaunched on the BBC's 'minority interest' channel at 6.00 p.m. on Friday 20 September, the opening episode (*Trapped in the Sky*) attracted an audience of nearly 7 million, a figure which reportedly astonished the Corporation's schedulers and programme controllers.

It also astonished merchandisers, who were caught on the hop by the unprecedented interest in THUNDERBIRDS products during the months leading up to Christmas 1991. Many manufacturers cursed their failure to react quickly enough to the programme's popularity and missed out on what should have been a dream Christmas for all THUNDERBIRDS merchandising licensees. Toy shops up and down the country were inundated with requests from parents for THUNDERBIRDS toys for Christmas, but virtually nothing was available. Some canny retailers imported models kits from Japan, which sold like hot cakes, but many parents had to endure the disappointment of their progeny come Christmas morning.

Interest in THUNDERBIRDS remained high throughout 1992 and, having been caught with their pants down once already, manufacturers were keen to make sure that they cashed in when the BBC repeated the series the following autumn (at Sunday lunchtimes from 4 October). Yet still they underestimated the enormous demand for related products, as a THUNDERBIRDS merchandise frenzy gripped the UK. In the latter months of 1992, THUNDERBIRDS proved to be the biggest merchandising success in the UK since *Star Wars* in the late 1970s, easily outstripping TEENAGE MUTANT NINJA TURTLES, BATMAN, HE-MAN and TRANSFORMERS.

The most popular items on the shelves were die-cast models of the various International Rescue craft produced by Matchbox, and the company's Tracy Island playset became the one toy that every child wanted for Christmas that year. Matchbox admitted that they had believed they were taking a huge gamble with the line and never expected such demand for their product. As a result, their production run was too small and stocks of the toys soon became scarce. At Toys 'R' Us, customers were rationed to a single set, while out on the street Thunderbird 2 models began changing hands for over £10 each (twice the

The Matchbox Tracy Island playset, the 'must-have' toy for Christmas 1992.

*PR for the new SCi
PlayStation 2 game for 2001
involved Gerry Anderson
and others appearing as
members of International
Rescue.*

recommended retail price). A female employee at a leading London department store was even reported to have offered a buyer sexual favours to acquire a set of the toys.

In January 1993, the BBC children's programme BLUE PETER came to the rescue by demonstrating how viewers could make their own Tracy Island playset (to scale with the Matchbox die-cast vehicles) from household rubbish. After successfully completing the model in a live broadcast, presenter Anthea Turner went on to tell viewers that a free twelve-page instructions leaflet was available from the programme. Within twenty-four hours, the BLUE PETER office was swamped by some 10,000 such requests and over the next ten days a further 100,000 were received from viewers. Faced with a printing bill of £15,000 that the programme could not afford, BLUE PETER editor Lewis Bronze was forced to call a halt to the offer and disappointed viewers were told that no more requests could be honoured. To placate those who missed out, in February BBC Video released the complete Tracy Island 'make' on a fifteen-minute video cassette, *Blue Peter Makes a Thunderbirds Tracy Island*. It was an instant best-seller.

Despite the immense popularity of the programme, the BBC oddly screened the series only once in its entirety. The second repeat run ended in May 1993 without the last six episodes being shown and these did not appear when a third, truncated run (seven episodes only) was broadcast over Christmas 1994. A couple of episodes were dubbed into French and Hindi as part of a BBC Schools language course and BBC Scotland presented a Gaelic version, TAIRNEARAN TAR AS (THUNDERBIRDS ARE GO). On satellite television, UK Gold screened all thirty-two episodes twice between August 1994 and September 1995.

*The new 'soundtech' range
of Thunderbirds toys from
Vivid Imaginations feature
the best-loved phrases from
the pilot of each craft.*

Five years later, THUNDERBIRDS reappeared once more, again on the BBC but this time in a new digital transfer prepared by the series' new owners, Carlton International Media. Each episode had been digitally remastered to improve the audiovisual quality. THUNDERBIRDS had never looked or sounded so good! To accompany this new broadcast came a whole new range of merchandise, including the first ever computer game and DVDs, as well as books, toys and gifts.

Just as popular with the British public as ever before, THUNDERBIRDS has proved its longevity and durability in a way that is unmatched by any other British television series made in the mid-1960s. This legacy is a fitting testimony to the imagination and skill of Gerry Anderson and his remarkable team at the Century 21 Studios in Slough, who set out to make a series the like of which had never been seen before and created a series that, more than thirty-five years later, remains truly unique.

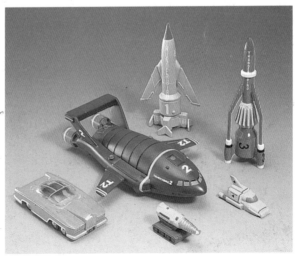

INDEX

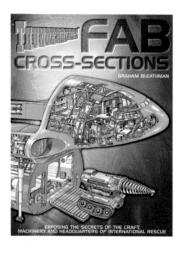

Also available from Carlton Books:

Thunderbirds FAB Cross-Sections
ISBN: 1 84222 091 8   £12.99

**Thunderbirds
Top Secret Annual 2001**
ISBN: 1 84222 094 2   £2.99

Brains's Puzzle Book
ISBN: 1 84222 096 9   £2.99

Thunderbirds Colouring Book
ISBN: 1 84222 107 8   £1.99

Lady Penelope Colouring Book
ISBN: 1 84222 106 X   £1.99

Thunderbirds Junior Story Books
The Cham-Cham
ISBN: 1 84222 098 5   £2.99

Martian Invasion
ISBN: 1 84222 100 0   £2.99

Day of Disaster
ISBN: 1 84222 099 3   £2.99

Cry Wolf
ISBN: 1 84222 097 7   £2.99

Available at all good book shops.
Or telephone 020 8324 5635.

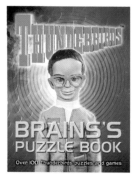

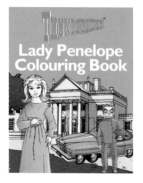

Available from Carlton Video, Thunderbirds on VHS and DVD:

VHS
VOL 1: Trapped in the Sky,
        Pit of Peril
        Cat No: 30074 20683   Sept 2000

VOL 2: Perils of Penelope,
        Terror in New York City
        Cat No: 30074 20693   Sept 2000

The Brains Behind Thunderbirds
        Cat No. 30074 20673   Sept 2000

VOL 3: Edge of Impact,
        Day of Disaster
        Cat No. 30074 21083   Nov 2000

VOL 4: Thirty Minutes After Noon,
        Desperate Intruder
        Cat No. 30074 21093   Nov 2000

From all good video retailers.

DVD
VOL 1: Episodes 1-4
        Cat No. 37115 00653 Sept 2000

VOL 2: Episodes 5-8
        Cat No. 37115 00663 Sept 2000

VOL 3: Episodes 9-12
        Cat No. 37115 00673 Sept 2000

VOL 4: Episodes 13-16
        Cat No. 37115 00683 Sept 2000

VOL 5: Episodes 17-20
        Cat No. 37115 00693 Nov 2000

VOL 6: Episodes 21-24
        Cat No. 37115 00703 Nov 2000

VOL 7: Episodes 25-28
        Cat No. 37115 00713 Nov 2000

VOL 6: Episodes 29-32
        Cat No. 37115 00723 Nov 2000